2/24

W9-AQG-562

OATH

AND

HONOR

Also by Liz Cheney

In My Time: A Personal and Political Memoir
(with Dick Cheney)

Exceptional: Why the World Needs a Powerful America
(with Dick Cheney)

Heart: An American Medical Odyssey
(with Dick Cheney and Jonathan Reiner, MD)

OATH
AND
HONOR

A Memoir and a Warning

LIZ
CHENEY

(L)(B)

Little, Brown and Company

New York Boston London

Little, Brown and Company
Hachette Book Group
1290 Avenue of the Americas, New York, NY 10104
littlebrown.com

First Edition: December 2023

Little, Brown and Company is a division of Hachette Book Group, Inc. The Little, Brown name and logo are trademarks of Hachette Book Group, Inc.

The publisher is not responsible for websites (or their content) that are not owned by the publisher.

Little, Brown and Company books may be purchased in bulk for business, educational, or promotional use. For information, please contact your local bookseller or the Hachette Book Group Special Markets Department at special.markets@hbgusa.com.

ISBN 9780316572064

Library of Congress Control Number: 2023944214

Printing 6, 2023

LSC-C

Printed in the United States of America

*For my parents, who taught me to love
America and read her history.*

*For Kate, Elizabeth, Grace, Philip, and
Richard — may you always live in freedom.*

For Phil, for everything.

CONTENTS

CONTENTS

CONTENTS

PART V

The Relentless March of Evidence

May to December 2022

CONTENTS

OATH

AND

HONOR

Prologue

THIS IS THE STORY OF the moment when American democracy began to unravel. It is the story of the men and women who fought to save it, and of the enablers and collaborators whose actions ensured the threat would grow and metastasize. It is the story of the most dangerous man ever to inhabit the Oval Office, and of the many steps he took to subvert our Constitution.

Since 1797, when George Washington voluntarily handed the power of the presidency to John Adams, every American president had fulfilled his solemn obligation to guarantee the peaceful transfer of power—until Donald Trump. When Trump lost the 2020 presidential election, he attempted to overturn the results in order to seize power illegally and remain in office. When the violent mob he had mobilized laid siege to our Capitol, he watched the attack on television and refused for more than three hours to tell the rioters to leave. Donald Trump's actions violated the law and the oath he swore to the Constitution.

Our founders built safeguards into our system of government to preserve our democratic process. But those safeguards require that men and women of goodwill—Americans elected to positions of public trust—put their duty to the Constitution above their party and above their loyalty to any one man. When our nation was tested after the presidential election of 2020, an alarming number of elected Republicans in Congress failed to do their duty. This is the story of how that happened, and why. It is a story that every American deserves to know.

The end of this story hasn't yet been written. The threat continues. The outcome now is in the hands of the American people and our system of justice. The methods Donald Trump is using to undermine our democracy are not unique to him. I saw authoritarian leaders use many of these same tactics in Eastern Europe, Russia, Ukraine, and across the Middle East when I was working for the US State Department. History is full of similar examples in countries around the world, but never in the United States—until now.

Like other aspiring autocrats, Donald Trump cannot succeed alone. He depends upon enablers and collaborators. Every American should understand what his enablers in Congress and in the leadership of the Republican Party were willing to do to help Trump seize power in the months after he lost the 2020 presidential election—and what they continue to do to this day. So strong is the lure of power that men and women who had once seemed reasonable and responsible were suddenly willing to violate their oath to the Constitution out of political expediency and loyalty to Donald Trump.

In the aftermath of January 6, one senior Republican congressman— who knew the danger Trump posed but would not speak out because he feared the political consequences—said to me: "Surviving is all that matters, Liz." It was a sad moment. Elected officials who believe their own political survival is more important than anything else threaten the survival of our republic, no matter what they tell themselves to justify their cowardice.

———

At the height of the Cold War in 1983, Ronald Reagan addressed the nation from the Oval Office. He said this about our duty to defend freedom:

> It is up to us in our time to choose, and choose wisely, between the hard but necessary task of preserving peace and freedom, and the temptation to ignore our duty and blindly hope for the best while the enemies of freedom grow stronger day by day.

The threat we face today is different but no less perilous. Our duty remains the same. It is up to each one of us to take seriously our obligation to safeguard the miracle of American freedom. We must abide by our duty to the Constitution, and demand that our political leaders do the same. Politicians who minimize the threat, repeat the lies, or enable the liar are not fit for office. Most importantly, we cannot make the grave mistake of returning Donald Trump—the man who caused January 6—to the White House, or to any position of public trust, ever again.

PART I

The Plot Against America

ELECTION DAY 2020 TO JANUARY 5, 2021

1. THE ONLY THING THAT MATTERS IS WINNING

Two DAYS AFTER THE 2020 election, House Republican Leader Kevin McCarthy told me he had talked to Donald Trump. "He knows it's over," McCarthy said. Trump just needed some time to process the loss. "He needs to go through all the stages of grief," McCarthy added.

For Trump, the stages of grief seemed to involve tweeting in all caps. Shortly after 9:00 a.m. on November 5, he tweeted: "STOP THE COUNT!" An hour later, at 10:09 a.m.: "ANY VOTE THAT CAME IN AFTER ELECTION DAY WILL NOT BE COUNTED!"

Thirty minutes later, Trump retweeted himself: "STOP THE COUNT!"

Shortly after noon: "STOP THE FRAUD!"

Donald Trump had been told repeatedly by his top campaign advisers, including on Election Day itself, that early returns on Election Night could show him leading initially, but that those numbers were likely to change as absentee and mail-in votes were counted. This happened in every presidential election. In many states, Election Day votes were counted first, and a larger percentage of Republicans than Democrats voted on Election Day. This was even more likely to be the case in 2020 because Trump had spent months, against the advice of his political advisers, urging Republicans *not* to cast absentee and mail-in votes and to vote in person on Election Day instead.

Donald Trump knew there would be a "red mirage," in which he seemed to be ahead at the outset. He helped create that red mirage. Despite this, he claimed the phenomenon was evidence of major fraud.

"We were up by nearly 700,000 votes in Pennsylvania. I won Pennsylvania by a lot. And that gets whittled down," he said in remarks from the White House briefing room on November 5. "Likewise, in Georgia, I won by a lot, a lot, with a lead of over, getting close to, 300,000 votes on Election Night in Georgia. And by the way, [that] got whittled down, and now it's getting to be to a point where I'll go from winning by a lot to perhaps being even down a little bit." The same was happening in Michigan and Wisconsin, he claimed. "They're trying to steal an election. They're trying to rig an election and we can't let that happen."

Trump's fraud claims also included repeated assertions about nefarious-sounding "ballot dumps." He tweeted that his lead in key states "started to magically disappear as surprise ballot dumps were counted. VERY STRANGE..." In another tweet, he said, "Mail-in ballot dumps were devastating in their percentage and power of destruction." We now know that Trump was aware this claim was false, too. Bill Stepien, Trump's campaign manager, told the Select Committee to Investigate the January 6th Attack on the United States Capitol that he had personally informed Trump that "periodic release of ballots would occur." Once again, Trump was taking something he knew to be a routine feature of the counting process and making it seem criminal.

When McCarthy and I spoke on November 5, we discussed the fact that although the election hadn't yet been called for Joe Biden, it seemed likely that would happen soon. When Biden's tally in the Electoral College reached 270, the dynamic would shift and people would start looking toward the future, the next administration, and the new Congress.

McCarthy appeared to be dealing in reality. This made it all the more surprising when I saw his appearance on Fox News just a few hours later: "President Trump won this election," Kevin proclaimed, "so everyone who is listening, do not be quiet! Do not be silent about this! We cannot allow this to happen before our very eyes." McCarthy knew that what he was saying was not true.

Every candidate has the right to bring legal challenges in court if they have evidence of fraud or irregularities in an election. That is what I expected to happen next. But even as the Trump team was beginning to discuss and file these suits, there were signs that Trump and his supporters might not accept the outcome of any legal challenges.

One of the first hints I saw of this came only a couple of days after the election in a tweet by Trump supporter and radio personality Mark Levin. I had known Mark for many years. He had supported me in the past. During the 2016 primaries, Mark initially supported Ted Cruz. At one point, before Trump's 2016 nomination, Mark had declared himself "Never Trump." But all that had changed over the past four years. Mark had become an ardent defender of Trump, sometimes signaling what people inside Trump's orbit were thinking.

On November 5, 2020, Levin tweeted this in all caps:

REMINDER TO THE REPUBLICAN STATE LEGISLATURES, YOU HAVE THE FINAL SAY OVER THE CHOOSING OF ELECTORS, NOT ANY BOARD OF ELECTIONS, SECRETARY OF STATE, GOVERNOR, OR EVEN COURT. YOU HAVE THE FINAL SAY — ARTICLE II OF THE FED CONSTITUTION. SO, GET READY TO DO YOUR CONSTITUTIONAL DUTY.

When I saw Levin's tweet, I wondered what exactly he was talking about. The legislatures had already had their "final say" under Article II of our Constitution, which provides that each state legislature directs the *manner* in which their state appoints presidential electors. Levin surely knew that every state legislature had already done so, and the *manner* they all chose was a popular vote. Each of the state legislatures had also specified a detailed *manner* in which to resolve any election disputes — through recounts, audits, and lawsuits, if necessary. If a presidential candidate disputes the election in any state by saying it was fraudulent or illegal, and the issue is not resolved by recounts or other procedures, the proper way to proceed under our Constitution is to file a lawsuit. And once that lawsuit is over and the courts' judgments are final, the election issues are resolved.

Now, however, it seemed that Levin was suggesting the state legislatures should ignore the laws they themselves had passed specifying the manner in which election disputes would be resolved, ignore the outcome of balloting in their states, and simply switch the results from Biden to Trump. Even conservative law professor John Eastman—who later worked with Donald Trump and would play a major role in January 6—confided to a colleague before the 2020 election that state legislatures could *not* change the outcome after the fact:

> Article II [of the Constitution] says the electors are appointed "in such manner as the Legislature thereof may direct," but I don't think that entitles the Legislature to change the rules after the election and appoint a different slate of electors in a manner different than what was in place on election day.

We were only two days past the election, and already Trump and his key supporters were inventing ways to ignore the lawful outcome of that election.

Early the next morning—Friday, November 6—I texted Adam Kinzinger, a Republican member of Congress from Illinois and an Air Force veteran who had flown missions in Iraq and Afghanistan. Adam and I had worked together on national security issues. He was no-nonsense and unafraid of speaking out, even in the face of party pressure.

As ballot counting continued in key states, the networks had yet to call the election for Biden. I thought it would be called soon—and once that happened, I believed Republicans in Congress would accept the results and move on. However, Levin's tweet and other public statements by Trump and his supporters made me think we needed to be prepared in case attempts were made to pursue paths like the one Levin was suggesting. I asked Adam to help me pull together a list of Republican members we could count on if it became necessary to step forward publicly and put a stop to the nonsense. Kinzinger readily agreed.

I had been elected two years earlier by my colleagues to serve as Chair of the House Republican Conference. The conference chair is the third-ranking Republican in the House, responsible for communications and messaging for the Republican Conference. As conference chair, I also convened the weekly conference meetings for all House Republicans.

Our weekly meetings, sometimes conducted by phone, normally involved a couple of hundred participants, including Republican members of Congress and congressional staffers, as well as staffers from the White House office of legislative affairs. Occasionally, we would ask guest speakers, including key officials from the Trump administration, to present on a particular topic. Kevin McCarthy sometimes had Trump dialed in, secretly listening to our discussions. Kevin didn't inform the entire conference when Trump had joined a call unless Trump planned to speak, but it wasn't difficult to tell when Trump was listening in. When certain members were particularly lavish in their praise for Trump, I suspected that Kevin had alerted them we had a presidential eavesdropper.

Our first post-election call of 2020 was at 1:00 p.m. on Friday, November 6. Following our opening prayer, we moved into leadership reports, where Kevin, Republican Whip Steve Scalise, and I briefed the membership. Our discussion that day focused on how well House Republicans had performed in races across the country. Though projected to lose seats, we had gained 15, leaving Democrats with a narrow nine-seat majority.

After leadership reports, we opened up the call for questions or comments from other members. Most commended the House Republicans' success on Election Night, and a number of them described what had happened in their own districts or states. Not a single member of Congress— including those from the states Trump was already saying had been stolen from him—suggested that their own election had been rigged or was flawed in any way. There were questions about the process the Trump campaign was likely to pursue going forward, and some discussion of possible audits, recounts, or election-related litigation.

After Kevin's appearance on Fox News the night before, I had heard from several colleagues unhappy that he was echoing Trump's stolen-election claims. One member addressed this when it was his turn to speak: "There's a legal process for contesting results, and Trump has the right to go through that," he said. But, he warned, "we can't have people on TV saying this was rigged when we don't have any evidence of that." McCarthy knew this was a direct criticism of him, and he responded by claiming he hadn't said the election was stolen. His denial was impossible to reconcile with the video of his Fox News appearance.

When it was Jim Jordan's turn to speak, the Ohio congressman—perhaps Trump's closest ally in the House—was dismissive of the discussion about the legal process for challenges and recounts. Jordan was not interested in understanding or discussing the rules. He didn't seem to think the rules mattered.

"The only thing that matters," Jordan said, "is winning."

As we now know, Trump's own campaign leadership was meeting with him to tell him he was not, in fact, winning. At a meeting on Friday, November 6, and again on Saturday, November 7, they informed the president that he had almost certainly lost.

Things got weirder over the weekend.

On Saturday, former New York City mayor–turned–presidential lawyer Rudy Giuliani held a press conference on behalf of the Trump campaign at Four Seasons Total Landscaping, a small business located between a crematorium and an adult bookstore in a strip mall outside Philadelphia. The site was a perplexing choice. Did someone think they were reserving space at the Four Seasons Hotel and end up at the strip mall by mistake? That's what Donald Trump seemed to believe when he issued his first tweet about the event and then had to correct it, adding the word *Landscaping* a few minutes later.

The owner of Four Seasons Total Landscaping appeared equally mystified. "We don't really know how it happened," the owner's son said a week later. "We heard it might've been a mistake or something. We just kinda picked up the phone and said yes and cleared some stuff out and managed to make it happen." The landscaping company capitalized on its newfound notoriety, offering MAKE AMERICA RAKE AGAIN and LAWN AND ORDER T-shirts for sale by the next week.

Watching news coverage of the event, my first thought was, *Is this a joke?* It quickly became clear that it was not. Here was Rudy Giuliani, the lawyer for the president of the United States, standing in a strip-mall parking lot making wild and false claims of election fraud. Giuliani had led New York City as our nation recovered from the attacks of 9/11. I had visited the remains of the World Trade Towers with him in the weeks after the attack. Now, as I watched the press conference, I kept thinking how far Rudy Giuliani had fallen. How had we gotten to a point that a spectacle like this was being held on behalf of the President of the United States?

Though they weren't saying so publicly at the time, the leadership of the Trump campaign had essentially the same reaction that I did.

To make matters worse for Donald Trump, the networks called the presidential race for Joe Biden just as Giuliani's Four Seasons press conference was airing. Maybe now, I thought, Trump will concede.

Instead, two days later, Trump announced personnel changes at the Pentagon that were unprecedented for a lame-duck president, and added to growing concerns about just what he might be planning. On November 9, Trump fired his secretary of defense, Mark Esper. I had known Mark for many years. We'd first worked together in 2008, when Tennessee Senator Fred Thompson ran for president and Mark and I were foreign-policy advisers to his campaign. I respected Mark and knew he was trying to do the right thing in a very tough set of circumstances.

I was serving on the House Armed Services Committee at the time, charged with overseeing the Department of Defense (DOD). Esper's firing was deeply disquieting.

The period of transition from one administration to the next is a time of heightened potential vulnerability for the United States. What happens at the Pentagon is especially important. Ensuring stability and a smooth transition is crucial. No lame-duck president focused on securing the nation would replace his top civilian leaders at DOD days after losing an election. Yet that's what Trump was doing.

Eric Edelman, a tremendously skilled and effective career ambassador who had served presidents of both parties at the highest levels of government, including in the White House, in the State Department, and as undersecretary of defense for policy, described it to me this way: "This is getting very serious, very dangerous, and very worrisome, even for folks who are disposed to remain calm." Esper believed he had been fired in part because he had made it clear that he would not stand for any use of the military to contest the outcome of an election.

Trump's appointment of Chris Miller to replace Esper was a further troubling sign. Despite a lengthy career in special operations, Miller lacked any expertise or relevant background in dealing with what had become our nation's greatest challenge: the threat from great-power competitors China and Russia. He had no familiarity with the huge array of policy challenges facing the Defense Department, its acquisition process, or its sprawling bureaucracy.

Although Chris Miller had briefly been placed in charge of the National Counterterrorism Center, he had never managed anything close to the scale of DOD. He was quite possibly the least-qualified nominee to become secretary of defense since the position was created in 1947.

At the same time, Trump moved to install other loyalists in what seemed an effort to ensure the inexperienced Miller could be guided and his decisions shaped to suit Trump's whims.

Kash Patel was appointed on November 10 to serve as Chris Miller's chief of staff. As far as I knew, Patel had no military experience. He had never served in any capacity at the Defense Department. But Patel was a Donald Trump loyalist. The president had reportedly attempted to appoint Patel to several other positions throughout the government, including as deputy CIA director and deputy FBI director, only to meet strong resistance—including threats of resignation—from the agency professionals who would have had to work with Patel.

Douglas MacGregor, a retired colonel who regularly spreads pro-Putin propaganda on American airwaves, was named senior adviser to the secretary of defense. Trump had nominated MacGregor to be US ambassador to Germany a few months earlier, but MacGregor failed to win confirmation. Now he was installed in the upper echelons of the Pentagon.

Trump also named retired Brigadier General Anthony Tata to be acting undersecretary of defense for Policy. Tata was yet another Trump nominee unable to win Senate confirmation. In this case, Trump was appointing him to the very position for which the Senate had refused to confirm him just a few months earlier.

Taken together, these appointments were deeply troubling. Trump had lost the election. Why was he appointing inexperienced loyalists to the most senior civilian positions in the Pentagon at a moment when stability was key? Why was he making these moves if he intended to begin an orderly and peaceful presidential transition to Joe Biden?

It was an ominous sign of things to come.

2.   PUT UP OR SHUT UP

THE HOUSE REPUBLICANS WERE SCHEDULED to meet again on November 17, 2020, to elect our leadership team for the 117th Congress. There were rumors that the Freedom Caucus—a group of Republican members of the House who had become very pro-Trump—was considering nominating candidates to run against Kevin McCarthy, Steve Scalise, or me for one of the top leadership posts.

Early in my first term, Jim Jordan, who was then chair of the Freedom Caucus, had tried to get me to join the group. Sitting down in an empty seat beside me at one of my first House Republican meetings, Jordan asked if I would consider becoming a Freedom Caucus member. Cynthia Lummis, my predecessor as Wyoming's congresswoman, had been a member, but I had told Wyoming voters that I did not intend to join. I wasn't comfortable with a number of things about the group, including their rule requiring every member of the caucus to support any position that was held by 80 percent of the membership. It didn't seem right to me for a member of Congress to agree to have their vote bound by anything other than their obligations to their constituents and to the Constitution.

Jordan did make a memorable pitch to me to join the group, though. It went something like this: "Would you consider joining the Freedom Caucus? We don't have any women, and we need one." Tempting as this offer was, I took a pass.

My voting record was more conservative than those of many members of the Freedom Caucus, a supposedly "conservative" group. But a number of its members were hypersensitive to any criticism I made of

Donald Trump. They had been grumbling about my public opposition to things such as Trump's July 2020 suggestion that we could postpone the presidential election. They were angry when I challenged Trump's refusal in September to commit to a peaceful transfer of power. And they seemed especially upset when I tweeted a picture of my dad wearing a mask in June of 2020, at the height of the Covid-19 pandemic, along with the caption "Real Men Wear Masks."

As it turned out, nothing came of their threats to challenge our leadership team. Kevin McCarthy, Steve Scalise, and I were each reelected to our positions without opposition.

Later that night, Donald Trump fired Chris Krebs, director of the Cybersecurity and Infrastructure Security Agency at the Department of Homeland Security. Appointed by Trump himself, Krebs had spent two years working to harden America's election systems from outside interference. In the aftermath of the election, Krebs repeatedly countered Trump's false stolen-election claims. On November 12, Krebs had issued a joint statement with other state and federal election officials explaining that "the 2020 election was the most secure in American history" and that "there is no evidence that any voting system deleted or lost votes, changed votes, or was in any way compromised."

Trump fired Krebs via tweet, just as he had fired Defense Secretary Esper a week earlier. Trump claimed, without any evidence, that "there were massive improprieties and fraud," and that glitches in machines had switched millions of votes from Trump to Biden.

Krebs did not go silently. After his dismissal, he confirmed repeatedly and publicly what federal and state election experts had concluded. In response, Joseph DiGenova, one of Donald Trump's lawyers, raged in an interview that Chris Krebs should be "drawn and quartered and taken out and shot at dawn."

———

The Republican National Committee headquarters occupies prestigious real estate on Capitol Hill, half a block from the Cannon House Office Building and next door to the Capitol Hill Club. On Thursday,

November 19, Rudy Giuliani, Sidney Powell, Jenna Ellis, Joseph DiGenova, Victoria Toensing, and Boris Epshteyn—a group of lawyers representing Trump—held a press conference in the headquarters building to lay out yet more false claims of massive voter fraud. Chris Krebs called the event "the most dangerous 1 hour 45 minutes of television in American history."

Giuliani opened the press conference by explaining that his assembled group was "representing President Trump and we're representing the Trump campaign." There were many lawyers working on this, he said, but "we're the senior lawyers." Giuliani promised that he, Powell, and Ellis were about to present "evidence we've collected over the last two . . . weeks."

He did not do that. Instead, Giuliani proceeded to make sweeping claims that Trump had won Wisconsin "by a good margin"; that he had carried Pennsylvania by "300,000 votes"; and that there had been "over-votes in numerous precincts of 150%, 200%, and 300%" in certain Michigan and Wisconsin counties. Giuliani proclaimed 682,770 ballots cast in Pennsylvania to be "null and void." In some precincts, he alleged, the number of votes cast was more than double the total population of those precincts.

As Rudy's litany of lies continued under the glare of the camera lights, he began to sweat. Pulling a handkerchief from his pocket, he repeatedly wiped his face as he claimed that there was "evidence of massive fraud"—and that the election had, therefore, been "irredeemably compromised."

As Giuliani turned to point to a map of the United States on an easel beside the podium, brown rivulets of what seemed to be hair dye streamed down the side of his face. He kept going. "In the states that we have indicated in red," he contended, "Georgia, Pennsylvania, Michigan, Wisconsin, Nevada, and Arizona, we more than double the number of votes needed to overturn the election in terms of provable illegal ballots." His "evidence" for this massive fraud consisted of 10 affidavits. He couldn't produce more, he said, because people feared going public, but he claimed the campaign had "a thousand, at least." Rudy failed to explain how even 1,000 "affidavits" would be adequate to justify throwing out the votes of tens of millions of Americans. Instead, he insisted he had additional secret evidence—"aspects of this fraud that at this point I really can't reveal."

The hair dye dripping down his face made it challenging to focus on what Rudy was saying. But as he introduced Sidney Powell, he made this attention-grabbing pronouncement: "I don't think most Americans know that our ballots get calculated, many of them, outside the United States... and it's being done by a company that specializes in voter fraud." According to Giuliani, America had used "largely a Venezuelan voting machine, in essence, to count our vote...[if] we let this happen, we are going to become Venezuela."

What is he talking about? I thought. Was Sidney Powell going to provide evidence for this claim?

Powell stepped up to the microphone and explained that America's entire election system had essentially been hacked by Dominion voting machines and Smartmatic technology software, which, she said, was software "created in Venezuela at the direction of Hugo Chavez." She described an "algorithm" that she said had switched votes from Trump to Biden, and that had "trashed" Trump votes. According to Powell, we learned about this only because Donald Trump got so many votes, the whole system broke. But we needed to be aware, she warned, that this same sinister "source code" resided in voting machines all across the country.

Her evidence for these assertions? "[O]ne very strong witness, who has explained how it all works." This witness's affidavit, she said, was attached to pleadings that lawyer Lin Wood had filed in a lawsuit in Georgia.

Then, her voice breaking with emotion, Powell said this was all "stunning, heartbreaking, infuriating, and the most unpatriotic acts I can even imagine for people in this country to have participated in..." She claimed that "President Trump won by a landslide. We are going to prove it, and we are going to reclaim the United States of America for the people who vote for freedom."

Immediately following Powell's remarks, Jenna Ellis stepped up to the podium to say that the assembled lawyers were an "elite strike-force team that is working on behalf of the president and the campaign." Rudy reiterated that he and Sidney were "in charge of this investigation."

The whole performance was too bizarre for words. My daughter Elizabeth, who had been following the litigation closely and was increasingly disgusted with what Trump's lawyers were doing, texted me that night: "Mom, I think it's safe to say that Rudy Giuliani's hair dye dripping down his face today was an act of God."

It quickly became apparent, even to hard-core Trump supporters such as Tucker Carlson, that Sidney Powell had no evidence to back up her claims. Three days after the press conference, Ellis and Giuliani issued a statement saying Sidney Powell was "not a member of the Trump Legal Team. She is also not a lawyer for the President in his personal capacity."

Rush Limbaugh, a steadfast Trump supporter, said of the press conference, "They promised blockbuster stuff and then nothing happened."

Ultimately, all three of the lawyers who spoke at the press conference — Giuliani, Powell, and Ellis — would be sanctioned by courts, censured, or have their license to practice law suspended. And each would be indicted because of their lies about the election.

Sidney Powell responded to a defamation lawsuit against her by arguing that "no reasonable person would conclude that the statements were truly statements of fact."

Jenna Ellis admitted she engaged in "professional misconduct" by spreading falsehoods about the 2020 election, and she was censured.

And a court in New York reached this conclusion about Rudy Giuliani: "[Giuliani] communicated demonstrably false and misleading statements to the courts, lawmakers, and the public at large in his capacity as lawyer for former President Donald J. Trump and the Trump Campaign in connection with Trump's failed effort at reelection in 2020."

But the damage had already been done. Millions of Americans — including tens of thousands of my own constituents — believed these lies, and they believed in the people telling them. One constituent called the performance "clear-eyed and determined." This person said that Powell struck her as "forthright" and noted that the Trump lawyer had been "shaking with righteous anger. Very persuasive." Then she added: "Of course the talking heads will dismiss them. F*** them."

We were in dangerous territory. The president and his legal team were making outlandish and false claims that struck at the heart of our electoral process. Millions of Americans believed them. And the Trump campaign continued to send emails and run ads, spreading these same falsehoods all over the country. Donald Trump was doing it nearly every time he spoke publicly.

I knew how perilous this was. I knew it had to stop. The next day, November 20, I issued a statement calling on President Trump to put up or shut up:

America is governed by the rule of law. The president and his lawyers have made claims of criminality and widespread fraud, which they allege could impact election results. If they have genuine evidence of this, they are obligated to present it immediately in court and to the American people. I understand that the president has filed more than thirty separate lawsuits. If he is unsatisfied with the results in those lawsuits, then the appropriate avenue is to appeal. If the president cannot prove these claims or demonstrate that they would change the election result, he should fulfill his duty to preserve, protect and defend the Constitution of the United States by respecting the sanctity of our electoral process.

I did not know it at the time, but the lawyers in the Trump campaign and at the Trump White House agreed with me. Despite that, the intense public reaction to my statement was a sign of things to come. I heard from many constituents that they believed I was "going after Trump" and that I was betraying Wyoming. Emotions were running high.

Some of the anger stemmed from desperation about the damage Biden policies might do to our state. Our biggest industries—fossil fuels and ranching—are profoundly impacted by policies set in Washington, DC. The federal government owns nearly 50 percent of the land in Wyoming, as well as two-thirds of the state's subsurface minerals. Whether the issue was grazing cattle on public lands, securing permits for oil and gas leasing, or sustaining our coal industry, there was a widespread sense that a Biden administration would impose policies that would ruin people's lives. If the Democrats had truly stolen the election, as Trump and his representatives alleged, no one in Wyoming would take that lying down.

The Republican National Committee's own lawyer, Justin Riemer, also sounded the alarm about the lies being told by the president's lawyers. In a message to Trump spokesperson Elizabeth Harrington on November 28, Riemer said, "What Rudy and Jenna are doing is a joke and they are getting laughed out of court. They are misleading millions of people who have wishful thinking that the president is going to somehow win this thing." He was right. Ultimately, the January 6 investigation found dozens of people in the White House, the Trump campaign, and throughout the Trump administration who agreed with what Riemer said.

A few days after I issued my November 20 statement calling on Trump to produce evidence of fraud and respect the sanctity of our elections, my chief of staff, Kara Ahern, got a call from a staffer in the White House. He informed her that I was off the guest list for the White House congressional holiday party. Invites to these parties are highly coveted by most members of Congress, but I hadn't gone during any of the previous years I'd been in Congress, and I hadn't planned to attend this one. I was amused that whoever gave the instruction to disinvite me thought I'd view it as a punishment.

When the news of my blacklisting broke in *Politico,* I got a wonderful text from my colleague Ken Buck, a congressman from Colorado who was a former prosecutor and had worked as a staffer for my father on the Iran-Contra committee in the 1980s. Ken told me he was having Christmas ornaments specially made that year bearing this Ronald Reagan quote:

> To a few of us here today, this is a solemn and most momentous occasion; and yet, in the history of our Nation, it is a commonplace occurrence. The orderly transfer of authority as called for in the Constitution routinely takes place as it has for almost two centuries and few of us stop to think how unique we really are. In

the eyes of many in the world, this every-4-year ceremony we accept as normal is nothing less than a miracle.

I wasn't the only one who recognized how dangerous this moment was becoming. But the truth was not breaking through. Far too many people were hearing only Donald Trump's lies. I was spending hours on the phone and in person talking to constituents about what was really happening. Conspiracy theories were everywhere, and they stretched beyond what was happening in the election. One afternoon, I called two constituents who had long been supporters of mine. They lived in different parts of Wyoming and didn't really know each other, but they had obviously been reading the same dangerous garbage online. They both began their separate calls with me asking whether I was aware that the chief justice of the United States Supreme Court was operating a child sex-trafficking ring in his basement. Of course that's not true, I told each of them. But how could I be *sure* it wasn't true, they each wanted to know.

I was dumbfounded. These were two relatively reasonable individuals—not people I would have guessed would be susceptible to crackpot claims like this. So ludicrous was the accusation that I wasn't sure where to begin to knock it down. It was becoming clear that the truth no longer really mattered.

When House Republicans convened by phone on December 1, Texas Representative Louie Gohmert, himself a purveyor of crackpot claims, got in the queue to speak. He had a message for me: "I want you to know," he said, "that had I seen your statement attacking Trump, I never would have supported your reelection to leadership. I would have recruited someone to run against you."

Sometimes it was best to let members vent in these calls or meetings with the entire Republican Conference. We did not respond to every complaint or criticism, but I decided not to let this attack stand. "Which part of the statement do you have a problem with, Louie?" I asked. "Surely you don't disagree with the part that says America is governed by the rule of law, or the part that says claims of widespread criminality must be backed up by evidence, or the part that says the president is obligated to respect the sanctity of our election process?"

As it turned out, Louie's commitment to those concepts was not exactly rock-solid: A few weeks later he sued Vice President Mike Pence, urging a federal court to rule that Pence could refuse to count certain states' electoral votes when he presided over Congress's upcoming joint session on January 6. When his lawsuit was dismissed, Gohmert claimed that the only option left was to take to the streets and get violent.

Gohmert later said that he hadn't actually been calling for violence. But there was no question that he had been spreading the worst lies and then implying that all the institutions of American democracy had failed. Gohmert was suggesting to people that their country was being stolen from them and there was only one way to save it.

3. SOMEONE IS GOING TO GET KILLED

IN THE UNITED STATES, OUR courts adjudicate claims of election fraud. Elections can't be overturned based merely on accusations, or because someone says they *believe* there has been fraud. Sufficient evidence is required, and the fraud must have occurred on a scale that could change the result. That's the rule of law. If he had a basis, Donald Trump had the right to bring election challenges in court. What neither he nor any other candidate has the right to do is ignore the rulings of those courts.

Donald Trump and his supporters were certainly trying to use the courts, filing more than 60 lawsuits. Throughout November and December, my husband, Phil, and I were watching the outcomes of those lawsuits in federal and state courts. Trump's losses in these cases began in the first half of November and continued over the following weeks. The results were the same almost everywhere: in state courts and in federal courts, including before federal judges appointed by Donald Trump himself. Never did any of Trump's allegations of fraud—including supposed fraud by Dominion Voting Systems, by Smartmatic, or by any other voting machine or software company—prove to be true. None of it was backed up by evidence.

Dozens of courts reviewed the Trump allegations, and dozens of courts rejected them. In a Nevada court, for example, the Trump legal team had a full opportunity to call witnesses and put on its case. At the time, Kayleigh McEnany, speaking for the campaign, celebrated that particular case as "the most important case" and an opportunity for Trump to prove that the election had been stolen from him. Yet despite the stacks of paper McEnany waved around on Sean Hannity's show, Trump and his team did not have any real evidence. They lost in the Nevada trial court, and they lost again in the Nevada Supreme Court. Ultimately, Trump and his allies lost 61 out of 62 cases. Their only victory, in Pennsylvania, involved an insufficient number of votes to impact the outcome of that state's election.

By December 1, Donald Trump's attorney general, Bill Barr, had had enough of what he later called "bullshit" election claims. Barr told the Associated Press that the Department of Justice had been investigating the allegations of fraud, and "we have not seen fraud on a scale that could have effected a different outcome in the election." This made Trump so angry that he reportedly threw his lunch at a wall in the White House. Undeterred, the next day Trump posted a 45-minute speech to Facebook, repeating his false claims of election fraud.

Across the country in early December, state election officials were facing increasing pressure as a result of Trump's continued false claims as they prepared to certify the results. In Georgia on December 1, election official Gabe Sterling held an extraordinary press conference in which he pleaded with the president personally to stop inciting threats and violence: "[S]top inspiring people to commit potential acts of violence. Someone's going to get hurt. Someone's going to get shot. Someone's going to get killed and it's not right."

A Georgia reporter tweeted out video of Sterling's plea and warning. At 10:27 p.m. that night, Trump responded. He didn't condemn the threats of violence. He didn't call for a stop to them. He doubled down. Retweeting the video of Sterling's speech, Trump repeated the very lies that Sterling had warned about: "Rigged Election. Show signatures and envelopes. Expose the massive voter fraud…"

I already had some sense at the time that Trump was pressuring state legislators. For example, he had invited Republican leaders of the Michigan State House and Senate to the White House in November. This visit caused enough alarm that, upon leaving their meeting with Trump, these lawmakers issued a statement reaffirming that they would not overturn the results of the Michigan election by flipping their electoral votes to Trump from Biden. However, Gabe Sterling's stark and direct warning about the potential for violence alerted me that Trump was doing far more than I had initially recognized. As Sterling made clear, Trump and his team were provoking violent threats.

————

The following week, the entire House Republican Conference was dragged into Trump's frivolous claims. This time in front of the United States Supreme Court.

On Monday, December 7, the state of Texas petitioned the Supreme Court, challenging the results of the presidential election in Georgia, Michigan, Pennsylvania, and Wisconsin—all four states won by Joe Biden. Although the Texas solicitor general would normally represent the state before the Supreme Court, he was not listed on the brief, which was instead filed by Texas Attorney General Ken Paxton.

A number of conservative Republicans raised public concerns about the constitutionality of the claims that Paxton was making. Texas Senator John Cornyn, who had previously served both as the state's attorney general and as a justice on its supreme court, said:

> I frankly struggle to understand the legal theory of it. Number one, why would a state, even such a great state as Texas, have a say-so on how other states administer their elections? We have a diffused and dispersed system and even though we might not like it, they may think it's unfair, those are decided at the state and local level and not at the national level.

Congressman Chip Roy, a Texas Republican and member of the House Freedom Caucus, said: "The case itself represents a dangerous violation of federalism."

A conservative legal analyst and former federal prosecutor noted that "every claim raised in Texas's complaint has already been rejected by other courts; in particular, the Third Circuit Court of Appeals and the federal district court in Pennsylvania." Noting that the Texas solicitor general had not signed the brief, this analyst pointed out that the lawsuit is "so frivolous and so blatantly political that the top appellate lawyers in his office evidently declined to endorse it."

The attorneys general for each of the states targeted by Texas—including Georgia's attorney general, who was also chair of the Republican Attorneys General Association—explained that the claims in the Texas brief were false, and that, in fact, each state had conducted its election in the *manner* determined by its state legislature. A spokesman for Georgia Attorney General Chris Carr said: "With all due respect, the Texas attorney general is constitutionally, legally, and factually wrong about Georgia."

On Wednesday morning, December 9, Representative Mike Johnson of Louisiana—who would become Speaker of the House in 2023—sent an email to Republican members of the House with the subject line ****Time-sensitive request from President Trump.**** "President Trump called me this morning," Johnson reported, "to express his great appreciation for our effort to file an amicus brief in the Texas case..." (An *amicus brief* is a way for people not directly involved in a case to express support for one side or the other.) In boldface and underlined red text, Johnson went on to say, **"He specifically asked me to contact all Republican Members of the House and Senate today and request that all join on to our brief."** According to Johnson, Trump would be paying close attention to who did and did not sign on: "He said he will be anxiously awaiting the final list to review."

Twenty minutes after Johnson's email went out, I started hearing from fellow members of Congress. They were angry with Mike's implied threat—that he would be collecting names and showing them to Trump. In addition, Mike was vice chair of the House Republican Conference, and he had included his official signature block in the email. Members wanted to know if this meant his effort was a leadership initiative. I assured them it was not.

When I called Johnson, he maintained that he had not intended to pressure people with his comment about President Trump reviewing the list. The amicus brief was, he said, simply meant to help President Trump "exhaust all legal remedies" and "show support for him."

The draft brief itself had not yet been distributed. But in his email seeking signatories, Johnson provided this description:

The simple objective of our brief is to affirm for the Court (and our constituents back home) our serious concerns with the integrity of our election system. We are not seeking to independently litigate the particular allegations of fraud in our brief (that is not our place as amici). We will merely state our belief that the broad scope of the various allegations and irregularities in the subject states merits careful, timely review by the Supreme Court.

Mike was seriously misleading our members. The brief did indeed assert *as facts known to the amici* many allegations of fraud and serious wrongdoing by officials in multiple states.

Early the next morning, Johnson emailed the draft brief to Republican members, along with a note explaining that more than 105 House Republicans had "expressed an interest in participating." Not one of them had seen the brief.

In his cover email, Johnson again asserted that the objective of the brief was simply to make clear "our serious concerns with the integrity of our election system." But then he added a new inaccurate claim: "As we point out, the record clearly shows that the Defendant states violated [Article II, Section 1 of the Constitution]." This was apparently an attempt to say that state officials had violated the state laws—passed by state legislatures—governing how they could act in administering elections. But virtually all of those claims had already been heard by the courts and decided *against* Trump, including by federal judges whom Donald Trump himself had appointed.

As I read the amicus brief—which was poorly written—it became clear Mike was being less than honest with our colleagues. He was playing bait and switch, assuring members that the brief made no claims about specific allegations of fraud when, in fact, it was full of such claims. I texted Johnson:

Mike—Just read the brief. Can you share with me who wrote it? I'm confused because contrary to our discussion and to your cover email, the brief recites and affirms as facts known to the amici allegations of serious wrongdoing and fraud by many state officials, including Republicans. I thought the strategy was to support the president's rights to have his claims heard, not to assert facts in a federal court without personal knowledge.

In addition to misleading our members, it seemed to me that making such assertions to a court—with no personal knowledge or basis in fact—would present ethical questions for anyone who is a member of the Bar.

By this point, Johnson's effort was raising serious red flags, including in other Republican leadership offices. Kevin McCarthy's general counsel, Machalagh Carr, agreed with me and said she would be discussing these issues with McCarthy. Here is how she described the brief:

> The amicus brief is not a simple support document to tell the Court to allow the President to make his legal argument. It makes serious claims about the integrity of the election, and attempts to cast doubt on the legality of actions many election officials have taken. The allegations of fraud and impropriety cannot be squared with the historic gains we see in the House Republican Conference. Moreover, many of the allegations in the Amicus have already been ruled on by lower courts (and the Supreme Court has refused to intervene as well). These are not undisputed facts, these are serious allegations claiming people have violated the Constitution.

On the morning of December 10, Carr texted me that she had spoken with McCarthy and was "99% sure" he would *not* be signing on to the brief. She said McCarthy was also going to call Johnson and recommend that Johnson tell all the members who had asked to be included to "actually read the brief." McCarthy's chief of staff, Dan Meyer, described the brief to my chief of staff, Kara Ahern, as "a bait and switch." Members of Steve Scalise's staff likewise told my staff that they had advised Scalise not to sign.

House Republicans were holding a press conference that morning on the Capitol steps to highlight the damage Covid was doing to small businesses. As we gathered in the hallway outside the House chamber before the press event, McCarthy walked over to me and said, "Hey, I'm not signing on to the Texas brief. It federalizes too much."

"Good," I told him. "That's the right decision. We shouldn't be doing this."

When news broke a few hours later that the brief had been filed, I was glad to see that McCarthy had been true to his word. He hadn't signed on. As the day wore on, reporters noted that he refused to respond to questions about whether he agreed with the brief.

Then, less than 24 hours later, a revised version of the amicus brief was filed. It bore the names of 20 additional members. Among them was *Kevin McCarthy.*

Mike Johnson blamed a "clerical error" for the initial omission of these additional names. A "clerical error" was also the rationale given to the Supreme Court for the revised filing. In fact, McCarthy had first chosen not to be on the brief, then changed his mind, likely because of pressure from Trump.

A few hours after the revised brief was filed, the Supreme Court rejected the Texas lawsuit, which wasn't a surprise. One conservative legal analyst described the ruling this way, "The justices unanimously found no merit in the risible lawsuit that Texas petitioned to file against four battleground states won by Biden." He went on to note that, contrary to claims being made by Trump and his allies, even the two justices who thought the Court should have heard the case, Justices Alito and Thomas, agreed that the relief Texas was seeking should be denied.

Mike Johnson and our Republican leaders had played a destructive role. Johnson had convinced 125 other Republican members of Congress to sign on to an amicus brief that many had never read—a brief, moreover, that made numerous false factual and constitutional claims. Members signed on in the hope that it would show support for Trump—and out of fear of political retribution if their names were not on the list. Some who had shown an initial inclination to do the right thing, like

Kevin McCarthy, lost their fortitude when they faced public criticism—and, I assumed, private pressure from Trump.

Former House Speaker Paul Ryan told me he was glad I had not signed the brief, which he called an "ugly episode and low point of anti-conservatism." He was right.

I was surprised by the way Mike Johnson had conducted himself. I had worked closely with Mike over the last several years. We were elected to Congress together. His office was next door to mine in the Cannon House Office Building. I had encouraged him to run for conference vice chair. I considered him a friend.

But the amicus-brief episode revealed a side of Mike I had not seen before. He appeared especially susceptible to flattery from Trump and aspired to being anywhere in Trump's orbit. When I confronted him with the flaws in his legal arguments, Johnson would often concede, or say something to the effect of, "We just need to do this one last thing for Trump." He would then continue championing his arguments in public or with our colleagues. Worse, he was telling our colleagues he was a constitutional law expert, while advocating positions that were constitutionally infirm.

Mike Gallagher of Wisconsin, who had been elected to Congress the same year that Johnson and I had, described Johnson's behavior during this period as "destructive." Jamie Comer, Republican from Kentucky, texted me that he didn't think "Mike Johnson's lawsuit gimmick was helpful to our Conference."

After posing several questions to Mike, I ultimately learned that a team of lawyers who were also apparently advising Donald Trump had in fact drafted the amicus brief. Mike Johnson had left the impression that he was responsible for the brief, but he was just carrying Trump's water.

A couple of days after the Supreme Court rejected the Texas case, Mike and I spoke by phone. Although we had disagreed on the advisability and legality of the brief, I still hoped we might work together to forge a path forward, especially as we handled the constitutional issues related to the upcoming counting of electoral votes on January 6. He said he agreed with me that we were facing a perilous moment, and we needed to be aware of how serious and grave these constitutional issues were. I hung up thinking that the episode with the amicus brief might have chastened Johnson. Perhaps he could be counted on to help steer us through the coming weeks responsibly.

Shortly after our call, Mike texted me to thank me for the outreach and to reiterate that he agreed with me about the peril of the moment. Then he attached a statement he had issued about the Supreme Court's rejection of the Texas petition—a statement that attacked the Supreme Court and misrepresented what it had just done. Mike's statement ended on this ominous note:

> So much for the rule of law. The chaos will continue now. This should concern every American—no matter what party you're in. Heaven help us.

This was ludicrous. Conservatives held a 6-to-3 advantage on the Supreme Court, and three of those conservative justices had been appointed by Donald Trump. Not one of them had agreed with Mike—*not one*.

I told Mike his statement was wrong, and that it was dangerous to accuse the Supreme Court of throwing out the rule of law: "Our words matter and we need to take care to be truthful and not increase the peril." The Court's recent ruling was straightforward and unsurprising, and limited to whether one state could bring an original action for alleged failures by other states to comply with their own election laws. Of course, Texas could not do that. Johnson was criticizing the Supreme Court for doing what it is bound by the Constitution to do. This was reckless and wrong.

Once again, Johnson said he didn't disagree with me. But then he sent me a Fox News Poll showing that 77 percent of Trump voters and 68 percent of Republicans believed the election had been stolen from Trump. "These numbers are big," Johnson remarked. "And something we have to contend with as we thread the needle on messaging."

Of course, Donald Trump's public campaign to spread false allegations of massive election fraud had *created* those polling numbers. And when members of Congress and other elected Republicans echoed his stolen-election claims, or accused the Supreme Court of throwing out the rule of law, those falsehoods had an impact on polling results because some people believed the lies.

This was about something far more important than messaging. "The issues we are dealing with now go to the heart of the survival of the republic," I responded to Johnson. "We can't play politics."

Once the Supreme Court ruled on the Texas suit, Donald Trump appeared to have no further recourse in the courts. He had lost almost every case, and the election litigation was all but over.

Everything could have ended at this juncture. Nearly every one of Donald Trump's senior advisers thought he should concede. Instead, Trump resolved to escalate this into what soon became a constitutional crisis.

4. THE BLOOD OF PATRIOTS & TYRANTS

ON SATURDAY, DECEMBER 12, SITTING at my kitchen counter, I opened my laptop and began watching coverage of the "Women for America First" rally being held on Freedom Plaza in Washington, DC. This was one of several pro-Trump rallies being held in the District that day. As the lawsuits by Trump and his allies kept failing, including on December 11 in the Supreme Court, Trump had continued to make blatantly false claims that the election was rigged and stolen. He often tweeted more than 20 times in a single day, repeating his debunked assertions. And his false ads alleging election fraud were only reinforcing those lies. Furious with the Supreme Court, Trump continued to launch assaults on justices, judges, and elected officials across the country. Shortly before the Freedom Plaza event began, he tweeted, "WE HAVE JUST BEGUN TO FIGHT!"

What was he talking about? What was he urging people to do? This was no longer about getting his day in court. He'd had his day, and he lost. With each new tweet, he seemed to be making it clear that he did not plan to abide by the rulings of the courts. I wanted to see exactly what the speakers were telling people to do on Trump's behalf.

Just after President Trump did a flyover in the presidential helicopter, *Marine One*, Katrina Pierson, a senior adviser for the Trump campaign, took the stage. She exhorted the crowd to "fight like patriots," claiming that the courts and all the institutions of government had been "weaponized against us." She said:

We the people will determine how this ends. We will use our system, the system that was founded by our forefathers, the system that was designed to protect us from exactly what is happening today. We will utilize that system to the very end, and then if that doesn't work, we will take our country back.... If you think for one second that sleepy Joe Biden is going to fake his way into the White House, then you haven't been paying attention.... We are the cavalry.

The phrase "utilize that system to the very end, and then if that doesn't work, we will take our country back" was striking. In a constitutional republic, a candidate can utilize the system to the very end, and if that doesn't work, they concede. What Pierson was suggesting was something else entirely—and it sounded unconstitutional.

General Michael Flynn, who had received a presidential pardon from Donald Trump less than a month earlier, spoke shortly after Pierson. When Flynn stepped up to speak, he said he was absolutely confident that Donald Trump would remain president. He then took aim, as Pierson had, at the rule of law: "The courts do not decide who the next president of the United States of America will be. We the people decide."

Of course the people had already decided, but speaker after speaker at the rally suggested that Americans were going to rise up—that there was some action they could take that would change the results. Some invoked religion, calling Donald Trump "our anointed one," proclaiming that "a group of wicked men...have stolen our Republic" and that "this is our 1776" as they called on listeners to rise up in an ultimate fight of good vs. evil. One speaker quoted Thomas Jefferson—"The tree of liberty must be refreshed from time to time with the blood of patriots & tyrants"—and then suggested that meant the election results could not stand, claiming, "If we do not rise now as a people, we will never rise again in this country."

I played some of the comments back for my husband when he walked into the kitchen. "It sounds like they're advocating the violent overthrow of the government," Phil said.

Members of several militant groups—including the Oath Keepers, the Three Percenters, and the Proud Boys, all of whom would be involved in the violent attack on the US Capitol on January 6—participated in that day's pro-Trump rallies. Photos taken on the afternoon of December 12 show General Mike Flynn walking side by side with Stewart Rhodes and other Oath Keepers at the US Capitol. Rhodes was later convicted of seditious conspiracy (plotting to overthrow the US government) for his role in the events of January 6.

At the other end of Pennsylvania Avenue, Proud Boys leader Enrique Tarrio was visiting the White House that day. Tarrio, who would also later be convicted of seditious conspiracy for his involvement in January 6, posted a picture of himself at the White House on the social-media platform Parler, claiming that he had received "a last minute invite to an undisclosed location." The White House denied that Tarrio had met with the president, or that he had been invited by the White House. A spokesman said he was merely on a "public White House Christmas tour."

Someone invited him, and someone cleared him in, even if it was just for a tour. And Tarrio himself thought the visit was significant, saying, it "shows we've come a long way." It was hard to believe this was a coincidence.

In an email to McCarthy counsel Machalagh Carr the next morning, December 13, I summed up the situation this way: "I am deeply concerned, having watched the speeches at the Trump rally on the Mall yesterday, and listening to the President's continued claims, that this has gone far beyond petitioning a court for relief. Speakers on the Mall were calling for rebellion."

The Electoral College met in all 50 states on Monday, December 14, to formally cast their votes for president and vice president. As had been clear for weeks, Joe Biden and Kamala Harris won, and it was not even close. Many Republicans in the House and Senate—including Wyoming senators Mike Enzi, John Barrasso, and I—issued statements affirming that the election was over.

I texted Senate GOP Leader Mitch McConnell to ask if he was going to issue a statement. He called me to say he would be speaking on the Senate floor the next day, acknowledging that the election was over and congratulating President-elect Biden and Vice President-elect Harris. He told me he also alerted White House Chief of Staff Mark Meadows and House Republican Leader Kevin McCarthy before he spoke.

Leader McConnell's remarks on December 15 could have served as a model for Donald Trump—had Trump been inclined to respect the sanctity of our election process and the obligations of his oath to the Constitution. McConnell devoted the first eight minutes of his ten-minute address to detailing the major accomplishments of the Trump administration. Then he turned to the presidential election:

> Six weeks ago, Americans voted in this year's general election. The legal and constitutional processes have continued to play out. Yesterday, electors met in all 50 states. So, as of this morning, our country has officially a President-elect and a Vice-President-elect. Many millions of us had hoped the presidential election would yield a different result. But our system of government has processes to determine who will be sworn in on January the 20th. The Electoral College has spoken.

In other words, it was over.

I didn't know it at the time, but many senior members of Trump's White House staff, including his White House Counsel, also recognized the election was over. They believed it was time for Trump to concede. Trump's Secretary of Labor Gene Scalia, son of the revered conservative Supreme Court Justice Antonin Scalia, called Trump after the Electoral College met and told him that "what had to be done was concede the outcome." Trump refused. He and his allies in Congress had other plans.

Jim Jordan was using his position as ranking Republican on the House Judiciary Committee to help carry out those plans. On December 17, a Republican member of the committee called to alert me that Jordan had convened a meeting of all the committee's Republican members the night before. The purpose of the meeting was to discuss what would happen on January 6 during the joint session when Congress counts electoral votes. By this point, we knew that some House members would likely object to certain states' electoral votes, but no senators had yet announced their intention to object. (Without a senator's support, objections would have no impact because they couldn't be debated or voted on.)

Jordan had reportedly told the Judiciary Committee Republicans that Senator Josh Hawley from Missouri would likely join the objectors. I knew that Mitch McConnell had been working hard to keep any senators from objecting, so I texted him to let him know what Jordan was saying about Hawley.

A few days later, Hawley announced publicly that he would object, becoming the first senator to do so—and paving the way for a protracted joint session, at the very least. Hawley was also setting the stage for whatever Trump had planned for that day.

In the days since I had watched Mike Flynn speak at the December 12 pro-Trump rally, I had been paying particular attention to any additional public comments Flynn was making. On December 17, Flynn was interviewed by Greg Kelly on Newsmax. In one segment of the interview, Kelly said:

> So, I hear some murmurings, you know, about the staff shake-up at the Pentagon. They're putting people in place who might not be opposed to aggressive action.

Kelly then asked Flynn what the president's options might be. Flynn said:

> [Trump] could immediately, on his order, seize every single one of these [voting] machines around the country, on his order. He could also order... within the swing states, if he wanted to, he could take military capabilities and he could place them in those states and basically re-run an election in each of those states.

Flynn went on to say that "martial law" had been imposed "64 times" in the past. But it certainly had never been imposed to "basically re-run an election" in swing states. Flynn noted that, "We have a constitutional process" that has to be followed. But the constitutional process had already *been* followed. Governors had certified the votes in each state, and the Electoral College had already met and voted. What exactly was Flynn urging Trump to do?

————

I sent a portion of Flynn's statement to a retired Army four-star general with whom I had worked closely for a number of years. His response: "Good God. That is completely delusional and grossly irresponsible."

Flynn's Newsmax interview prompted the press to make inquiries to the Department of Defense. In response, Secretary of the Army Ryan McCarthy and Army Chief of Staff General James McConville issued a statement repeating what the Chairman of the Joint Chiefs, General Mark Milley, had said several months earlier: "There is no role for the US military in determining the outcome of an American election."

The DOD statement — which was factual and should have been unobjectionable — enraged Donald Trump. He instructed the director of White House personnel, Johnny McEntee, to call Acting Secretary of Defense Chris Miller, apparently to convey the message that if any further statements like this were made, the officials would be fired. Secretary McCarthy later testified to the Select Committee that Miller had called him from an airplane on the morning of Saturday, December 19 to deliver that message. McCarthy said he understood he would be fired if any other statements like this were issued. After he spoke with McCarthy, Miller called McEntee back and confirmed that he had delivered the message, whereupon McEntee wrote a note to President Trump: "CHRIS MILLER SPOKE TO BOTH OF THEM AND ANTICIPATES NO MORE STATEMENTS COMING OUT (IF ANOTHER HAPPENS, HE WILL FIRE THEM.)"

By the time the January 6th Select Committee obtained McEntee's note to Trump, it had been ripped into four pieces — most likely by Donald Trump, trying to destroy any record of it.

Had I known about the note and the exchange of calls between McEntee and Miller at the time they were occurring, I would have been even more alarmed. McEntee's calls leave little doubt that Donald Trump was in fact considering deploying our military for some election-related purpose. These calls, and McEntee's note, also coincided with a now-famous White House meeting on December 18.

News of the highly contentious December 18 meeting broke the next day. Flynn had been at the White House, along with Sidney Powell and Rudy Giuliani, and it was clear that an angry fight had broken out in front of Trump. White House Counsel Pat Cipollone, White House lawyer Eric Herschmann, and Staff Secretary Derek Lyons discovered soon after the meeting began that Flynn, Powell, and others were in the Oval Office. The White House officials rushed to crash the gathering, and a great deal of furious yelling ensued, with Trump's White House lawyers aggressively objecting to every course of action that the visitors were recommending—which, we learned later, involved some of the ideas that Mike Flynn had proposed in his December 17 Newsmax interview.

In the early hours of December 19, when the meeting finally ended, Donald Trump summoned his supporters to Washington, DC, tweeting: "Big protest in D.C. on January 6th. Be there, will be wild!"

———

Marjorie Taylor Greene had not yet been sworn in to Congress when she joined several Republican members for a January 6 planning meeting with Donald Trump on December 21, 2020. I was alerted to the meeting when Machalagh Carr forwarded me a tweet by a Capitol Hill reporter: "SPOTTED in the West Wing today: GOP members like @mtgreenee, @mattgaetz, @Jim_Jordan, @RepMoBrooks, @replouiegohmert. They met with the president, multiple sources told me."

Mike Johnson also texted me about the meeting. He had been trying unsuccessfully to reach members of the Freedom Caucus that day. "Just realized why they wouldn't call me today," Johnson texted. "Fox News reporting a group of Members just had a strategy meeting with Trump at the WH..." He forwarded a video that Marjorie Taylor Greene had just tweeted out.

Speaking to the camera, Greene says:

Just finished with our meetings here at the White House this afternoon. We had a great planning session for our January 6th objection. We aren't going to let this election be stolen by Joe Biden and the Democrats. President Trump won by a landslide. Call your House reps. Call your senators from your states. We've got to make sure they're on board, and we already have a lot of people engaged. Okay, stay tuned.

In her tweet, Greene said, "We have a rapidly growing group of House Members and Senators. Jan 6 challenge is on." I responded to Johnson:

Hope they understand the personal legal peril for each of them of plotting to overthrow the results of an election by, for example, urging POTUS to impose martial law in swing states.

"Yep," Johnson responded. "At least Jenna is starting to see the light." (Johnson was forwarding me an article quoting Jenna Ellis saying she did not support invoking the Insurrection Act.)

Over this same period, I had been reading Ted Widmer's book *Lincoln on the Verge,* about Abraham Lincoln's train trip to Washington to be sworn in as president in 1861. Widmer describes the scene at the US Capitol on February 13, 1861, when the electoral votes were counted. Pro-Southern militias were gathering in Washington, raising concerns they might attempt to invade the Capitol and stop the vote count. Vice President John Breckinridge of Kentucky, who would later become the Confederate secretary of war, was to preside over the proceedings. Some feared that he would fail to do his duty—that he might refuse to recognize Lincoln's victory when the electoral votes were counted. Another fear was that Southern sympathizers might attempt to steal the votes as they were carried through the Capitol Building from the Senate to the House, preventing them from being counted (and thus stopping Lincoln from being officially declared president). Police were searching the Capitol basement each night for bombs.

This made for chilling reading in December of 2020. I remember thinking, *At least this isn't 1861.* With all the uncertainty about what Trump was doing, I took some comfort—false, as it turned out—in the idea that at least we didn't have to be concerned about a Capitol invasion.

Yet I was worried about all the plans the president and some of my colleagues seemed to be making to disrupt our joint session. What did President Trump expect to do with the crowd of supporters he was summoning to Washington? Would they try to disrupt or delay the electoral count on January 6? How? Would there be a bomb threat? If someone called in a bomb threat and the Capitol was evacuated, were arrangements in place for Congress to meet somewhere else? How would we ensure we could complete our work?

On December 22, I reached out to both Mitch McConnell and Kevin McCarthy to discuss these concerns and find out if adequate security plans were in place. I texted McCarthy shortly before 8:00 p.m.: "Things seem to be going off the rails fast, and a potentially dangerous set of circumstances developing. Can you give me a call." A few hours later, he responded that he was just getting out of surgery. We were unable to connect that night.

Mitch McConnell and I spoke around 8:00 p.m. We discussed what we were hearing and seeing. We were both aware of what Trump had been saying, and I told him about watching the incendiary speeches at the December 12 rally—the attacks on the rule of law, and the open calls for people to rise up and fight. He too was worried. He had been tracking plans to ensure that Congress could meet in joint session away from the Capitol, if necessary. He also said there would be significant security at the Capitol, including a large contingent of Secret Service agents because Vice President Pence would be in attendance.

Trump's behavior that night was increasingly erratic. He had posted a video calling the Covid relief package, which his administration had supported, a "disgrace" and detailing what he called "wasteful and unnecessary items." Many of the line items that Trump attacked were the same ones he had asked Congress to fund in his official budget. Now he was using them as justification to threaten to veto the bill.

Staffers in the White House office of legislative affairs were contacting Hill staffers to distance themselves from the president's behavior. One sent the video to my chief of staff, Kara Ahern, along with a note that said, "...we got Tipped off about 5 min b4 this dropped and tried [to] kill it but... I'm sorry."

At 8:08 p.m. on the 22nd, Trump posted a video attacking Ruby Freeman and her daughter, Shaye Moss, two poll workers in Georgia. The video repeated false claims about ballot counting in Georgia and accused Freeman and Moss of illegal activity. Trump's unfounded public attacks against Freeman and Moss resulted in terrifying harassment and death threats, ultimately putting both women in serious danger.

An hour later, Trump posted a 10-minute video to Facebook. Speaking from the diplomatic reception rooms in the White House, he went on an angry tirade, making the same false claims that had been disproven time and time again about a "thundering Trump victory," a "monstrous fraud," and "big and very illegal ballot drops."

We convened a call of the Republican Conference on December 23. Many members were angry. After the administration had requested funds for some of the very programs that Trump was now criticizing and gotten Republican members to sign on to a negotiated deal, Trump was hanging everyone out to dry — blaming members for supporting a deal his own treasury secretary had negotiated. At the same time, Trump was suddenly attacking members for supporting $600 Covid checks, arguing they weren't large enough.

McCarthy told us that he had talked to Trump, and that he was trying to convince him not to veto the spending bill. But Trump was still threatening to do so.

While our conference call was underway, I started getting texts from members alerting me to another potential crisis: "Did Trump just veto the NDAA?" asked one.

Indeed, he had.

The NDAA, or National Defense Authorization Act, is the annual legislation authorizing the activities of every branch of our military. Because it is crucial legislation for the defense of the nation, it has passed on a bipartisan basis every year since 1961. In 2020, the NDAA passed the House by a vote of 295 to 125. Trump vetoed the bill because he was angry it did not include language related to liability protections for social-media companies. In other words, he vetoed a bill that authorized every program necessary for defending the United States because it didn't include controversial language unrelated to defense.

Congress overwhelmingly voted to override Trump's veto, by a margin of 322 to 87 in the House and by 81 to 13 in the Senate. Unwilling to stand up to Trump in support of the NDAA, Kevin McCarthy announced that he was following a principle most of us had never heard him mention before: that he would never vote to override a veto by a president of his own party. Kevin stayed in California rather than casting a vote.

Trump's erratic behavior with respect to the NDAA and the Covid relief package came against the backdrop of his refusal to concede the election and his replacement of the top civilian leadership at the Pentagon with inexperienced loyalists. Every day he was rage-tweeting stolen-election claims he knew were false, and he had followed up his December 19 tweet—the one calling his supporters to Washington for a "wild" protest on January 6—with many additional tweets repeating that invitation and stressing how important January 6 would be.

As state and federal courts continued to rule against him, Donald Trump ignored the rulings and plotted with his supporters in Congress. I wasn't sure exactly what they were planning. At times, it was like looking down from an airplane and trying to see the ground through heavy cloud cover. Occasional glimpses would come into view, but never the whole picture. What I was seeing was concerning enough that, as 2020 came to a close, I was working to determine what else I could do to intervene and stop him.

5.   THE OATH

As HOUSE REPUBLICAN CONFERENCE CHAIR, I was receiving daily questions from Republican members about all the lawsuits that Donald Trump and his allies had lost. Trump was ignoring these rulings. Members of the White House Counsel's office, White House staff, senior Trump officials in the Department of Justice, and members of Trump's presidential campaign were privately saying almost exactly what I was saying to my Republican colleagues—that Trump had had his day in court, and he had lost. The law firms that were initially part of his campaign's election-litigation team had quit. They refused to participate in the claims being made by Rudy Giuliani, Sidney Powell, and others.

Members were also asking me what would actually happen on January 6 in our joint session to count the electoral votes. Some of the confusion had been caused by Mike Johnson's amicus filing in the failed Texas case. Some of it was coming from our colleagues, including in the Freedom Caucus, who were claiming that Congress had the power to undo the election, to overrule the courts, and to choose the next president on January 6. That, of course, was nonsense. But it was obvious that President Trump, Rudy Giuliani, and others were pushing Republican members in that direction.

This was far more than a political debate. The question before us as we approached January 6 was whether we were going to abide by the oath we had all sworn to the Constitution.

———

Our founders risked everything in the revolution of 1776. But by the late 1780s, most knew very well that the Articles of Confederation—the first compact binding the new American states together—was failing. The men designated by their states to convene in Philadelphia in 1787 knew the lengthy history of failed efforts at democracy and representative government. As they debated a new Constitution, they were realistic about human motives—they knew that greed, partisanship (which they called *factionalism*), and the temptation of accumulated power might doom American freedom and the nascent American government. The framers of our Constitution therefore spent much of the summer of 1787 searching for the best and most durable way to secure our nation's newly won liberty.

In Article VI of our Constitution, the founders required that every member of Congress, all state legislators, and "all executive and judicial Officers" of the federal and state governments take an oath to support and defend the United States Constitution. For elected representatives, the oath must supersede any duty to represent their constituents. They must represent constituents' interests solely in a manner that complies with the representatives' paramount duty to the Constitution.

The president's oath is arguably the most consequential. The president has tremendous power to enforce his will—not only as our commander in chief, but as the constitutional officer who can command the actions of critical executive branch agencies. The founders had utmost confidence in the wisdom and grace of George Washington. But they were not convinced that every future president would be so honorable. This is why Article II of our Constitution details precisely what the president must pledge: to "faithfully execute the Office of President of the United States" and to "preserve, protect and defend the Constitution of the United States."

Under our Constitution, the president is selected by a separately organized group of Americans, called Electors, chosen nowadays through popular election in each state. The founders were concerned that a faction in Congress might conspire to control the selection of a president. They granted Congress what is, in most circumstances, only a ministerial role: counting the electoral votes that have been certified and transmitted to Washington by the individual states. As Alexander Hamilton explained in *Federalist 68,* "No senator, representative, or other person holding a place of trust or profit under the United States" can serve as a member of the Electoral College.

On more than one occasion, Supreme Court Justice Antonin Scalia lectured on what he regarded as the most important features of our Constitution—what he called the "real constitutional law." In the course of his remarks, Justice Scalia would read from one country's expansive bill of rights, which featured a long list of impressive-sounding protections of individual freedom. "Wonderful stuff," he would say, before disclosing that he'd been reading the text of the 1977 constitution of the communist Soviet Union. And that's when Justice Scalia would begin to explain what truly protects American freedom: the "structural provisions of our Constitution, principally the separation of powers and federalism." He would explain that no bill of rights, standing alone, is sufficient to ensure liberty:

> They are what the Framers of our Constitution called "parchment guarantees," because the real constitutions of those countries—the provisions that establish the institutions of government—do not prevent the centralization of power in one man or one party, thus enabling the guarantees to be ignored. Structure is everything....
>
> Those who seek to protect individual liberty ignore threats to this constitutional structure at their peril.

I believe that Donald Trump's decision to attack the lawfully certified Electoral College results and to ignore the rulings of our courts was an assault on the structural constitutional safeguards that keep us free.

———

As January 6 approached, I knew I needed to circulate a concise explanation of all these issues to my Republican colleagues. Over the Christmas holiday, I recruited my husband, Phil, to help me draft a memorandum for the House Republican Conference. It would clarify what the Constitution required of us on January 6, and explain how the courts had ruled in the election challenges. Phil had served in the US Department of Justice, as the general counsel of two federal agencies, and he had litigated constitutional and federal regulatory issues for many years as a partner in a law firm. I also spoke with several of my colleagues, as well as current and former staff members.

Phil and I spent several days rereading the principal judicial rulings in the election litigation. We walked through all the constitutional arguments, and reread the Federalist Papers that addressed these issues. None of this was a close call. Over a few days we compiled a 21-page memorandum that spelled it out succinctly. The simple conclusion: Congress does *not* have the authority to undo an election by refusing to count state-certified electoral votes. Period.

As the Constitution requires, Congress's role in this specific context is ministerial only: Congress counts the certified electoral votes. The 12th Amendment is very clear in these circumstances: "The President of the Senate shall, in the presence of the Senate and House of Representatives, open all the certificates and the votes shall then be counted; The person having the greatest number of votes for President, shall be the President. . . ." As our 21-page memo explained:

> Nothing in the Constitution remotely says that Congress is the court of last resort, with the authority to second-guess and invalidate state and federal court judicial rulings in election challenges. Indeed, the Constitutional text reads: "The person having the greatest Number of [Electoral College] votes for President, shall be the President." It does not say: "The person having the greatest Number of [Electoral College] votes for President, shall be the President, *unless Congress objects or Congress wants to investigate.*" The Constitution identifies specifically the *only* occasions when Congress can take any non-ministerial action — when no Presidential candidate has a majority of the electoral votes. . . .

Thus, the Constitutional text tells us very clearly what Congress' role is and is not.

In addition to the constitutional text, the Electoral Count Act of 1887 made clear that Congress was obligated to accept as "conclusive" each governor's official certification of the election outcome in their respective state. Congress had received only *one* official certified electoral slate from each state; those certifications were conclusive.*

After laying out the Constitution's requirements, our memorandum also summarized the outcomes of many of the key state and federal cases, including rulings against Trump by judges he had appointed. Many judges had been very clear about how unfounded Trump's fraud allegations were. One federal judge said this: "Allegations that find favor in the public sphere of gossip and innuendo cannot be a substitute for earnest pleadings and procedure in federal court. They most certainly cannot be the basis for upending Arizona's 2020 General Election." Another said, "[C]alling an election unfair does not make it so. Charges require specific allegations and then proof. We have neither here."

A number of other cases also addressed a common Trump argument — that state election officials had acted in a manner inconsistent with laws passed by the state legislatures. These issues were also resolved against Donald Trump: state officials were acting well within the authority expressly granted them by the legislatures. Only one case — which, as mentioned, had involved too few votes to impact the election outcome — came out in Trump's favor. There was no lawful way for Trump to prevail in the presidential election of 2020 once those 61 cases had concluded.

---

* While the Electoral Count Act had another provision allowing objections in other contexts, it did not apply here, and could not apply here consistent with the Constitution's clear text.

6. THE SECRETARIES OF DEFENSE

ON DECEMBER 26, AS PHIL and I worked on our memo, a column by *Washington Post* reporter David Ignatius caught my attention. Ignatius, a longtime journalist who was well-sourced at the Pentagon, reported that senior government officials feared that Trump was "threatening to overstep the constitutional limits on his power." One possibility Ignatius reported was that Trump might attempt to stay in power by using violence on January 6 as an excuse to invoke the Insurrection Act. Trump could then, Ignatius reported, take steps like the ones retired General Mike Flynn detailed in his December 17 Newsmax interview, including deploying the military to rerun the election in swing states.

Ignatius suggested the personnel changes Trump had made at the Pentagon since he lost the presidential election could be a sign that "pro-Trump officials might be mobilizing to secure levers of power." The potential domestic turmoil was occurring against a backdrop of danger overseas, including the Iranians firing rockets at the US Embassy compound in Baghdad and the upcoming anniversary of the US killing of Iranian Quds Force commander Qasem Soleimani. There was growing alarm about the potential for escalating violence overseas, as well as about what might happen here.

The possible scenario — described by Ignatius as "a multifaceted campaign by die-hard Trump supporters to use disruptions at home and perhaps threats abroad to advance" Trump's interests — was dangerous. And while Ignatius's concern was well-founded, his suggested solution did not seem realistic. Ignatius wrote: "[A] delegation of senior Republicans should visit [Trump] at the White House and insist, emphatically: Biden has won. This must stop."

As soon as I read the Ignatius piece, I texted Eric Edelman, and I called my dad to make sure he saw the piece, as well. The next morning, December 27, I went to my dad's house, and we called Eric together. We agreed that the concerns Ignatius described were well-founded. The question was what could be done.

Was there a group of elected Republicans who could deliver a stern warning to Trump in private? There were two problems with this.

First, there wasn't exactly a long line of Republican officials eager to take on such a mission. Most who understood the peril of the moment were quietly keeping their heads down, just hoping to get through to the Inauguration on January 20, after which Trump would be gone.

Second, even if we could come up with the right group, it was unlikely to do any good. By the end of December, it was clear that privately urging Trump to do the right thing was fruitless. He didn't care. I had had several firsthand experiences of sitting in the Oval Office, calmly trying to tell Donald Trump what he did not want to hear. I knew how he would respond. A private approach would not work. We needed a *public* warning to Trump, *and* to his new appointees at the Pentagon. And it needed to come from a leader or group of leaders who could not easily be ignored.

We decided to try to mobilize the former secretaries of defense. There were 10 living secretaries. What if all 10 of them would sign a letter of warning? It would be unprecedented, and it seemed our best chance of delivering a clear warning to the current leadership of the Defense Department, and to Trump himself. We divided up the list of former secretaries and started making calls.

Because Phil and I were still working on our legal memo for the House Republicans, Eric agreed to produce an initial draft of the letter. He also sought the assistance of Eliot Cohen, a scholar, historian, and expert on civilian-military relations. As we edited the draft, we knew the letter needed to leave no doubt that any official who attempted to utilize the military to overturn an election would be personally accountable for a grave attack on the republic.

With my dad on board, we divvied up the remaining nine former secretaries. I agreed to contact Mattis, Panetta, and Rumsfeld. Eric, meanwhile, would reach out to Secretaries Carter, Cohen, Esper, Gates, Hagel, and Perry. I also called retired General Jack Keane, former vice chief of staff of the Army. Keane had served as a trusted adviser to my dad for many years. We'd spoken in the weeks since the election, including about Mike Flynn's statements, and now I wanted his advice on this matter too. I explained what we were doing, and asked for his help in connecting with Jim Mattis.

A short while later I spoke to General Mattis. I described what we were seeing and hearing and why we thought this unprecedented public statement was necessary. He agreed immediately and told me where to send the draft letter for his review.

Next I texted Jimmy Panetta, a friend and colleague who had been elected to the House of Representatives in 2016, the same year I was. I told him I had a time-sensitive matter I needed to discuss with his father, former Defense Secretary Leon Panetta, and I asked Jimmy if he could put us in touch. Less than 15 minutes later, Secretary Panetta called me. Like my dad and Secretary Rumsfeld, Panetta had been a congressman and White House chief of staff as well as secretary of defense. He had been following developments at the Pentagon since the election. He did not hesitate to join our effort.

Eric Edelman contacted me not long after. He had reached former Secretary Bob Gates, who had served as defense secretary in both the George W. Bush and Obama administrations. "If Cheney's on, I'm on," Gates told him.

When the draft of the letter was done, we began sending it to the former secretaries for their edits and approval. My dad decided that he also wanted to call Don Rumsfeld and read the letter to him over the phone. Their relationship stretched back over 50 years. They were very close, and the gravity of this unprecedented public warning was something my dad wanted to discuss with Rumsfeld directly.

As my dad dialed Rumsfeld's home in Taos, New Mexico, I took a seat across the desk from him. It was New Year's Eve. A fire was burning in the fireplace in my dad's study. The sword his great-grandfather had carried through four years of the Civil War hung above the mantel. The

Presidential Medal of Freedom, which President George H. W. Bush had awarded him for his leadership in Desert Storm, hung on the opposite wall. We were surrounded by family photos, historical maps, and his beloved books about our nation's history.

Rumsfeld came on the line, along with his daughter Marcy. As I listened to my dad read the letter, the gravity and peril of the moment were palpable. He began:

> As former secretaries of defense, we hold a common view of the solemn obligations of the U.S. armed forces and the Defense Department. Each of us swore an oath to support and defend the Constitution against all enemies, foreign and domestic. We did not swear it to an individual or a party.
>
> American elections and the peaceful transfers of power that result are the hallmarks of our democracy. With one singular and tragic exception that cost the lives of more Americans than all of our other wars combined, the United States has had an unbroken record of such transitions since 1789, including in times of partisan strife, war, epidemics, and economic depression. This year should be no exception.

The secretaries noted that election audits and recounts had occurred, challenges had been addressed by the courts, results had been certified, and the Electoral College had voted. Therefore, "The time for questioning the results has passed; the time for the formal counting of the electoral college votes, as prescribed in the Constitution and statute, has arrived." The letter then quoted the same Defense Department statement that had, a week or so earlier, apparently prompted Donald Trump to threaten to fire the secretary of the Army and the Army chief of staff:

> As senior Defense Department leaders have noted, "there's no role for the U.S. military in determining the outcome of a U.S. election." Efforts to involve the U.S. armed forces in resolving election disputes would take us into dangerous, unlawful and

unconstitutional territory. Civilian and military officials who direct or carry out such measures would be accountable, including potentially facing criminal penalties, for the grave consequences of their actions on our republic.

Accountability, and potential criminal penalties—that was the sober but necessary point.

Transitions at the Department of Defense are consequential for the security of our nation. There can be no partisanship as authority is handed from one administration to the next. The former secretaries reminded the acting secretary of defense *by name* of his solemn duty to ensure a full, cooperative, and transparent transition of presidential power:

Acting defense secretary Christopher C. Miller and his subordinates—political appointees, officers and civil servants—are each bound by oath, law and precedent to facilitate the entry into office of the incoming administration, and to do so wholeheartedly. They must also refrain from any political actions that undermine the results of the election or hinder the success of the new team.

We call upon them, in the strongest terms, to do as so many generations of Americans have done before them. This final action is in keeping with the highest traditions and professionalism of the U.S. armed forces, and the history of democratic transition in our great country.

When my dad finished reading, he paused. Rumsfeld said he would sign on. Then Marcy spoke up, her voice breaking with emotion: "Thank God someone is finally doing something."

The next day, Phil, the kids, and I went to my parents' house for a New Year's Day lunch. As we were leaving, my father came outside to the driveway. He walked around to the passenger side of my car and gave me a hug. Then he looked at me and with steel in his voice said, "Defend the republic, daughter."

"I will, Dad," I said. "Always."

7. JUST HUMOR HIM

AT 3:00 P.M. ON JANUARY 1, we had a call for House Republicans, including new members who had just been elected for the first time. We discussed arrangements for the January 3 opening session of the 117th Congress, as well as the January 6 joint session when the House and Senate would meet together to count the electoral votes.

Following opening remarks by Kevin McCarthy and Steve Scalise, I told members I would be circulating a memo summarizing the rulings in the key election-litigation cases and detailing our constitutional obliga- tion to count the electoral votes on January 6. I explained why we had no authority to object to electoral votes. And I stressed to members that this was likely the most consequential vote we would ever cast. The election was over. Trump had had his day in court and lost. The Electoral College had met and voted. We had a single certified slate of electors signed by the governor of each state. Objecting to these electors would be claiming for Congress the right to overturn elections and select the president. Nothing in the Constitution gave us that authority. Those who were objecting might be trying to tell themselves it was no big deal, but in reality it could not have been a bigger deal. We could not act in a way that we knew to be contrary to the Constitution. I urged all our members to think very care- fully about the ramifications of objecting to electoral votes.

As I was speaking, colleagues on the call began texting me messages of support for the position I had outlined, and gratitude for my willingness to explain why we could not vote to object. Typical was this text from Kelly Armstrong of North Dakota: "Thank you. Thank you. Thank you."

When I finished, Kevin McCarthy spoke up again. "Liz is speaking only for herself," he said. He wanted everyone to know that my views did not reflect a formal leadership position. This naturally led members to press Kevin for *his* views. If Liz is not speaking for leadership, they wanted to know, then who is? Do your views differ from hers?

Kevin tried to dodge the questions, but members would not let him off the hook. We were facing a historically consequential vote. I had just explained why the Constitution did not authorize us to object. Members justifiably wanted to know what the House Republican leader's position was. How could he be refusing to answer?

As members continued to press him, Kevin adopted a surprising approach: He lashed out at those asking for his view. Referring to the individualized card each member of Congress uses to cast their votes in the machines on the House floor, Kevin suggested anyone asking for his view should hand over their voting card. "If you're so concerned with what I think," he bristled, "why don't you just give me your voting cards? I'd be happy to vote for you."

The queue of members in line to ask questions started to grow. Members who had already spoken were getting back in line, requesting more time to speak; they were angry that Kevin was being so evasive—and so condescending—about his position. "Stop talking about our voting cards, Kevin," one said. "No one wants to give you their voting card. You're the leader. This is a crucial vote. We have a right to know your view on it."

While the tense exchange was underway, Adam Kinzinger texted me: "Kevin is scared to death." He was right; Kevin never did answer the question that day.

The incoming freshmen members were particularly worried about what they should do. They had not even been sworn in yet, and they were going to have to cast what would likely be the most important vote of their careers in an atmosphere of intense political drama and pressure. They were looking for guidance. I heard from several of them that Kevin was advising them to object and telling them the vote really wasn't a big deal. Objecting was the safe thing politically. It would keep Trump happy, and, besides, what harm could it do? McCarthy was also describing the potential political cost to members who refused to object—telling them he would be unable to protect them from primary-election challenges.

When I heard what Kevin was telling freshmen members, it reinforced what I had earlier concluded about his refusal to explain his position on our conference call. Kevin McCarthy was essentially telling members of Congress to ignore their constitutional obligations and, instead, do what Trump wanted. It was no wonder he preferred to deliver this message in small groups only.

By contrast, former Speaker Paul Ryan issued a public statement that left no doubt about the potential danger of objections to electoral votes. He said, in part:

> All our basic rights and freedoms flow from a fidelity to the Constitution and the rule of law. This principle is not only fundamentally American but a central tenet of conservatism. Under our system, voters determine the President, and this self-governance cannot sustain itself if the whims of Congress replace the will of the people. I would urge members to consider the precedent that it would set. Efforts to reject the votes of the Electoral College and sow doubt about Joe Biden's victory strike at the foundation of our republic. It is difficult to conceive of a more anti-democratic and anti-conservative act than a federal intervention to overturn the results of state-certified elections and disenfranchise millions of Americans.

Ryan had heard about my presentation on the January 1 House Republican call and told me he regretted that it took the No. 3 person in leadership to say the right thing. I appreciated his clear and unequivocal public statement and hoped it would remind more of our members what was at stake and what their duty required.

Over in the Senate on January 2, Ted Cruz, along with Senators Blackburn, Braun, Daines, Johnson, Kennedy, and Lankford—as well as Senators-elect Hagerty, Lummis, Marshall, and Tuberville—announced that they would object to electors from "disputed states." They released a joint statement containing no evidence of any fraud or irregularities. Nor did they name the states whose electors they would be voting to throw out, saying instead that they would "reject the electors from disputed states." They would be doing so because of the "unprecedented allegations" of fraud and irregularities in the 2020 election.

It was true that there had been unprecedented *allegations* about the 2020 election. Donald Trump and his allies had spent months making these allegations, spreading stolen-election lies they knew to be false. The senators cited a poll showing that 39 percent of Americans *believed* "the election was rigged." In other words, these 11 senators were taking the position that because Donald Trump had successfully spread falsehoods about election fraud, and because a poll showed many people believed those falsehoods, Congress could refuse to do what the Constitution explicitly required.

Cruz proposed a 10-day "audit" that would have violated both the Constitution and the Electoral Count Act. The text of the 12th Amendment clearly requires that the counting process occur immediately, including in this directive: "The President of the Senate shall... open all the certificates and the votes shall *then* be counted." Ted Cruz and his fellow senators surely knew that. They also surely knew about all the state audits, recounts, and litigation that had already addressed—and rejected—Trump's allegations. And they knew that no new multistate "audit" could ever be conducted in anything close to 10 days, much less that the "commission" they were proposing could meet to review and report on the audit results during that period. A later re-audit of Arizona's votes, for example, required *several months* and found no election fraud.

Had Congress attempted to follow Cruz's proposal, chaos would have ensued—potentially with no presidential transition on January 20 and no constitutional process to resolve the crisis. As we know now, Cruz had coordinated this proposal with the White House. Our Select Committee investigation later uncovered text messages about the "audit" scheme between Ted Cruz and White House Chief of Staff Mark Meadows.

As is typical for Cruz, he was grandstanding for his own benefit. It was one of the worst cases of abandonment of duty for personal ambition

I've ever seen in Washington. Judge J. Michael Luttig, for whom Ted Cruz had clerked after law school, described it this way: "Such is Republican politics of the moment, that presidential and congressional aspirants will purchase the former president's blessing and approval at any price."

On January 3, I circulated my 21-page memo to all my House Republican colleagues. The memo provided members with detailed information making clear there was no ambiguity about our constitutional obligations. If they objected to certified state electoral slates now, they would be doing so *knowing* that their actions were unconstitutional and *knowing* that the courts had already concluded there was no legal or factual basis for doing so.

8. MORE SINISTER THAN I WAS PREPARED FOR

THE 117TH CONGRESS FORMALLY CONVENED on January 3, 2021. The proceedings that day had already been touched by tragedy. Luke Letlow, a 41-year-old father of two young children who had been elected in Louisiana's 5th District, had died of complications from Covid just days before he could be sworn in. And Tommy Raskin—the beloved son of Maryland Congressman Jamie and his wife, Sarah—had died by suicide on December 31, 2020.

As conference chair, it was my responsibility on January 3 to give the speech nominating Kevin McCarthy as the Republican candidate for Speaker. This was a pro forma task, but I wanted to acknowledge the unimaginable losses suffered by the Letlow and Raskin families, and call on our common humanity—at a time that felt dangerous and hate-filled—to be kind to one another and remember we are all God's children. I included this quote from an 19th-century Quaker missionary in my remarks:

> I expect to pass through this world but once. If, therefore, there can be any kindness I can show or any good thing I can do my fellow being; let me do it now. Let me not defer or neglect it, for I shall not pass this way again.

When I finished speaking, Democratic Leader Steny Hoyer came over to me. "Jamie Raskin is here," he said. "He's in my office. Can you come see him?"

I followed Steny up the aisle and out of the House chamber to the majority leader's office next door. Jamie was there, surrounded by several of our colleagues. I could not imagine the crushing pain he was feeling. All I wanted to do was give him a hug. I reached out to embrace him. "No hugs!" I heard from the corner of the room, as one of our colleagues stepped out from behind a desk to intervene. Covid had made even that basic human comfort impossible.

After a few moments with Jamie, I walked back into the Republican cloakroom next to the House floor. While I was in the cloakroom, Phil called to tell me he had just talked to Acting Attorney General Jeff Rosen, an extremely capable lawyer and a principled man. During the Bush administration, Phil and Jeff had both served as Senate-confirmed general counsels for federal agencies. They worked together often, shared similar policy views, and had been friends for nearly 20 years.

The previous day, Phil and I had called Jeff to relay our security concerns surrounding January 6. It was increasingly clear that efforts were underway to disrupt or delay the counting of the electoral votes, and we worried that a bomb threat or some other tactic might be used to halt the count. Phil mentioned the security measures that had been put in place around the White House in the aftermath of 9/11. Jeff told us that they were planning to have extra Justice Department security assets available at a nearby military base. These could be quickly mobilized in case the US Capitol Police required assistance. He also said they were actively tracking the numbers of people coming into the city in an effort to predict how big the crowd was likely to be.

Twenty-four hours later, Jeff reached out to Phil to speak again. Without divulging any details, Jeff said he was going to a White House meeting that evening and he thought he might be fired. Later we would learn far more about what transpired in the Oval Office that night. Trump had replaced Rosen with Jeffrey Clark in the position of acting attorney general because, unlike Rosen or other DOJ leadership, Clark was willing to issue the type of Justice Department statement that Trump wanted—a statement indicating that the 2020 presidential election had likely been corrupted.

The rest of the Department of Justice senior leadership said they would resign if Clark took over from Rosen. So did Trump's White House Counsel. Facing the prospect of widespread resignations at the Justice Department, in the White House Counsel's office, and perhaps elsewhere in his administration, Trump ultimately backed down and abandoned the Clark appointment.

At about 1:00 in the afternoon of the 3rd, audio of President Trump's January 2 phone call with Brad Raffensperger, Georgia's Republican secretary of state, became public. This was the infamous call in which Trump pressured Raffensperger to "find" enough votes to flip the state from Biden to Trump. To his credit, Raffensperger calmly resisted every effort Trump made, explaining point by point why Trump was wrong— even when Trump suggested that Raffensperger and his counsel were risking criminal liability.

When I saw reports about the call, I assumed the audio of Trump pressuring state officials to violate the law and overturn the election would mean the end of most of the objections in the House. I couldn't imagine members would continue to do Trump's bidding. A short time later, after what we all assumed was significant pressure from Donald Trump, Kevin McCarthy announced he would be voting to object. I was certain that Kevin did not believe the objections were constitutional, nor that they could be justified by any genuine fraud in the election. His chief counsel clearly did not think so. But this had never really been about principle for Kevin.

Throughout this period I had also been in touch with Texas Congressman Chip Roy. Chip was firmly opposed, on constitutional grounds, to the effort to object to electoral votes. He was also willing to speak out.

At the beginning of a new Congress, a resolution is passed authorizing the Speaker to swear in new members. Normally this resolution passes by a voice vote, but in 2021 Chip Roy demanded a recorded vote. He was right to do so. If members were going to object to electoral votes on the grounds that elections in certain states had been tainted by fraud and irregularities—or on the grounds that certain states had administered the 2020 elections in a way that violated the US Constitution—how could members of Congress from those states simultaneously agree to recognize the legitimacy of their own elections and seat themselves? If there was systemic fraud, how could it be that their own elections — on the same ballots — were not likewise tainted? Chip wanted members on the record voting to seat themselves. This would show how baseless their claims about "constitutional infirmities" or fraud in the election really were. Only two members, Morgan Griffith of Virginia and Andy Harris of Maryland, voted against the resolution to seat the members.

When Chip texted me just before 5:30 to alert me he was going to call for a recorded vote, I told him it was the right thing to do. I also told him I understood there was "more bad stuff going on at DOJ" right now. We learned later that evening that Jeff Rosen had survived the White House meeting and had not been fired.

While I was in the cloakroom that afternoon, I also checked my email. The Trump campaign hadn't taken me off their email distribution list, so I received an invitation for a "briefing call for surrogates" about plans for the joint session on January 6. According to the email, the briefers would be "Rudy Giuliani, Personal Attorney to President Trump; Jenna Ellis, Senior Legal Advisor; and Jason Miller, Senior Advisor." The call was intended to prepare supporters to go on TV to defend Trump's strategy. I wanted to hear what Trump's team was telling them.

That evening I received a text from a well-known conservative legal analyst. He had been critical of Trump's strategy but hadn't fully recognized the danger of what was happening. Now he texted me to say, "You were right. I thought this was just a clown show. Wrong. I mean, it IS a clown show, but it's more sinister than I was prepared for."

9. FAKE ELECTORS

JENNA ELLIS KICKED OFF THE January 4 Trump "surrogate" call with a claim that seven states had "dueling slates of electors." This was a dangerous lie. Every state had certified a single slate of electors. Each governor had already transmitted that certified slate to Congress. In no state were there two official slates. The only way any state would have what Ellis was calling "dueling slates of electors" would be if the Trump campaign had created fraudulent slates and sent them in.

In the seven states with supposed "dueling electors," Jenna reported, there was "clear evidence" that the states had "violated their own laws." This too was a lie: There was no such evidence.

According to Jenna, this is where Vice President Mike Pence came in. Under our Constitution, the vice president is also president of the Senate, and presides over the joint session to count electoral votes. In the scenario Ellis described, when Pence was presiding, he could either refuse to open or refuse to count the electoral votes from states with multiple "dueling slates." Pence could do this, Ellis suggested, based on the objections that she expected would be made by Republican members of the Senate and House.

Ellis gave some examples of what Pence could say. For example, she suggested, Pence might announce, "I don't have in front of me a certification from these states" or "Which of these two slates have been certified as correct?" Then the vice president could refuse to count any votes for those states. This would, of course, have thrown our nation into turmoil.

Of course, this was not legal. There were no "dueling" slates of legitimate electors. Each state had submitted a single slate, certified by the governor as required by law. If Jenna Ellis or others on the Trump team had sent fraudulent slates of electors to Congress, they would be in serious legal jeopardy. And of course, contrary to Ellis's claim, the Trump campaign had provided no "clear evidence" that any state had violated its own laws. In fact, Trump and his supporters had gone to court scores of times and lost 60 out of 61 cases.

I had been hearing the false claims of fraud and the lies about what was constitutionally permissible on January 6 for weeks now, but this was the first time I had heard such a detailed description of how Donald Trump and his supporters actually planned to put their false claims into action. Ellis's description of what they anticipated the vice president would do was alarming: Was Mike Pence really going to stand at the dais in the House of Representatives and try to steal the 2020 election?

Then Jenna explained that some Republican members of Congress were already aware of these plans. She was saying out loud that this was a plan to obstruct or delay the lawful counting of electoral votes. And that some members of Congress were in on it.

Next she turned the call over to Jason Miller, a senior adviser for the Trump campaign. Miller described what he called "an uptick in activity" in calls from state legislatures to "address concerns." That was not even remotely true. The Trump campaign had been trying for weeks to coax state legislatures to change their votes. It was already well publicized that not a single one had done so. Miller described support for Trump's plan in Congress, saying it "goes all across the spectrum, from Jim Jordan to Elise Stefanik."

That's a pretty narrow spectrum, I thought. Although Elise Stefanik had once been a reasonable and thoughtful member of Congress, she had undergone a dramatic transition into a Trump sycophant over the past 18 months. There was no longer any difference between her and members like Matt Gaetz. I suspected Jim Jordan was deeply involved in this scheme. Was Elise also involved in the fake electoral slates and the Pence plan? I kept listening.

Jason Miller said that Republican objectors would be "calling out details of fraud and irregularities" and "working to overturn election results." Yet Miller *knew* then, as he was saying these things, that the campaign had no genuine evidence to prove the election had been stolen. Indeed, Miller was scrambling at the time to try to find any basis to support the Republican objections.

Pausing, Miller said, "What's the harm? What are the Democrats so afraid of?"

The harm? How about the shattering chaos that would ensue if the vice president refused to count certified electoral votes? We would be in completely uncharted territory. We would have no playbook. Having just lost a lawfully certified election, Trump was attempting to seize power unconstitutionally. If Pence had gone along, as one of the January 6 Select Committee witnesses later suggested, the conflict would very likely have been settled in the streets.

What Trump's team was describing on this call was illegal. It was destructive. And they all knew by then that the stolen-election allegations were "complete nonsense" and "BS," as Attorney General Barr and other Justice Department officials had repeatedly said. Yet here they were, trying it anyway.

As soon as the call ended, I went back inside the Capitol to the Office of the House Parliamentarian. The Parliamentarian is a nonpartisan career official, responsible for maintaining the precedents of the House and providing guidance to members on House rules and procedures. Jason Smith had recently been appointed to the post. Both he and his predecessor, Tom "Wick" Wickham, were in the office when I arrived. Wick had retired at the end of 2020 after a 25-year career in the Parliamentarian's office. He agreed to stay on to advise on issues connected to the upcoming Joint Session on January 6. When I was first elected, I had taken every opportunity I could to learn from Wick. I had gone to see him many times, including one snowy day when we sat in his office just off the House floor and talked about how the events of 9/11 had changed congressional operations.

Now I was rushing to Wick's office to get urgent answers. What could we do if, during the joint session, the vice president opted simply not to count legitimate votes? What if he took illegal action while he was presiding? What procedure could we follow to ensure this didn't happen?

Nobody knew the rules of the House better than Wick and Jason, but the answers were not comforting. They explained that because the electoral-vote count takes place in a joint session, the proceedings that day would not be governed by the rules of the House. No debate would be allowed. In the event the vice president abandoned his constitutional duty, the only real recourse would be to move to adjourn.

I was not at all certain that a motion to adjourn would work. What if Pence denied that motion in the joint session, then went forward with Trump's plan? "You need to talk to the Senate, too," Wick said. "It will take coordinated action to adjourn and block any attempt like this."

I hoped Vice President Pence would not abandon his oath. I didn't trust Donald Trump or my colleagues who had been conspiring with him. The description by Jenna Ellis and Jason Miller of what Trump and his campaign were urging Pence to do made it clear: We needed to be prepared.

I left Wick's office and walked through the Speaker's lobby, across the chamber, and into the House Republican cloakroom to call Mitch McConnell. I suppose I should have talked to Kevin McCarthy first. He was the House Republican leader and I was the House Republican Conference chair—the third-ranking member of leadership. Calling the Senate leader about something this crucial without first looping in the House leader was not standard procedure, but I had known Mitch McConnell for decades. And, by this point, I simply did not trust Kevin McCarthy to do the right thing. The stakes were too high. I thought Kevin might have been in on Trump's plan. I was hearing from other members of Congress that Kevin had been coordinating closely with Jim Jordan in the planning for January 6. And just the day before, McCarthy had announced that he would vote to object to Electoral College votes.

I stepped inside one of the phone booths in the Republican cloakroom and placed a call to Mitch. "I was just on a Trump surrogate call with Jenna Ellis and Jason Miller," I told him. "They claim there are dueling slates of electors, and they say this means Pence can reject electors." I described my conversation with Wick, and told Mitch we needed a joint plan to ensure we were prepared for what Trump and his allies in Congress were planning.

McConnell agreed. He asked me to coordinate with his chief of staff and members of the Senate Parliamentarian's office.

A short while later, I spoke with a member of McConnell's staff and a staff member from the Senate Parliamentarian's office. I walked them through what I had just heard on the Trump surrogate call: "They are submitting Trump electors from states Biden won, with no basis in law and counter to the outcome of the elections in those states. They are suggesting that Pence will rely on the fake slates and refuse to count the actual certified electors from those states, claiming he isn't in possession of a clear certified slate of electors."

I wasn't sure if they had heard about this scheme before, but it was clear that the Parliamentarian had already received a number of the fraudulent electoral slates. I told them my view was that these fraudulent slates should not be placed in the mahogany boxes that hold the certified electoral votes and are carried into the House chamber every four years during the joint session to count the votes. If the fake electoral slates made it into the boxes, as Donald Trump and his team intended, I didn't know what might happen.

Only later would I learn that Vice President Pence and his counsel, Greg Jacob, had also been meeting with the Senate Parliamentarian during this period to address the counting process and the fake electoral slates. As the Select Committee investigation later showed, Pence and Jacob worked with the Parliamentarian's office to craft the very specific language the vice president used in the joint session. That language, as it was ultimately edited, made clear there was only a single slate of duly certified electors for each state. Only later did I understand that the fake electoral slates were not in the mahogany boxes that were carried through the Capitol and into the House chamber for the count.

As I left the Capitol on the evening of January 4, I had a terrible feeling in the pit of my stomach. I kept replaying in my mind the discussions of the last few days. There was little doubt about what was happening: Donald Trump was trying to prevent Congress from fulfilling our constitutional duty. He was trying to seize power through illegal and unconstitutional means. And some of my Republican colleagues were helping him.

A lot now rested in Mike Pence's hands. It was clear he was under enormous pressure from Trump to violate the law and the Constitution. Would he withstand the pressure, or would he fold? I didn't know if we could count on him.

Paul Ryan summed up the situation this way in a text shortly after midnight on January 5: "I worry he breaks but think he will not."

10. POWDER KEG

House Republicans convened in person in the auditorium of the US Capitol Visitor Center for one final meeting the day before the January 6 joint session. The purpose of the meeting was to discuss electoral-vote objections. Mike Johnson spoke first, in support of objections. Chip Roy followed, in opposition. We spent more than an hour discussing the legal, constitutional, and political issues surrounding objections. Although it was a courteous debate, some members believed that the fact we were having the debate at all was the problem, since there was no basis for these objections in either the law or the Constitution. Mike Gallagher described the dangerous slippery slope we were on in a text to Adam Kinzinger and me:

> So we've accepted the premise that the debate is appropriate. We accepted the idea that Jan 6th is a significant part of the election process, which it is not. It is ministerial. Now our next big fall-back will be hey it's no big deal if we vote yes on the objection… which means we've endorsed the principle that Congress has a role in litigat[ing] election fraud claims.

For Mike Johnson's presentation, he read from a letter he planned to issue later that day: "We will vote to sustain objections to slates of electors submitted by states we believe clearly violated the Constitution." He claimed that the "well-established rules and procedures" in four states — Georgia, Michigan, Pennsylvania, and Wisconsin — had been "deliberately changed," and that this constituted a "usurpation of the [state] legislatures' sole authority." Of course, he ignored the rulings of the state and federal courts that had rejected those claims in each of those states.

Johnson was asserting that Congress should—absent any constitutional authority, or legal or factual basis—reject the rulings of the courts and throw out the duly certified electors from each of these states. He admitted that Congress had no "express authority or ability to independently prove the many allegations of fraud in the four subject states," but then asserted, "Since we are convinced the election laws in certain states were changed in an unconstitutional manner, the slates of electors produced under those modified laws are thus unconstitutional."

Convinced? By what? All we had before us were allegations and legal theories rejected by our nation's courts. Even the Trump campaign itself was not "convinced." We had no evidence of anything, nor any means of evaluating evidence and adjudicating disputes.

Mike repeatedly held himself out as a "constitutional lawyer." I know many constitutional lawyers, including many conservative constitutional lawyers. Not a single one of them agreed with Mike.

Others were equally stunned by Mike Johnson's arguments. Later that night I heard from Kevin McCarthy's chief counsel, Machalagh Carr. She told me she had made clear to Johnson that his letter was wrong, and that he knew it was. She said she "pushed back very strongly" when they discussed it that afternoon:

> He knows he is wrong on the fundamental constitutional principle. And his argument—that he has some sort of power to individually determine—absent due process of any sort—that a state didn't meet their constitutional obligation, and then that the remedy should be that—without any process whatsoever the federal congress gets to overturn the will of the people—is astonishing.

And as other members pointed out, there was an additional flaw in Mike's argument: Why was he objecting only to electors from states that Biden had won? Voting rules in other states, such as Texas and North Carolina, had also been changed because of Covid. If this was a violation of the US Constitution, why then was Johnson objecting only to states where Trump had been defeated?

Indeed, in almost every state, the question was whether the state legislature had delegated sufficient legal authority to the election officials to make these Covid changes. As one federal district court judge (and Trump appointee) explained, "Whatever actions the [Wisconsin] Commission took here, it took under color of authority expressly granted to it by the Legislature." Another federal judge, also appointed by Donald Trump, explained that an action taken by the Georgia secretary of state "is a manifestation of Secretary Raffensperger's statutorily granted authority. It does not override or rewrite state law." Under Mike's theory, simple legal issues about the scope of an official's delegated authority, which had already been resolved by a host of courts, had now become a basis to attempt to throw out the will of the voters and seize the presidency. Mike knew about these and many other similar judicial rulings, but he did not care.

When Chip Roy responded, his message was direct and to the point.

First, he said, we have no constitutional authority to reject electoral votes. We have one certified slate of electors from each state. The 12th Amendment is clear: Under these circumstances, we count. The framers did not intend Congress to select the president.

Second, even if you believed Congress did have this constitutional power, the claims about election fraud are false. Chip then detailed a number of assertions being made that were patently untrue. He warned that if Republicans were to go down this path, we would be ensuring that Democrats will do the same in every presidential election from here forward.

Roy then reminded the members gathered in the Capitol Visitor Center auditorium that every one of us but two had voted to accept the results of our own elections just two days earlier. There was no way that could be consistent with rejecting electors who had been chosen in the same election, under the same rules and procedures. If you believed that there was a systemic constitutional flaw in how the elections were conducted in these four states, then Republicans elected in those states in those same elections could not legitimately be seated.

Jim Jordan spoke next. He made his entire presentation based on the wrong section of the Constitution. Presidential elections are governed by Article II. Yet Jim kept invoking, with great enthusiasm, the language of Article I, Section 4, saying, "Article I, Section 4—time, place and manner determined by the legislatures in the states thereof..." Article I, Section 4, governs elections for Congress; it has nothing to do with presidential elections. Jim also made assertions about fraud in certain states, claiming that Democrats had committed it because they knew they couldn't beat Trump.

Many members spoke eloquently about our constitutional obligations and what was really at stake. Dan Crenshaw of Texas cautioned members planning to object that they should stop saying this was not about overturning an election: This was quite literally about overturning an election, Crenshaw insisted, because that is precisely what an objection is.

Our founders had explicitly prohibited members of Congress from assuming this authority. In *Federalist 68*, Alexander Hamilton explained why:

> And they have excluded from eligibility to this trust, all those who from situation might be suspected of too great devotion to the President in office. No senator, representative, or other person holding a place of trust or profit under the United States, can be of the numbers of the electors.

Not only did the framers reject the idea of Congress as a body selecting the president, they prohibited individual members from serving as electors—specifically because, according to Hamilton, these members might exhibit too much "devotion" to an incumbent president. Once again, I was struck by how prescient the framers were.

Mike Gallagher from Wisconsin raised a fundamental question. Many of the objectors had been claiming that we needed to have a debate about the election in order to give Americans confidence in the election. He pleaded with our colleagues to think about the people coming to the nation's capital for January 6. Those people were praying that Congress would overturn the election and make Donald Trump the president for four more years, and they were angry. Did members really think that a debate about objections on the House floor tomorrow would satisfy the droves of people descending on the city? How long, Gallagher wanted to know, will it be before we are prepared to tell these people the election is over?

Gallagher thought this was a powder keg. So did I.

Debbie Lesko of Arizona had an even more direct question about the thousands of people coming to Washington the next day: She asked that leadership come up with a safety plan for members. Lesko said she was especially worried about "Trump supporters who actually believe that we are going to overturn the election, and when that doesn't happen—most likely will not happen—they are going to go nuts." She wanted a transportation plan to get members of Congress home with a police escort.

McCarthy assured Lesko he would be meeting with the Sergeant at Arms to discuss this and make sure things were covered. They'd been preparing ahead of time, Kevin said, and security precautions were already heightened, including the closure of many local streets.

That night, Eric Trump, the president's son, appeared on Sean Hannity's show on Fox News. He said there would be consequences for any member who did not do what his father wanted, threatening that "any senator or any congressman ... that does not fight tomorrow ... their political career is over." I received a text from a senior Republican House member who had just watched the interview: "Eric Trump is on Hannity threatening/promising primaries for anyone who does not object. Where is our leadership? Is this what our party has become? I'm beyond disgusted."

I told him freshman members were reporting to me that Kevin McCarthy was making the same threat in meetings with them: "Kevin knows this is unconstitutional, but Trump has threatened him, so he feels he has to object and wants as many people with him as possible." I agreed it was disgusting.

Privately, Sean Hannity had texted Mark Meadows that same day: "I'm very worried about the next 48 hours." Yet here was Hannity, making things even worse by giving the president's son a platform to threaten members of Congress.

The next day would set a match to Donald Trump's powder keg.

PART II

The Attack

JANUARY 6, 2021

11.   THE OATH DOES NOT BEND OR YIELD TO POPULAR SENTIMENT

FOR MOST OF OUR HISTORY, the counting of electoral votes by Congress has been an uneventful, though important, constitutional proceeding. Before 2021, the vote count I had the most distinct recollection of was January 6, 2001. That year, Vice President Al Gore and his wife, Tipper, invited our family to tour the vice president's residence at the US Naval Observatory. My parents would be moving in after my father was sworn in as vice president on January 20, 2001.

Vice President Gore met us at the front door of the 19th-century mansion in Northwest Washington. Although it was a Saturday, he was wearing a suit and tie. The rest of us were dressed more casually. He smiled as he explained the business attire: "I'm on my way to preside over the counting of electoral votes for your victory, Cheney," he said. There was no bitterness in Vice President Gore's voice as he left to carry out his constitutional duty.

It had been a hard-fought campaign and one of the closest presidential elections in history. A few weeks earlier, on December 13, 2000, after multiple rounds of litigation, Al Gore had conceded the race, saying, in part:

Almost a century and a half ago, Senator Stephen Douglas told Abraham Lincoln, who had just defeated him for the presidency, "Partisan feeling must yield to patriotism. I'm with you, Mr. President, and God bless you." Well, in that same spirit, I say to

President-elect Bush that what remains of partisan rancor must now be put aside, and may God bless his stewardship of this country.

The election was over, Gore said:

Resolved, as it must be resolved, through the honored institutions of our democracy...I know many of my supporters are disappointed. I am, too. But our disappointment must be overcome by our love of country.

Al Gore's concession speech was both gracious and patriotic—one of the best concession speeches ever given by a presidential candidate.

By any measure, the presidential election in 2000 had been far closer than the 2020 contest. President George W. Bush's victory in 2000 had ultimately come down to just over 500 votes in Florida, with a razor-thin Electoral College margin of 271 to 266. By contrast, Donald Trump lost in 2020 by more than 70 electoral votes. His nationwide popular-vote deficit of seven million represented a 5 percent gap—not even close. Trump would have needed tens of thousands more votes across at least three different states to reverse his Electoral College loss.

But by January 6, 2021, Donald Trump had consumed a good portion of almost every day in a rage: inventing and spreading lies about election fraud, preying on the patriotism of his supporters, and telling them they had to "fight like hell" if they wanted to save their country. He had summoned them to Washington for a "big protest" on the day of the congressional vote count, promising them it would be "wild."

The United States had never seen anything like this.

Some of my Republican colleagues in the House were preparing to use Trump's stolen-election lies as the basis for an unconstitutional attempt to overturn the election results. Historian Timothy Snyder has described the deep damage this was doing to our country: "Making [Trump's] fictions the basis of congressional action gave them flesh."

A sinister feeling was in the air in the days before January 6, 2021.

Most members of Congress recognized the potential for danger. I didn't know exactly what might happen, but security was a real concern.

For more than seven years, while my dad was vice president, I was a Secret Service protectee. The brave, patriotic, and professional men and women of the Secret Service had kept my family and me safe. I have stayed in touch with many of them for nearly 20 years.

A few days before January 6, I called one of these former agents, a person who had headed multiple protective details, and asked for security advice. He helped me arrange for private security on January 6. Another retired agent would drive me to and from the Capitol and remain on standby throughout the day. And in the days that followed January 6, a number of other former agents provided a private security detail. These were some of the same people who had protected my family when the threat we faced was from al-Qaeda terrorists. Now they were protecting me again — this time in the face of threats from our fellow citizens, mobilized to violence by an American president.

Before heading for the Capitol on the morning of January 6, I was watching news coverage of the statements Trump had made over the last 48 hours. He had been tweeting repeatedly about the "thousands of people pouring into D.C.," suggesting the outcome of the election could change on January 6, and threatening that the crowds "won't stand for a landslide election victory to be stolen." He was also spreading the lie that the "Vice President has the power to reject fraudulently chosen electors." I wanted there to be no doubt about the responsibilities of Congress that day, so I put out this statement:

> We have sworn an oath under God to defend the Constitution. We uphold that oath at all times, not only when it is politically convenient. Congress has no authority to overturn elections by objecting to electors. Doing so steals power from the states and violates the Constitution.

As we drove down the George Washington Memorial Parkway to Capitol Hill, I was working to make sure Republicans who were not objecting to electoral votes would be given time to speak during the floor debate. Normally, debate on the floor is equally divided between Democrats and Republicans. In this case, we needed to ensure that the objectors would not monopolize all the Republican speaking slots.

I also called in to a local Wyoming radio station, KGAB, to do an interview about the day's upcoming proceedings. It was clear from the host's questions that disinformation about what Congress could do on January 6 had taken hold. I described how America's presidential-election process works, and how allegations of fraud had already been addressed in the courts. I also explained that Congress had no authority to overturn an election. If we do this, I said, four years from now there will be nothing to stop the Democrats from saying they disagree with the electors Wyoming has chosen—then substituting their preferred candidate for ours.

When we arrived on Capitol Hill, we parked in the Cannon House Office Building garage, and I walked through the underground tunnel to the Capitol. I got on the elevator in the basement to ride up to the second floor, where the House chamber is located.

The elevator stopped on the first floor. When the doors opened, my friend Joyce Hamlett was standing there. Joyce had worked in the Capitol for over 35 years. Since 2007, she had been the "Keeper of the Mace." The mace is one of the oldest objects in the Capitol, and one of the most important symbols of our nation's government. As she stepped into the elevator shortly before noon on January 6, Joyce was carrying the large silver mace in her gloved hands.

A little over four feet long, the mace is made of 13 ebony rods (representing the 13 original states) wrapped by two interwoven silver bands—an ancient Roman design meant to symbolize the strength of *unity*. Topped with a silver globe and an eagle with outstretched wings, the mace represents the power and authority of the House of Representatives, and is carried into the chamber whenever the House is in session. It stands on a pedestal on the rostrum near the Speaker. The current mace dates from 1841. The original was destroyed when the British invaded and burned the Capitol in 1814.

I was honored to be riding with Joyce that morning. We had spent a lot of time talking together in the well of the House over the previous difficult months. Today, the House and Senate would meet and perform our constitutional duty. To mark the occasion, I took a picture of Joyce holding the mace.

Neither of us would have predicted that a few hours later, Joyce would be forced to rush the mace off the House floor to protect it from an irate mob of our own countrymen.

The House chamber was cold when I walked in that morning. The temperature had been lowered in preparation for the bright television lights and additional people, including the senators and staff members, who would be attending the joint session. Inside the Republican cloakroom, members were signing their names on sheets of paper spread out on tables against the wall. I asked what they were doing. A cloakroom staffer explained that they were signing the electoral-vote objections. The signature sheets were arranged by state, in alphabetical order from left to right, Arizona to Wisconsin.

This was purely for show. Each objection is made by a single member of Congress. If a senator joins, there is debate and a vote. Every House member would be recorded voting on any objection a senator joined. Signing these pieces of paper was therefore meaningless—except as yet another public display of fealty to Donald Trump.

Most of the members taking part in the sheet-signing ritual knew it was a farce. Among them was Republican Congressman Mark Green of Tennessee. As he moved down the line, signing his name to the pieces of paper, Green said sheepishly to no one in particular, "The things we do for the Orange Jesus."

I shook my head and walked to the other end of the room. Ryan O'Toole, a member of Kevin McCarthy's cloakroom staff, let me use his computer to finish the remarks I planned to make during the upcoming debate on objections. Shortly after January 6, Ryan would quit working for McCarthy and come to work for me.

While I was sitting at Ryan's desk, my dad called me.

"Are you listening to Trump?" he asked. Trump was speaking at a rally on the Ellipse, but I hadn't been listening.

"He just told the crowd they should 'get rid of the Liz Cheneys of the world.' He has created a serious threat to your security."

I stepped into a cloakroom phone booth for privacy and slid the door shut. "You are in danger," my dad said. "You need to be aware of that as you think about whether to go forward with your remarks."

My dad's voice was steady — and deadly serious. I knew he was angry and worried as a father, and I knew that his heart was breaking for our country. The president of the United States was attempting to utilize an angry crowd as a weapon to threaten Congress, to prevent us from carrying out our constitutional duty.

My father knew immediately and unequivocally that Trump's speech was likely to cause violence. And now Trump had targeted me directly.

I listened to what my dad was saying, but I think we both knew what the answer had to be. There was no world in which I would let Donald Trump threaten or bully me into abandoning my duty.

"I can't stay silent out of fear, Dad."

"Okay," he said. "I understand. But please call me as soon as you're speech is done." I said I would and I told him I loved him.

The next time I talked to my father, I was being rushed from the House chamber as the violent mob mobilized by Trump stormed through the Capitol.

———

The remarks I had written for that day, but never got the chance to deliver, said this:

Madam Speaker, I rise in opposition to the objection. Let me begin by noting how disappointed I am at having to rise today to address this issue. I wanted the election to turn out differently. But I'm bound by a solemn oath, given before God, to preserve, protect, and defend the Constitution. I cannot comply with that oath only when it is convenient politically. Our oaths are not given to any specific president. They are given to preserve the Constitutional structure that has governed our republic for over

230 years. The oath does not bend or yield to popular sentiment, mob rule, or political threats.

We do not compromise our oath. It compels us to adhere to the Constitution and rule of law . . . always.

What the Constitution requires here is not a mystery. It is clear from the plain text of Article II and the 12th Amendment. The states and the people have the authority to choose the president, not Congress. Some have suggested that we should read more into the Constitution than it says—inferring authority the framers did not give us. We do not have some secret unwritten constitutional authority to overturn elections, impose our will, contradict state law, and contradict the rulings of the courts. If we assert that we do, we are creating a tyranny of Congress, stealing power from the states, and striking at the foundations of our republic.

In the years to come, historians and scholars will take account of what we say here today. They will credit those who stood true to the text of the Constitution and honored their oaths.

————

Later, as television coverage began to show Donald Trump's armed mob surging through metal security barriers, attacking police officers, and scaling the walls outside the Capitol Building, my dad feared that the Capitol Police were losing control. He thought that it had become too dangerous for me to remain on the House floor, so he called my chief of staff, Kara Ahern. "You need to go get Liz," he said. "She isn't safe."

Kara and my special assistant, Will Henderson, worked with the retired agent providing my security that day to find a way to evacuate me. But it was already too late. The Capitol had been breached.

12.   THIS IS BECAUSE OF YOU!

SHORTLY BEFORE 1:00 P.M., BEFORE the mob had invaded the building, Vice President Pence and Leader McConnell led the members of the United States Senate in a procession from the Senate side of the Capitol through the Rotunda and Statuary Hall and into the House chamber. At the head of the procession, members of the Senate staff carried the large mahogany boxes, bound with leather straps, that held the electoral votes. As the Senate staffers entered the House chamber and placed the boxes on the rostrum in the well of the House, I hoped that the fraudulent electoral slates that Jenna Ellis and Jason Miller had described two days before had been removed from the boxes.

The vote count proceeded quickly through Alabama and Alaska, with no objections. When the time came to count Arizona's electoral votes, however, Paul Gosar and Ted Cruz stood to object. The vice president declared the joint session in recess, and the senators returned to their chamber. Both houses would now meet separately to debate the Arizona objection.

At 1:15 the Speaker gaveled the House back into session. I was on the list of members scheduled to speak during this debate, but a number of others were ahead of me. I finished the draft of my remarks, printed them out in the cloakroom, and walked onto the House floor to listen to the debate.

Member after member on the Republican side made the same arguments that we'd been hearing for days. Members who bragged about their conservative beliefs, and their fidelity to the plain meaning of the text of the Constitution, were now arguing that Congress should claim power found nowhere in the Constitution to disregard the will of the people and overturn an election.

As I listened to Mike Johnson claim that Arizona "clearly violated" the Constitution in its selection of presidential electors, it occurred to me that I had never heard him raise a concern about Arizona's elections before. The amicus brief that he and the other members had filed concerned only Georgia, Michigan, Pennsylvania, and Wisconsin. And Johnson's January 6 statement explaining his support for the objections had likewise dealt only with those four states. To my knowledge, Johnson had never made a single argument to our conference challenging the election in Arizona. Yet now he was on the floor of the House, arguing that we should ignore the rulings of federal and state courts in Arizona and throw out the results of Arizona's election, thereby disenfranchising millions of voters.

Arizona now seemed to be Mike's target because it starts with an *A*, and therefore came first in our debate. He had apparently developed what he called "a genuine belief" that Arizona's election violated the Constitution because it provided an earlier speaking slot—and thus an opportunity to appear on camera earlier in the day. Mike's "expert" constitutional analysis seemed to come with a surprising amount of flexibility. It was a weapon he could wield to disenfranchise any American.

Inside the House chamber, we were focused on the debate and couldn't see what was happening outside. Most of us weren't aware how large a crowd had been forming. However, Lauren Boebert, a freshman member from Colorado, gave the impression she was in touch with people in the crowd. Shortly before 2:00 pm, during her floor remarks supporting the objections, she announced, "I have constituents outside this building right now!"

As the debate went on, I took a seat on the center aisle, a few rows from the front of the chamber and near one of the podiums on the Republican side where I planned to give my remarks. Chip Roy of Texas, who was also going to speak in opposition to the objections, was sitting in front of me. Jamie Raskin of Maryland was across the aisle on the Democratic side. Members were on edge.

At about 2:15, the Speaker recognized Paul Gosar of Arizona to speak. Gosar began to repeat all kinds of unproven allegations, none of which had gone anywhere in the Arizona lawsuits: "Over 400,000 mail-in ballots were altered, switched from President Trump to Vice President Biden," he said, "or completely erased from President Trump's totals." He said the proof of this was "in the counting curves." It wasn't clear exactly what that meant. If Gosar really believed there was enough fraud in the Arizona election to overturn it and throw out millions of votes, I wondered how he could have voted—as he did less than 72 hours earlier—to recognize his own victory and officially seat himself.

Shortly after Gosar began, there was a commotion at the front of the chamber. Speaker Pelosi's security detail evacuated her. This development was live-tweeted by Lauren Boebert: "The Speaker has been removed from the chambers." It seemed to some of my colleagues that Boebert was rooting for the rioters to succeed. Was she updating them on their progress so far?

I had never seen or heard of a Speaker being evacuated from the chamber. It was clear we were facing a security threat, and there was no question what had caused it. I looked over at Representative Jason Smith, sitting in the front row. Jason had been one of the members arguing in favor of objections. The C-SPAN cameras captured me as I pointed at him and said, "You did this." I was angry. "*You* did this."

A few moments later, Dean Phillips, a Democratic member from Minnesota, yelled at my Republican colleagues from his seat in the House gallery: "This is because of you!"

Jim McGovern, chairman of the House Rules Committee, took the chair as the Speaker departed. He tried to calm everyone, and said if we could get order in the chamber, we could continue the debate. But restoring order was not possible.

A Capitol Police officer from one of the protective details ran down the center aisle. Democratic Leader Steny Hoyer was surrounded by his detail and evacuated from the chamber. The Republican and Democratic whips, Steve Scalise and Jim Clyburn, were ushered out as well. McGovern asked members to take their seats. A minute or so later, however, he declared the House in recess "pursuant to clause 12(B) of rule 1," a provision adopted by the House after the 9/11 attacks to allow for a recess in an emergency situation.

I stood up and turned around to look at my colleagues sitting behind me. Many of them were there because they were supporting the objections. I was sad and angry at what was happening—at what they had caused. Did they realize what they had done?

As I sat back down, Raskin was still opposite me, looking down at his phone. "Liz," he said, "there is a Confederate flag flying inside the United States Capitol."

I couldn't believe it. That hadn't happened, even during the Civil War. "My God, Jamie—what have they done?" We later learned that, at this same time, senior staff in the White House were begging President Donald Trump to tell the rioters to halt the violence and leave the Capitol Building. He refused.

I went over to speak to Keith Stern, who managed the House floor for the Democrats and was controlling speaking time for members who were opposed to objections. If we were able to resume debate, I knew it would be crucial for a member of Republican leadership to speak soon against what the objectors were doing. I asked Keith to move me up in the order. "You'll be next," he told me.

I went back to the Republican side just as a police officer moved to the microphone and made an announcement:

We have had a breach of the Capitol Building, that's going to be going into a lockdown of both chambers, the House and the Senate. Capitol Police is responding to the area where the individuals have breached the building, and we will advise you of further information once it becomes available to us. Please remain calm and remain seated. You can move around inside, but please do not try to leave at this time until we give you further instructions.

As the officer concluded his announcement, the unmistakable sound of rioters pounding on doors outside the chamber was getting louder and louder. Inside, Capitol Police were slamming doors shut and locking them. We were being locked in.

Dozens of members were on the House floor. Another 30 or so, along with reporters, were in the gallery above. A handful of plainclothes and uniformed Capitol Police were in the chamber with us. And several members of Congress who had served in the military or law enforcement were preparing to help guard the doors.

McGovern announced there was another update and asked for everyone's attention. Paul Irving, who was then the House Sergeant at Arms, approached the microphone and said this:

> Everybody, you need to be prepared to get down under your chairs if necessary. We have folks entering the Rotunda and coming down this way. So, we'll update you as soon as we can, but just be prepared. Stay calm.

People were saying that our chairs were bulletproof; we could take cover behind them. Markwayne Mullin of Oklahoma had been sitting a few rows in front of me, and now he edged closer.

"Do not lie down or try to take cover," he warned me. "You will not be safe in here if they breach the chamber. Get out of here, fast. Go out that door," he said, pointing at the door to the right of the Speaker's chair next to the historic portrait of Lafayette.

"Got it," I said, my anger growing.

Jim Jordan approached me. "We need to get the ladies off the aisle," he said and put out his hand. "Let me help you."

I couldn't believe what I was hearing. *Get the ladies off the aisle?* Really?! He and his coconspirators in the White House and Congress had provoked this attack on the heart of American democracy, and now he thought I needed or wanted his help?

I swatted his hand away.

"Get away from me. You f—ing did this."

As Jim scurried off, there was another announcement from the Capitol Police:

> We have tear gas in the Rotunda. Please be advised there are masks under your seats. Please grab a mask, place it in your lap, and be prepared to don your gas masks.

The Capitol Rotunda is not far from the House chamber—less than a minute's walk out the door. With each subsequent police announcement, the mob rampaging outside was getting closer and closer.

I had not been aware that there were gas masks under the seats in the House chamber. I reached under my seat and pulled out a black pouch. Inside the pouch was a box that contained another bag. I tore open the bag and took out the rescue hood inside. I looked up to see Gosar, still standing in front of the podium where he'd been delivering remarks. Now he was afraid, and fumbling with his gas mask. "How do you open this?" he was repeating over and over. I grabbed the pouch from him, opened it, and handed it back.

Once opened, the air filters on the masks automatically engaged and began emitting a high-pitched, motorized whine. The noise would drone on in the background for hours throughout that terrible day.

The chaos in the chamber was growing as members tried to put on the hoods. Ruben Gallego, a former Marine, jumped onto a table on the Democratic side and started shouting instructions to people about how to open the packaging and when to put on the hoods. I remember him yelling, "Whatever you do, *do not* hyperventilate!" This was helpful information, but it hadn't occurred to me that hyperventilation was a possibility until Gallego said it.

There was an awful din in the chamber by this point. As the whine of the gas masks mingled with the sounds of members calling loved ones and preparing to fight the mob, the pounding outside the doors seemed to grow louder. I remember thinking it sounded like the mob had a battering ram. Their jeering violent shouts and chants were echoing off the marble hallways outside the chamber.

The House chaplain, Margaret Kibben, went to one of the microphones and began to pray:

While you prepare, I will pray. Almighty God, we ask that you provide peace if you can. You have been our ever defender and strength. We call upon you today that even as we walk this tough path. Each one of us has an element of fear and anxiety.

May we lay it down before your feet, God, that you will spare us from it.

I bowed my head in prayer. I am a firm believer in the power of prayer. I have seen it work in my own life and in the life of our nation. But at that moment, I couldn't help thinking that we needed to pray *quickly* so we could prepare to confront the violent mob right outside the chamber door.

In the gallery above the House floor, Jason Crow of Colorado, a former Army Ranger, was doing just that. He later described instinctively shifting into combat mode and going through a mental checklist to secure the perimeter and get the dozen or so fellow members seated up there with him into a small group in a defensive position. He instructed members in the gallery to remove their official congressional pins, making them harder to identify if the mob broke through. As he helped other members get their gas masks ready for use, Crow described looking up and seeing "one of the most shocking things" he had ever seen: Capitol Police officers barricading the chamber doors—with members still in the chamber. Crow later said this was when he realized we were very likely in deep trouble:

> There was a moment where I was going to ask one of the officers for his firearm. Because I've used firearms before against people, I know that I'm capable of doing what's necessary to protect myself and protect others, but I didn't know whether the officers were.... My experience in combat is that you never know who is willing to actually pull that trigger and do what's necessary. But I knew that I could.

———

Suddenly people were running in the aisle at the back of the chamber. The mob was battering the doors to the chamber itself, attempting to invade. Members of Congress and plainclothes Capitol police officers were rushing to find whatever they could—benches, desks, chairs—to barricade the door and defend the chamber of the House of Representatives.

The rioters had shattered the glass panels of the chamber doors, perhaps with flagpoles topped with spears. Police officers drew their guns.

Troy Nehls, a freshman member and former sheriff from Texas who helped barricade the doors, told an interviewer in the days after January 6 that the Capitol Police would have been justified in opening fire:

> The guards are saying, "Stop banging on that. Don't come through that door. We will shoot you." And I felt that it would have been totally justified in doing so.

Members were told to evacuate the chamber. "We need everyone out!" officers instructed.

What sounded like gunshots—but was likely the sound of glass shattering—filled the air. People began yelling: "Shots fired! Shots fired! Get down!" A member of Congress, his voice filled with fury, yelled at the mob, "Stop it! You sons of bitches, stop!"

"They won't listen," someone told him in response.

There was only one person they would have listened to—the man who provoked this attack; the man who mobilized the violent mob and sent them to the Capitol; the man who for months fed his supporters lies that the election had been stolen from him; the man who told them that they had to fight like hell to save their country. That man was sitting in his dining room at the White House two miles away watching television coverage of the attack on the United States Capitol. Donald Trump refused to tell his mob to leave.

"We've got to get you guys out of here!" a police officer ordered.

Descending the stairs to the first floor, we passed officers in the hallway holding their long guns. "Move as fast as you possibly can," someone instructed. I saw former House Parliamentarian Tom Wickham (Wick) as we were rushing down the stairs. Two days earlier we'd been contemplating parliamentary rules and procedures we could employ if Vice President Pence had refused to count electoral votes. Now an armed mob was hunting members of Congress and the vice president through the halls of the Capitol.

"Move it, move it, guys. They're coming."

"They are right behind us. We need to move!"

"We've got to go. Seriously. Move, move, move, move. They are right behind us."

While members of Congress and staffers were still evacuating the House floor through the west end of the Speaker's lobby, rioters were attempting to break through the doors about 100 feet away at the east end of the long hall outside the House chamber. Those doors, like the ones in the chamber itself, had been barricaded with desks and chairs piled on top of each other. Video shows the mob taunting Capitol Police officers standing between them and the east doors. Rioters were chanting "F*ck the Blue!" while others were striking at the glass in the doors with flagpoles and helmets and whatever else they had to try to break through. Three members of uniformed Capitol Police were forced to withdraw, leaving only a single plainclothes officer standing between the violent mob and members of Congress still evacuating at the other end of the lobby.

The plainclothes officer drew his weapon and issued multiple warnings for the mob to get back, to stop attempting to break through. Ashli Babbitt, wrapped in a Trump flag, ignored the warnings and began climbing through the broken window into the Speaker's lobby.

The officer fired. Babbitt can be seen on video falling backward just as law-enforcement officers in tactical gear arrived. Markwayne Mullin was still in the House chamber when this happened. He later recounted that the officer who shot Babbitt approached him, distraught, immediately afterward. Mullin later said in several interviews that the officer had no choice, and that his action saved lives:

> He had to take someone's life but in return he probably saved a whole bunch of people's lives. And that is a difficult thing for anybody to do that's never been in those situations...I commend that guy...that's why I hugged him. I said "Sir, you did what you had to do."

Ashli Babbitt was shot at 2:44 p.m. Approximately 20 minutes later, a

White House staffer wrote a note — later produced to the Select Committee — that read: "1x civilian gunshot wound to chest @ door of House cha[m]ber." The note was delivered to President Trump, who continued to sit in his dining room, watching the violence on television and refusing to tell the mob to leave the Capitol.

People died on January 6 because of Donald Trump's lies. Had it not been for the actions of courageous members of law enforcement, many more lives likely would have been lost.

———

At some point during this period, Phil called Acting Attorney General Jeff Rosen and told him we needed overwhelming force at the Capitol immediately. Trump had done nothing to tell the rioters to leave the Capitol. If he wouldn't do so, then a show of numbers would be critical to stem the violence. Of course, Jeff agreed. He had staged units in advance and was working on deploying them to the Capitol, even without any order from Trump.

As I rushed down the stairs and through the Capitol tunnels, I knew already that Donald Trump had to be impeached and removed from office. He was a clear and present danger. His actions, including mobilizing the violent mob that was now laying siege to the Capitol, were undoubtedly impeachable offenses. Every minute that passed without an unambiguous public statement telling the mob to leave the Capitol made the case for impeachment and removal even stronger. The president's unlawful conduct was endangering the republic.

13.   IT TURNED OUT THAT KEVIN
WAS LYING

WHILE THE HOUSE CHAMBER WAS being evacuated, Mike Pence and his family were rushed from his office on the Senate side of the Capitol into a basement garage. The mob was hunting the vice president and chanting "Hang Mike Pence!" Donald Trump poured gasoline on the flames, tweeting at 2:24 p.m.:

> Mike Pence didn't have the courage to do what should have been done to protect our Country and our Constitution, giving States a chance to certify a corrected set of facts, not the fraudulent or inaccurate ones which they were asked to previously certify. USA demands the truth!

In his speech on the Ellipse that morning, Donald Trump had told the angry crowd that Mike Pence could secure Trump's victory. Now, as the rioters were invading the Capitol, Trump was telling them that Mike Pence had refused to do what they all demanded. Our investigation later demonstrated how this tweet further inflamed the violent mob, causing rioters both inside and outside the Capitol to surge forward. Our investigation also showed that, at the moment Trump sent this tweet, he knew there was a violent attack underway at the Capitol.

Later, when I saw the video of the vice president and his family being evacuated down the stairs in the Capitol Building, I was reminded of a photo of my father being evacuated down the stairs in the White House as al-Qaeda attacked our nation on 9/11. This time, the life of our vice president was threatened not by terrorists flying hijacked planes but by a violent mob sent by the president of the United States.

As our group arrived outside the Ways and Means Committee Room, I spotted Hakeem Jeffries. Hakeem was chairman of the House Democratic Caucus, my counterpart on the Democratic side. I didn't know where the other leaders were, but I wanted to begin working with Hakeem to make sure we would get back into session and finish counting the electoral votes.

When I saw Hakeem in the hallway, he was carrying his gas mask in one hand and his coat and tie in the other. Next to him was Colin Allred of Texas, a former NFL linebacker. Both had removed their coats and ties in anticipation of having to fight their way out of the chamber. As we moved into the committee room, I told Hakeem we needed to prepare articles of impeachment against President Trump.

The Ways and Means Committee Room is large and ornate, with portraits of previous committee chairmen lining its walls. In 2018, House Republicans held our organizing conference meetings there, including the leadership elections in which I was elected conference chair for the first time.

Members of Congress, staff, journalists, and police officers filed through the doors, and began to take seats at large conference tables set up around the room. I walked over to one of the tables and put down my gas mask and bag. As I was pulling out a chair to sit down, a staff member came over and asked me to move to the front of the room: "You and Mr. Jeffries are the most senior elected-leadership officials still here. We'd like you to sit together on the dais." I agreed and Hakeem and I met again in the front of the room.

There were hundreds of members now gathered in the Ways and Means room. Kara Ahern and a number of other members of my staff had been evacuated from the Cannon House Office Building earlier, after a pipe bomb was found across the street at the Republican National Committee. They had moved to the House Republican Conference offices in Longworth, along with Representatives Nancy Mace and Dan Crenshaw. A second bomb was discovered at the Democratic National

Committee. House Speaker Nancy Pelosi, Senate Leader Mitch McConnell, and other senior congressional leaders had been moved off-site, to nearby Fort McNair.

The Capitol offices of both Speaker Pelosi and Leader McCarthy had been breached by the mob. A frightened Kevin McCarthy had begged President Trump to stop the violence. When that didn't work, he had appealed to Trump's adult children, also begging for their help. None of those efforts succeeded.

For a time that afternoon, after he had been shocked by the violence, McCarthy's public comments were reasonable. "I completely condemn the violence in the Capitol," he said in a television interview. "It is un-American. It has to stop. It has to stop now." He also said that he had been "very clear with the president that it must stop," and he said he told the president he needed to make a public statement telling people to stop. For a little while, at least, Kevin McCarthy was neither making political calculations nor appeasing Trump.

Our investigation would later show video of all the Senate and House leaders at Fort McNair: Pelosi, McConnell, Thune, Hoyer, Clyburn, Schumer, and Scalise, together in a room, talking to senior officials at the Defense Department and the Justice Department, talking to Mike Pence, working together to bring more law enforcement and security assets to the Capitol. It is difficult to find Kevin McCarthy in those videos or in any of those discussions. For a time, it appears that he was somewhere else in the building, perhaps alone or on the phone with someone else, while other leaders of both parties were working together to find a security solution.

Back in the Ways and Means room, the mood was tense. We had hundreds of members and staffers in the room. A group of members of the Freedom Caucus who had led the effort to object were gathered around one of the tables. Across the room, another member of Congress was dismantling a stanchion, apparently preparing to use the brass rod as a weapon, should it come to that. There were no televisions in the main room, but members were getting information and updates on their phones and from their families.

Hakeem and I decided we needed to address our colleagues. We wanted members to know we were operating in a nonpartisan way, united in our determination to get back into the chamber and complete our work. We also wanted them to know we would keep them updated, providing additional details as quickly as we could. And we reminded members not to reveal our location, particularly if they were speaking to the press.

As soon as we finished speaking, Bill Johnson of Ohio approached me and asked if he could offer a prayer. Given the tension in the room and the anger at the objectors, I was hesitant to have Johnson, an objector, make remarks. But I agreed that he could offer a prayer. Hakeem had not heard me approve Johnson's request, so when he saw Johnson move toward the microphone he stepped in to block his way. The two men began to argue. I explained that Johnson was just going to offer a prayer, and Hakeem agreed. Later on, I learned that many members in the room were offended by Johnson speaking at that moment, given the role the objectors had played in contributing to the events of that day.

Around 3:00 p.m., I received a text from Jenna Lifhits, who handled national-security issues on my staff. She sent me Abraham Lincoln's 1838 Lyceum Address. Speaking when he was only 28 years old about the "perpetuation of our political institutions," Lincoln famously warned of the danger of "mob law":

> At what point then is the approach of danger to be expected? I answer, if it ever reach us, it must spring up amongst us. It cannot come from abroad. If destruction be our lot, we must ourselves be its author and finisher. As a nation of free men, we must live through all time, or die by suicide.

The only way to fortify against this danger, Lincoln said, was for every American to pledge his life, his property, and his sacred honor to the Constitution and laws:

> Let reverence for the laws be breathed by every American mother, to the lisping babe, that prattles on her lap—let it be

taught in schools, in seminaries, and in colleges; let it be written in Primers, spelling books, and Almanacs;—let it be preached from the pulpit, proclaimed in legislative halls, and enforced in the courts of justice.

I would read this address many times in the coming weeks and months.

Looking at the Freedom Caucus members gathered in the committee room, I thought, surely, after this violence, all those who were objecting would stop. They must certainly recognize we had entered very dangerous territory. They would agree to unify to get our job done. I knew it would do little good for me personally to approach the Freedom Caucus members and ask that they drop their objections. But I asked several other members to speak to the group to see if they would agree—for the good of the country—to stop.

Markwayne Mullin walked up to the dais a short while later. He told me he had just come from the "triage room," where they were bringing police officers wounded in the day's combat with the Trump mob. He said it was devastating. Scores of law-enforcement officers had been seriously injured.

Mullin described their injuries in detail: broken bones, deep lacerations, an officer whose eye had been gouged by the mob, others who had been attacked with bear spray, pepper spray, and other irritants. The ongoing violence had blocked ambulances from reaching the casualties and transporting them to hospitals. It was sickening.

Markwayne went over to talk to the members of the Freedom Caucus. I thought maybe if they heard about what was going on, about the violent attacks on police officers, they would withdraw their objections.

I was wrong.

They would not.

A video taken that afternoon shows members of the group sitting at tables smiling, chatting, and smirking as if they had already accomplished something important that day—as if they were proud of what had happened. Jim Jordan's public statements, including in testimony before the

Rules Committee a few months later, suggest that he was actually on the phone with Donald Trump during this time, apparently still discussing how to stop the counting of electoral votes. The violence had not ended. Members of Congress were under threat in an undisclosed location. But Jim Jordan was evidently on the phone with Trump. Still, apparently, trying to help him stay in power.

Even if the House members refused to withdraw their objections, the matter would be settled if we could get the senators to withdraw theirs. Every objection required the support of at least one senator. Without that, there would be no further delay in counting electoral votes. Both chambers had been evacuated in the middle of the debate on the Arizona objection, so we would have to complete the remaining debate and vote on the objection. But if we could persuade every other senator to withdraw their objections, there would be no more debate.

At 4:10, I texted McConnell:

Can we get senators to withdraw their objections to the remaining states? We should go back in as soon as we can. Deal with az and then move forward unified as quickly as possible. This can't stand.

A few minutes later, Mitch responded: "That's exactly the plan."

Around 4:15, I spoke with Savannah Guthrie on NBC. It was important that the country know the attack on our Capitol would not stand, that we were united across party lines in our determination to go back into session and finish our job. I thought about my years working at the State Department, and how this attack on the US Capitol would be viewed by America's allies and adversaries overseas. They needed to know there had not been a successful coup in the United States, that we were resolved to finish counting the Electoral College votes, and that power would transfer lawfully.

Uncertainty remained about when we could reconvene. I've since seen some initial predictions that clearing and securing the Capitol could have required multiple days. At the time, I knew we had to find a way to go forward *that night,* regardless of the potential security risks to senators or members of the House. We could not afford to wait.

When I appeared live on NBC, I did not want to reveal our precise location, but I wanted people to know that a bipartisan group of legislators were together, and that we intended to finish our job:

> My Democratic counterpart, Hakeem Jeffries, and I have both made clear that we do not intend to allow mob violence to prevent us from carrying out our constitutional duty. Our institutions have got to be defended and protected. We have an oath to the Constitution. Sending an angry violent mob to disrupt proceedings at the Capitol cannot stand.

At 4:17, as the interview was underway, the White House tweeted out a video that President Trump had finally recorded three hours after the attack began. Savannah broke in to play the video. I was hearing it for the first time live on the air. This is what President Trump said:

> I know your pain. I know your hurt. We had an election that was stolen from us. It was a landslide election, and everyone knows it, especially the other side, but you have to go home now. We have to have peace. We have to have law and order. We have to respect our great people in law and order. We don't want anybody hurt. It's a very tough period of time. There's never been a time like this where such a thing happened, where they could take it away from all of us—from me, from you, from our country.
>
> This was a fraudulent election. But we can't play into the hands of these people. We have to have peace. So go home. We love you. You're very special. You've seen what happens. You see the way others are treated that are so bad and so evil. I know how you feel, but go home and go home in peace.

Finally, after three hours of violence and lawlessness, Trump was telling the rioters to go home. But he was simultaneously praising those same people—the ones who had been laying siege to the Capitol, the people who had attacked and seriously injured the police officers now lying on stretchers in the triage room.

When Savannah asked for my reaction, I didn't hide my anger:

When you have violent mobs storming the floor of the House of Representatives and the floor of the United States Senate and the president's response is to say he loves those people...it is absolutely counter to the Constitution and counter to the peaceful transfer of power and the values on which this republic was built.

I also said this:

The president's statement now, in my view, was completely inadequate. What he has done, what he has caused here, is something we've never seen before in our history. It has been 245 years and no president has ever failed to concede—to agree to leave office after the Electoral College has voted. What we are seeing today is a result of convincing people that somehow Congress was going to overturn the results of this election, a result of suggesting he wouldn't leave office. Those are very, very dangerous things. This will be remembered. This will be part of his legacy, and it is a dangerous moment for our country.

Shortly after I finished this interview, Hakeem and I addressed the assembled members again, along with House Sergeant at Arms Paul Irving. He updated members on efforts to clear the Capitol. I told the group I had been in touch with Leader McConnell, and that there was bipartisan and bicameral agreement that we needed to return to work to finish our job. I did not mention Kevin McCarthy because I had not talked with him since the violence began. Hakeem and I both stressed that we would not let the mob prevail: We would return to count electoral votes. When we finished, the room erupted in applause.

Meanwhile, all afternoon, President Trump and his allies had been busily making calls to senators, and perhaps to other members of Congress, trying to find ways to keep us from going forward with the count. President Trump's counsel, John Eastman, was still lobbying the vice president's counsel. The Trump team was still insisting that Mike Pence halt the counting of votes.

Annie Kuster, a Democrat from New Hampshire, approached me after we finished. "Thank you for making sure we get back tonight. Your dad would be so proud of you."

I appreciated Annie's kind words. At that point getting the count completed was a bipartisan—though not unanimous—priority.

At some point, a combination of developments made it clear that the tide was turning against the attacking mob. After Donald Trump's tweeted video at 4:17 p.m., a number of the rioters voluntarily left. Additional security, which ultimately included units of the National Guard, was being deployed. Around 5:35, Sergeant at Arms Irving informed the room that the Capitol would soon be secure. There was another round of applause. He asked members to remain in the committee room for the time being but said we would be able to resume our work that night.

Sometime around 6:00, I finally connected with Kevin McCarthy by phone. I stepped back into the anteroom behind the dais. Kevin told me the plan was to go back into session as soon as it was safe. He said he would give a speech "about America." He said he would condemn the violence, talk about how terrible the day had been, and urge us all to come together—not as Republicans or as Democrats, but as Americans. He said he did not plan to move forward with the objections.

In that moment, it sounded like we were on the same page.

I hung up with McCarthy and walked back out into the committee room. Kevin's counsel, Machalagh Carr, was sitting in one of the chairs at the dais.

"I just talked to Kevin," I told her. "He says he is going to speak when we first come back into session, condemn the attack, and urge us all to move forward in a unified way for the good of the country. He's going to talk about America and how we have to move beyond partisanship now. He's not going to keep objecting."

Machalagh looked at me and said, "Mr. Jordan just told me that *he* just got off the phone with Kevin, and Kevin told him the opposite. Jordan says Kevin is going to carry on with the objections."

That can't be right, I thought. There is no way that any leader would let these objections go on in the wake of the violent assault on the Capitol. The idea was so unimaginable that I assumed Jordan was lying.

I was wrong.

It turned out that Kevin was lying.

14.   THESE ARE THE THINGS
THAT HAPPEN

A LITTLE AFTER 6:00 P.M., I called in to Bret Baier's show on Fox News. Bret asked me to describe my personal experiences that day, but I thought it was more important to talk about the gravity of what was happening, and the threat the attack on our Capitol posed to our democracy. I also wanted to be absolutely clear about Donald Trump's responsibility for what had happened: "What's important is to recognize we have just had a violent mob assault the US Capitol in an attempt to prevent us from carrying out our Constitutional duties."

Donald Trump had "lit the flame" of this attack, I said, but he would not prevent us from doing our duty:

> The mob will not prevail. We have all taken an oath to the Constitution. It's an oath that doesn't bend to mob rule. It doesn't bend to political threats. It's an oath [taken] under God, and we will carry it out. What happened today can never happen again in the United States, and the president needs to take responsibility for it.

As I was on the air, Trump tweeted again. He certainly did not take responsibility. He did not condemn the violence, or call for the people who stormed the Capitol and brutally beat law-enforcement officers to be held accountable. Instead he justified the attack: "These are the things and events that happen when a sacred landslide election victory is so unceremoniously & viciously stripped away." Then Trump urged his supporters to "remember this day forever," as if it were something to celebrate.

What a monster, I thought. I said this to Bret: "The president is abusing the trust of the American people, and abusing the trust of the people who supported him."

As I was walking back into the committee room, I saw Madeleine Dean, a Democrat from Pennsylvania, standing by the door. I don't think Madeleine and I had ever spoken before, but I knew she had a reputation as a thoughtful and serious member. We looked at each other. I shook my head in sadness.

"Do they know they've gone too far?" she asked.

I knew she was talking about the objectors among the House Republicans. It was the same thought I'd had hours earlier as I stood in the House chamber looking at my Republican colleagues as the violence began.

"Some of them do," I said quietly. I didn't say what I actually feared: Some of them don't care.

Shortly before 7:00 p.m., Hakeem and I made our third announcement of the day: The House floor would reopen at 8:00 p.m. We would finish our work.

As we were addressing the members, Speaker Pelosi, Majority Leader Hoyer, and Majority Whip Clyburn arrived in the room. Hakeem and I stepped to one side while they addressed everyone. When Pelosi thanked Hakeem for his leadership that day, Hakeem spoke up to say that he and I had done it together.

Steny Hoyer came over to me when the remarks were finished. I respected Steny and knew how much he loved the institution of the House. Steny is a student of history. He is a gentleman. And he is trusted by members on both sides of the aisle.

"Steny," I said, "we need to finish this count and then we need to move articles of impeachment against Trump. He's a clear and present danger."

Democratic Congressman Tom Malinowski of New Jersey joined our discussion. We had spoken earlier in the day about getting back into session—and about articles of impeachment.

Steny asked me if I thought other Republican members realized the danger.

"Yes," I replied. "*Some* do."

I didn't know how many Republicans would vote to impeach, but I felt we had no choice. Other members of both parties had weighed in with me on this and shared my view.

As I walked out of the Ways and Means Committee room after 7:00 p.m., my phone rang. It was my daughter Grace. A cowgirl and barrel racer, Grace is normally tough as nails. But that night, as soon as I answered the phone, she began to cry. News coverage of the day's events had been terrifying, she said. She didn't know if I would be okay. I told her—with a little more confidence than I felt at that point—that she didn't need to worry, that the Capitol had been cleared and we were safe. The people who attacked us had not prevailed.

———

The House chamber opened up again around 8:00 that night. One of the first people I saw when I walked onto the House floor was Greg Pence, a freshman representative from Indiana and the older brother of Vice President Mike Pence. We met in the middle of the chamber on the Republican side of the aisle and gave each other a hug. What a sad and tragic day. I asked him how he was.

Greg told me that he had been with his brother all day. "You cannot imagine the pressure he's been under," Greg said. I told him how grateful I was that the vice president had done the right thing.

As we waited for the House to come back into session, I told my chief of staff, Kara, that I wanted to go to the Rotunda and Statuary Hall to see what damage had been done. We left the House chamber through the door that had been barricaded with furniture and guarded by police with guns drawn just a few hours earlier. The glass panels were shattered.

I wasn't prepared for what I saw when we entered Statuary Hall.

The original chamber of the House of Representatives, Statuary Hall is a room full of the history of our republic. Brass plaques on the floor mark the locations of the desks of presidents who served in the House, including Abraham Lincoln and John Quincy Adams. Statues of prominent Americans line the outer walls. On the night of January 6, law-enforcement officers in tactical gear were seated on the floor, leaning up against every statue and all around the walls of the room, exhausted from the battle they had fought to defend the Capitol. I walked around the room thanking them for what they had done.

One said to me, "Ma'am, I fought in Iraq and I have never encountered the violence I did out there today."

Then he repeated the point to make sure I understood: "It was medieval and bloodthirsty."

It was unfathomable that this was happening in the United States of America.

Kara and I walked to the Rotunda next, where more of the courageous members of law enforcement who had defended us that day sat on the floor and on benches beneath portraits depicting the most important events from the earliest days of our republic. Walking past statues of Lincoln and Washington, Grant and Eisenhower, I tried to thank every police officer. I asked other members of Congress to go to the Rotunda and do the same. Because of the bravery of the Capitol Police, the Metropolitan Police, and all the law-enforcement officers who fought the rioters that day, we and our republic were preserved. But the battle was far from over.

I also wanted to go to the Senate side of the Capitol to check on something that was personal to me. The hallways outside the Senate chamber are lined with busts of America's past vice presidents, each of whom also served as president of the Senate. My father's bust stood outside Leader McConnell's office. I wanted to see if it had been damaged or destroyed.

As we neared the door to the Senate majority leader's office, we noticed a group of reporters gathered there. I didn't want to attract attention, so I stayed back while Kara walked ahead to check on my dad's bust.

"It's fine," she reported. "Not damaged at all."

I wondered if we would be able to say the same about our republic.

15. HE WAS GOING TO LET THE TRAVESTY GO ON

Shortly after 9:00 p.m., Speaker Nancy Pelosi gaveled the United States House of Representatives back into session. I stood in the rear of the chamber, listening to her remarks. Members were filing in. We still had to finish the debate and vote on the Arizona objection. After Steny Hoyer finished his remarks and House Republican Leader Kevin McCarthy prepared to speak, I took a seat near the front of the chamber—close to where I'd been sitting a few hours earlier, when the attack happened. The House chaplain sat a few seats away. I hadn't given any more thought to Jim Jordan's claim that Kevin was going to continue objecting, mostly because I couldn't believe it was true.

McCarthy began his remarks by condemning the day's violence as "unacceptable, undemocratic, and un-American." There was a sustained ovation when he thanked members of law enforcement and the National Guard for defending us. McCarthy acknowledged the brutality of the attack on law enforcement, saying "many of them are injured right now." He also thanked the members of Congress who had helped Capitol Police "hold the line" and "ensured the floor of this chamber was never breached."

And then, as though none of that mattered at all, he said Republicans would continue the objections.

Despite the brutal violence, destruction, and death at the Capitol, despite the fact that Donald Trump's lies—the same lies Republicans were telling to justify the objections—had mobilized the mob and caused the attack, McCarthy was going to let the travesty go on. Kevin McCarthy lacked the courage and the honor to abide by his oath to the Constitution.

This wasn't leadership. It was cowardice, and it was craven. I wanted no part of it. I got up and walked out of the House chamber.

Several hours earlier, over in the Senate, Republican Leader Mitch McConnell had this to say about Republican objections:

> We're debating a step that has never been taken in American history, whether Congress should overrule the voters and overturn a presidential election.... The Constitution gives us here in Congress a limited role. We cannot simply declare ourselves a national board of elections on steroids. The voters, the courts, and the states have all spoken. If we overrule them all, it would damage our republic forever... If this election were overturned by mere allegations from the losing side, our democracy would enter a death spiral....
>
> I will not pretend such a vote would be a harmless protest gesture while relying on others to do the right thing. I will vote to respect the people's decision and defend our system of government as we know it.

What McConnell said that night in the Senate is what McCarthy should have said in the House. But Kevin McCarthy had an entirely different agenda—one based on personal ambition, not principle.

————

In the cloakroom, the objection sign-up sheets were spread across the tables again.

"Are many members coming in and taking their names off these lists?" I asked a staffer.

"Not really," she replied. "Maybe one or two."

I was still slated to speak during the debate that evening, but I felt that everyone had heard plenty from me that day and in the days leading up to it. I wanted us to get the counting done, and I didn't think another speech by me was necessary. So when Tom Reed, a New York Republican, and Josh Gottheimer, a New Jersey Democrat, approached me and asked if I would yield my time so they could make bipartisan remarks condemning the violence and calling for unity, I readily agreed.

After the House and Senate completed the debate and voted on the Arizona objection, the joint session reconvened and the counting proceeded. Some House members objected to other states, but no senator joined any of the objections—until we got to Pennsylvania. Missouri Senator Josh Hawley would not withdraw his objection. Once again, the joint session was forced to dissolve for a two-hour debate in each house.

Ultimately, despite the carnage of the day, eight United States senators voted to object to electoral votes in Pennsylvania or Arizona: Senators Cruz, Hawley, Hyde-Smith, Kennedy, Lummis, Marshall, Scott, and Tuberville. All told, 139 House members voted in favor of objections that evening, including Leader McCarthy and Whip Scalise.

Late that night, I crossed paths with Vice President Pence in Statuary Hall. He was surrounded by senators, Secret Service agents, and members of his staff. He stopped as I walked over to him. "Thank you, Mr. Vice President," I said, "for what you did for our country today."

Mike Pence did not say much in response, but his actions that day had been courageous. Had he succumbed to Donald Trump's pressure, our nation would have faced a far-worse constitutional crisis.

A few hours later, shortly before 4:00 a.m., Congress completed the counting of electoral votes: Joe Biden had defeated Donald Trump by a count of 306 to 232. The mob had not prevailed, but the danger wasn't over. The January 6 attack was an assault on our constitutional republic. As Congress finished our work early on January 7, President Trump still had not condemned the attack or committed to leave office.

PART III

A Plague of Cowardice

JANUARY 7 TO JUNE 30, 2021

16. IMPEACHMENT AND 25TH AMENDMENT ARE REAL

As dawn broke on January 7, 2021, Washington, DC, was a city under curfew. After the electoral count finished around 3:45 a.m., I slept for a few hours on the sofa in my office in the Cannon House Office Building, waiting for the curfew to lift so I could leave. I had been scheduled to do several television interviews that morning, but I canceled. I didn't want to be speaking to the press on so little sleep at such a moment of danger for the country. And I wanted to get home to see my family.

Trump administration officials had begun resigning even as the attack was underway. The deputy national security advisor to the president, Matt Pottinger, later told the Select Committee he decided to resign the moment he saw Donald Trump's 2:24 p.m. tweet targeting Vice President Pence. Deputy Press Secretary Sarah Matthews also resigned. "As someone who worked in the halls of Congress, I was deeply disturbed by what I saw today," she wrote in her resignation letter. She believed President Trump "should have been telling these people to go home and to leave and to condemn the violence that we were seeing." Instead, he was "pouring gasoline on the fire and making it much worse."

Secretary of Transportation Elaine Chao, wife of Senate Republican Leader Mitch McConnell, sent an email to employees at the Department of Transportation:

> Yesterday, our country experienced a traumatic and entirely avoid-
> able event as supporters of the President stormed the Capitol

building after a rally he addressed. As I'm sure is the case with many of you, it has deeply troubled me in a way that I simply cannot set aside.

Secretary of Education Betsy DeVos resigned the next day. In a letter to President Trump, she called the attack on the Capitol "unconscionable," adding, "There is no mistaking the impact your rhetoric had on the situation, and it is the inflection point for me." She warned that "impressionable children are watching all of this."

Five senior members of the national security council staff resigned, as did the White House social secretary and Melania Trump's chief of staff. Mick Mulvaney, who had previously served as Donald Trump's chief of staff and director of the Office of Management and Budget, resigned from his position as special envoy for Northern Ireland. In an interview on CNBC, Mulvaney said he called Secretary of State Mike Pompeo and told him, "I can't stay here. Not after yesterday. You can't look at that yesterday and think I want to be a part of that in any way, shape, or form."

On Capitol Hill, anger at the unprincipled Republican reaction to the violence led to staff resignations, including one of the most senior Republican staffers on the House Armed Services Committee, Jason Schmid. Twenty-one Republicans who would serve on the committee in the 117th Congress, including ranking member Mike Rogers, had joined Republican Leader Kevin McCarthy in voting to reject electoral votes *after* the mob attacked the Capitol. In his resignation letter, Schmid stressed the harm this had done to America's security:

Anyone who watched those horrible hours unfold should have been galvanized to rebuke these insurrectionists in the strongest terms. Instead, some members whom I believed to be leaders in the defense of the nation chose to put political theater ahead of the defense of the Constitution and the Republic. The decision to vote to set aside legitimate electors harmed the ability of every service member, intelligence officer, and diplomat to defend the nation and advance American interests.

Images of the attack on the US Capitol sparked horror around the world. I heard from many friends and colleagues overseas—people I had worked with during my time at the State Department. One friend from Egypt told me how traumatic it had been to see the images on January 6. He reminded me of a conversation we'd had in the aftermath of the 9/11 attacks about United Airlines Flight 93, the commercial airliner that had been hijacked and was headed for Washington, DC, when the incredibly courageous passengers on board sacrificed their own lives to take down the plane and stop the terrorists from killing even more people. Had Flight 93 made it to Washington, its target would likely have been the White House—where my parents and husband had been that day—or the Capitol Building. My friend told me he believed the Capitol had been the target because "there is no greater symbol of American freedom and democracy than the United States Capitol Building." Now, all these years later, he said it was hard to describe the anguish he had felt as he watched the Capitol come under attack.

I thought back to the speech President George W. Bush gave when he addressed the nation from the Oval Office on the night of September 11, 2001. He said, "Terrorist attacks can shake the foundations of our biggest buildings, but they cannot touch the foundation of America."

Terrorists couldn't shake the foundations of our republic, but what if an American president refused to guarantee the peaceful transition of power? What if he attempted to overturn an election in order to stay in power, ignored the rulings of the courts, mobilized a violent mob, and provoked them to attack and invade the Capitol? An American president willing to do those things was a threat unlike any we had ever faced before—a direct threat to the foundations of our republic.

———

Even President Trump's staunchest supporters seemed to understand that this was a moment of profound peril for the nation, for the president, and for those who had enabled him. We learned later that Fox News host Sean Hannity and White House Press Secretary Kayleigh McEnany, two of President Trump's most ardent public defenders, had been texting each other on the evening of January 7. They recognized that Trump needed to be isolated.

Hannity told McEnany, "Key now. No more crazy people."

She replied, "Yes 100%."

Hannity responded with a list of instructions and talking points for use with Trump that included: "1-No more stolen election talk. 2-Yes, impeachment and 25th amendment are real, and many people will quit. 3-He was intrigued by the Pardon idea!! (Hunter)..."

McEnany agreed, "Love that. Thank you. That is the playbook. I will help reinforce. THANK YOU for your help. You are doing a great service for your country!"

At that moment, even Hannity and McEnany seemed to understand the damage the president's lies had inflicted on the nation—and the consequences he might be facing. Many rumors were circulating, including that White House Counsel Pat Cipollone had instructed White House staffers to avoid Trump, apparently concerned that they might later find themselves being called as witnesses against Trump if they got caught up in a conversation with him.

The House and Senate were out of session, but leadership in both parties began meeting by phone to grapple with the aftermath of the attack and plot a course ahead. It became clear during this period that some House Democrats intended to propose a resolution referring to the Ethics Committee for possible expulsion all members of the House who had voted to object to the electoral votes—139 House Republicans had done so, even after the violence. The Democrats' resolution cited Section 3 of the 14th Amendment, which explicitly provides that:

> No person shall be a Senator or Representative in Congress, or elector of President and Vice President, or hold any office, civil or military, under the United States, or under any state, who, having previously taken an oath, as a member of Congress, or as an officer of the United States, or as a member of any state legislature, or as an executive or judicial officer of any state, to support the Constitution of the United States, shall have engaged in insurrec-

tion or rebellion against the same, or given aid or comfort to the enemies thereof.

When the resolution was formally introduced on January 11, there were 47 Democratic cosponsors, including a number of members who represented swing districts and had moderate voting records. The revulsion at what had happened was widespread; it was not confined to a narrow segment of the ideological spectrum.

House Republican leaders held our first call on Friday, January 8, with members of the Elected Leadership Committee (ELC), which consisted of about 10 members of leadership and at least as many staff members. In addition to McCarthy, Scalise, and me, ELC meetings usually included Tom Emmer, chair of the National Republican Campaign Committee; Mike Johnson, vice chair of the House Republican Conference; Gary Palmer, chair of the Republican Policy Committee; Drew Ferguson, the chief deputy whip; and Richard Hudson, secretary of the conference. Tom Cole of Oklahoma, the ranking Republican on the House Rules Committee, also participated, along with Guy Reschenthaler of Pennsylvania and Andrew Clyde of Georgia. Reschenthaler and Clyde were class representatives for members elected in 2018 and 2020.

House Democrats were meeting at the same time we were. They held the House majority, so the decision about whether and when to introduce articles of impeachment was in their hands. Based on the real-time reports we were getting from members on the Democrats' call, it sounded like there was almost certainly going to be an impeachment resolution.

McCarthy gave us an update on the security situation at the Capitol. With the Inauguration less than two weeks away, there would be increased security measures, including the deployment of an additional 6,000 National Guard troops. He had placed a call to Biden, but they hadn't yet connected. McCarthy told us that he planned to urge unity and healing. He said what Trump did was "atrocious and totally wrong," and "what he [Trump] said was not right by any shape or any form, inciting people."

Steve Scalise discussed the injuries sustained by members of the Capitol Police, and ways members could help the family of Capitol Police

Officer Brian Sicknick, who had died on January 7 after facing brutal attack on January 6 while protecting the West Front of the Capitol.

Republican members were angry, Scalise reported. They were concerned about what had happened, and about Trump's conduct. Scalise said we needed to address the question of what the post-Trump Republican House would look like. It seemed obvious to all that Trump could no longer lead the party.

Among leadership—at least at that time—there was no question that Donald Trump was culpable for January 6. The focus of our discussion was what the potential solution should be. We discussed the options we knew the Democrats were considering: impeachment; urging Trump to resign; or asking Pence to invoke the 25th Amendment, which authorizes the vice president and a majority of the Cabinet to determine that the president is no longer capable of discharging the duties of his office. Kevin said he was concerned about member security overall, and, in particular, he worried that if the House moved forward with impeachment, that would be divisive and would seriously increase the threat of violence against members.

After several participants on the call expressed concerns about the potential negative political ramifications of impeachment, Tom Cole spoke up. Tom had served in Congress since 2003, and members valued his insight and judgment. He said the Rules Committee had already begun looking at the grounds for impeachment, anticipating that any articles would have to move through Rules first before being voted on by the full House. He wanted everyone to be aware that there were real grounds here for impeachment. I made a note to call him after the call wrapped up.

When I spoke, I urged that we keep several things in mind as we talked to members of our conference. We needed to remember how serious this was, that there were likely going to be extensive and significant criminal investigations into what had transpired, and we needed to be clear about what the president had done. I also reminded people that Vice President Pence had been in the Capitol with his wife and daughter while the mob was hunting him. During that time, Trump had attacked

Pence on Twitter. Pence was a former House member, and many of our colleagues knew him well.

Richard Hudson, who had objected to the electoral votes along with most of the other members on the call, expressed desperation at the unfolding situation. Members of Congress who had objected were being blamed for the violence. Major corporate donors were threatening to cut off campaign contributions to all the objectors.

Indeed, some of the biggest corporate donors—companies such as McDonald's, Nike, Boeing, Wells Fargo, Blue Cross Blue Shield, and Marriott—had begun announcing that they would no longer contribute to members who had voted to object. This was an existential threat to Kevin McCarthy's leadership of House Republicans. Raising money and distributing it to Republican members and candidates was Kevin's principal strength. He would not be able to maintain his position as leader—much less ever become Speaker of the House—if he could no longer raise money.

Kevin had made a political calculation to object—thinking it would win him the favor of the far-right members who had sunk his chances of becoming Speaker in 2015, when Paul Ryan had been elected. McCarthy had lobbied other members to join him in objecting. Now they were facing the prospect of losing corporate donations to their campaigns, and it was Kevin's fault.

Later that night, a freshman Republican forwarded me a note that Andrew Clyde had sent to all the freshman members, "summarizing" our leadership call. Clyde claimed that "there was majority agreement that the President did not incite this violence..."

That was a lie.

I sent Clyde's message to Kevin and Steve. They both responded immediately.

Kevin said, "He sent this to all of them? This isn't what I heard or said."

Scalise said it was "completely inaccurate and [doesn't] represent what we discussed."

Kevin told me he instructed Clyde to issue a correction. The next morning, Clyde removed the dishonest sentence and sent the note around again. We had learned a lesson: We could not trust Andrew Clyde to be honest. A few months later, Clyde—who had been photographed trying to help barricade the doors on January 6 to stop the violent mob from invading the House chamber—said the day had looked just like "a normal tourist visit."

That afternoon, I also spoke to Tom Cole. He forwarded a memo prepared by an attorney who was a senior Republican staffer on the Rules Committee. In the cover note, the staffer explained that, having analyzed the impeachment power, the facts of the case, and the application of those facts to the constitutional requirements, "my conclusion, which I do not take lightly, is that I believe that President Trump's actions on January 6 constitute a high crime and misdemeanor within the meaning of Article II, Section 4 of the Constitution, and therefore constitute an impeachable offense."

The Republican staff memo went on to describe this in detail, and to explain how January 6 was very different from the first Trump impeachment. The memo did not focus solely on Donald Trump's Ellipse speech, or on the words of incitement in that speech. It was broader—including Trump's "rhetoric" before the election, and his efforts to pressure state officials, among other things. The memo's conclusion was clear and direct, finding that President Trump's conduct:

> . . . was a serious act, political in nature, that corrupted or subverted the political process and threatened the order of political society. As such, in my opinion, the House of Representatives is justified in pursuing the constitutional remedy of impeachment.

The political question of whether a president should be impeached with just 12 days left in office was, according to the memo, "a judgment call," but there was no question, according to this analysis, that the president's actions had constituted an impeachable offense.

17.   A VOTE OF CONSCIENCE

On Sunday night, January 10, a smaller group of House Republican leaders convened again by phone. By this time, we knew the Democrats planned to introduce a resolution calling on Vice President Pence to invoke the 25th Amendment. That would be followed by the introduction of a single article of impeachment.

We had heard that the 25th Amendment was genuinely being discussed among Trump Cabinet members, as Sean Hannity's January 7 text to Kayleigh McEnany also suggests. One Cabinet secretary told me that they had been trying to get Trump to convene a Cabinet meeting, but Mark Meadows had blocked it. Was the White House staff concerned that a meeting of the entire Cabinet would provoke further dangerous behavior from Trump? Were they trying to avoid gathering the vice president and the Cabinet together out of fear that they would take the opportunity to invoke the 25th Amendment?

Against this backdrop, Congress would be deliberating about both the 25th Amendment and impeachment. What would happen, Kevin asked staffers on the call, if this legislation passed after Trump had already left office?

At one point in the conversation, it appeared that McCarthy was saying that Trump might resign. I asked Kevin if that was a possibility. He said he'd had a few discussions about this. He didn't think Trump would step down, but then he said:

> I'm seriously thinking about having that conversation with him tonight... what I think I'm going to do is I'm going to call

him, this is what I think. You know it [the 25th Amendment resolution and/or impeachment] will pass the House, I think there's a chance it will pass the Senate even when he's gone and I think there's a lot of different ramifications for that.

Kevin said he did not want to be involved in any discussion about Pence pardoning Trump. "The only discussion I would have with him is that, 'I think this will pass and it would be my recommendation you should resign.'"

I was surprised by his answer. Maybe now that things have gotten so bad, I thought, Kevin has no choice but to do the right thing.

The Democrats had also made plans to move forward with an article of impeachment. The text of their resolution included language disqualifying Trump from ever again holding "any office of honor, trust, or profit under the United States." If Trump were impeached in the House, there would be a trial in the Senate and a two-thirds vote would be required to convict Trump and remove him from office. However, McCarthy said that he and Senate GOP Leader McConnell had spoken earlier that evening, and McConnell's view was that once Trump was impeached, we could pass a 14th Amendment ban on Trump running in the future by a simple majority vote.

Campaign Committee chair Tom Emmer weighed in to oppose impeachment on political grounds, and he suggested we consider a censure resolution instead. He proposed that Kevin could call Trump and see if Trump was willing to accept censure. I said I was opposed to any effort to seek Trump's permission for any course of action we might take. Kevin said he agreed with me, but I don't know whether or not he ultimately made the call Emmer suggested.

Kevin also echoed what Tom Cole said on our earlier call—that this impeachment was different from the previous one the Democrats had introduced. The magnitude of the attack on the Capitol was very serious, and he questioned whether a censure would be "letting Trump off." Eventually, Kevin said about Trump: "I've had it with this guy. What he did was unacceptable. Nobody can defend that, and nobody *should* defend it."

We talked about what information we would be providing to our members as we prepared for our call the next day with the entire conference. Jim Jordan had apparently already been calling other members, aggressively defending Trump. I recalled what Jordan had said at our last Republican Conference meeting on January 5: He had made a strident speech about the constitutional text governing presidential elections, based entirely on the wrong provision of the Constitution. It had been embarrassing. I also remembered that Jim had been at the December 21 White House meeting where Donald Trump's plans for January 6 were discussed. Jordan knew all along what Trump was planning, and, as we learned later, Jordan had talked to Trump from the Ways and Means Committee room while the violence was ongoing.

I strongly objected to any scenario where Jim Jordan would be making any presentation about our constitutional obligations to the conference. It was important that our conference not be seen as excusing what happened or advocating that people take a position on impeachment for political reasons. It was clear more evidence would come to light in the weeks to come, and any reflexive vote against impeachment now would ultimately be judged against all of that evidence.

Even since our last leadership call two days earlier, additional information had come out about the attack and Donald Trump's actions while the violence was underway. On January 9, Kellyanne Conway, former Trump campaign manager and White House communications adviser, tweeted out a CNN story describing the mob "hunting congressional leaders" and suggesting "there could have been a massacre" while Donald Trump was calling senators and urging them to continue objecting. "Don't avert your eyes & don't excuse this," she urged. "The more we see & learn, the worse it is."

We were also worried about death threats against members of Congress. Security at the Capitol had been dramatically bolstered. In addition to the 6,000 National Guard troops that would be deployed until after the Inauguration, towering, unscalable fencing now ringed many blocks of the Capitol complex. The FBI was providing briefings to House leadership about online planning that seemed to portend additional violence in Washington and around the country, and about continued threats against members of Congress.

We thought some in our party, like Matt Gaetz and Louie Gohmert, were potentially provoking some of those threats. Kevin committed to talk to them and to urge all members not to attack colleagues by name.

Mo Brooks of Alabama had given an incendiary speech to the crowd at the Ellipse on January 6, and some of our members were urging that he be stripped of his committee assignments. A few hours before the Capitol invasion, Brooks, yelling into the microphone, had directed the crowd to go to the Capitol, where they would find members of Congress. He said that Senators and House members opposed to the objections were choosing "to turn America into a godless, amoral, dictatorial, oppressed, and socialist nation in decline." Targeting those members, Brooks told the crowd: "Today is the day American patriots start taking down names and kicking ass!"

Brooks later admitted he had been warned on Monday, January 4, that there might be violence on January 6, so he was wearing body armor as he exhorted the crowd, "The fight begins today!"

———

The Democrats' impeachment resolution was introduced shortly before 1:00 p.m. on January 11. Although the impeachment article was titled "Incitement of Insurrection," it was not predicated solely on the words of incitement in the president's Ellipse speech. Having spent considerable time before January 6 trying to uncover what Donald Trump appeared to be planning, I knew Trump's actions attempting to overturn the election were far broader than that one speech. The impeachment article identified Trump's many false election claims "in the months preceding the Joint Session," as well as Trump's claims that the state electoral results "should not be accepted." It also cited Trump's "prior efforts to subvert and obstruct" the lawful results of the 2020 election. The article summarized Trump's conduct this way: Donald Trump "interfered with the peaceful transition of power and imperiled a coequal branch of Government. He thereby betrayed his trust as President, to the manifest injury of the people of the United States."

———

Over the next two days, I had extensive conversations with Republican members. There was widespread sentiment that we had to take action to hold Trump accountable. Kevin McCarthy reflected this in a letter he sent to the conference on January 11. He began by mourning the losses of Officers Brian Sicknick and Howard Liebengood of the US Capitol Police, then shared these thoughts:

> Having spoken to so many of you, I know we are all taking time to process the events of that day. Please know I share your anger and your pain. Zip ties were found on staff desks in my office. Windows were smashed in. Property was stolen. Those images will never leave us. . . . In the same breath, I have also heard profound resolve from our conference in the face of this evil.

The letter acknowledged the "evil" of January 6 but did not support impeachment. Instead, McCarthy identified other options to hold Trump accountable and ensure something like January 6 would never happen again. One possibility described in the letter was a potential "Resolution of Censure under the Rules of the House." Another proposal was the establishment of a "Bipartisan Commission to Investigate" January 6.

At the time, leading Republican members were preparing to introduce both of these bills. Brian Fitzpatrick of Pennsylvania was working with a group of members on the censure resolution. Fitzpatrick, a former FBI agent, is a thoughtful and responsible member of the House. Even when we disagreed, which wasn't all that often, I always knew Brian was taking his duties seriously and dealing in good faith. Early on January 11, he told me he planned to use essentially the same language from the article of impeachment but would relabel it as a *censure*—condemning Trump's actions but stopping short of calling for impeachment.

The censure resolution was ultimately very similar to the Democrats' article of impeachment, reciting basically the same unlawful conduct that merited impeachment: President Trump had made "false statements" both before January 6 and on that date, and he had incited the Ellipse crowd with statements such as, "If you don't fight like hell, you're not going to have a country anymore." Trump's conduct, the Republican resolution stated, "foreseeably resulted" in lawless action at the Capitol and was an attempt to interfere with the joint session's constitutional duty. Trump had "gravely endangered the security of the United States" and threatened the "integrity of the democratic system."

The Republican censure resolution said Congress "publicly states that President Donald J. Trump has acted in a manner grossly incompatible with self-governance and the rule of law" and "censures and condemns" Trump "for trying to unlawfully overturn the 2020 Presidential election and violating his oath of office." The resolution made no attempt to defend President Trump, nor to deny what had actually happened. We all knew the truth.

The second item in McCarthy's January 11 letter to the conference was a bill to create an independent commission to investigate January 6. The bill was introduced by Republican Rodney Davis, with more than 30 Republican cosponsors. Modeled on the bipartisan 9/11 Commission, the proposed January 6 commission would have equal numbers of members from both parties. The bill specifically required the new commission to "examine and report upon the facts and causes relating to the domestic terrorist attack of January 6th, 2021."

This was unambiguous. The Republican bill called January 6 a "domestic terrorist attack" because that's what we all believed it was. Most of us had witnessed it firsthand. And we had since seen public footage of the horrific violence against police. I told my colleagues: "The mob on the steps of the Capitol got hold of a police officer... and dragged him down the steps, beat him. You watch that and it's like Mogadishu." I was referencing Somalia's capital city, where members of the US military had been killed in 1993 and their bodies dragged through the streets. There was no question in my mind that there would be a major investigation into everything that had happened, and I said so.

The Republican independent-commission bill had a long list of cosponsors, including at least four members of the House Freedom Caucus: Ted Budd, Diana Harshbarger, Clay Higgins, and Ralph Norman. Every one of them signed on to legislation calling January 6 *a domestic terrorist attack*. Even a year later, Ted Cruz called January 6 "a violent terrorist attack on the Capitol." Of course, Tucker Carlson would force him to apologize for his momentary truthfulness the very next day, but in the immediate aftermath of the attack, virtually no one was pretending that January 6 was not a profoundly dangerous event.

———

As we began gathering material to distribute to House Republicans in preparation for our full conference meeting on January 11, Kevin McCarthy's chief counsel, Machalagh Carr, forwarded a Twitter thread by attorney Seth Abramson that analyzed Trump's Ellipse speech and concluded that the speech constituted "incitement." Abramson called the speech "one of the most dangerous presidential addresses in American history." Carr said his analysis *should be required reading for all House Republicans.*

I was fielding questions from members as they weighed supporting impeachment. One concern I heard repeatedly was this: Members believed Trump should be impeached, but they feared a vote for impeachment would put them—and their families—in danger. We were now entering territory where the threat of violence was affecting how members voted, preventing them from voting to impeach the president who had already unleashed violence.

The threats were real, and they were coming in the form of calls, voice mails, social-media posts, text messages, and letters to members' offices and homes. We were having discussions about where we could obtain body armor and whether official funds could be used to increase the security at our homes and district offices.

When one member (who ultimately voted against impeachment) told me that he knew what Trump had done was impeachable but he couldn't vote to impeach because "I am afraid it will put my wife and my new baby in danger," I absolutely understood his fear. But I also thought, "Perhaps you need to be in another job."

Other members said they believed Trump had committed impeachable offenses, but they complained about the timing of the vote. Some said it was rushed. Others claimed Trump would be gone soon, so we didn't really need to impeach him.

These arguments sounded like rationalizations to me. And, of course, the timing was out of our hands. The Democrats were in the majority. They controlled when and whether articles of impeachment would be introduced. Each member would have to choose how they wanted to be recorded by history.

Steve Womack of Arkansas gave the opening prayer when House Republicans met by Zoom on January 11. The deaths of Capitol Police Officers Sicknick and Liebengood were in the forefront of our minds. We prayed for comfort for their families as we honored their service and the service of all who defended us on January 6.

McCarthy echoed Womack's prayers for our Capitol Police officers. He described the mob breaking through the windows into his office. Rioters dressed in paramilitary gear had been photographed invading the Capitol with equipment, including zip ties, which presumably would have been used if they had taken hostages. Kevin stressed again that zip ties had been left in his offices. Every single person who did this has to be brought to justice, McCarthy said. And he left no doubt about Donald Trump's culpability:

> I've been very clear to the president. He bears responsibilities for his words and actions—no ifs, ands, or buts. I asked him personally today, does he hold responsibility for what happened? Does he feel bad about what happened? He told me he does have some responsibility for what happened. And he needs to acknowledge that....

Steve Scalise didn't beat around the bush, either. He said this was "no time to equivocate what happened, it was wrong. It was anarchy. It was insurrection...there's no excuse for what that was." I knew that Steve would not support impeachment. But at this juncture, at least, he wasn't trying to shade the truth about Donald Trump's conduct, or back away from the facts.

When I spoke, I wanted to make it clear that this wasn't a partisan issue. Republican leadership would not be "whipping" this vote or expecting members to adhere to a party line. Each member should do what they believed was right. "This has been a grave historical event," I said. "It's going to be a vote of conscience...not one about party, but one about the future of the republic."

Rodney Davis, the ranking Republican on the House Administration Committee, gave an update on security precautions around the Capitol. Davis and McCarthy had both described briefings they'd received from Capitol Police in the days before January 6, in which they'd been assured sufficient additional security measures were in place. Davis said the Capitol Police were monitoring different groups that planned to attend, and they thought the plan to push out the security perimeter and use bike racks for crowd control would work. These measures had worked a few months earlier, when there had been protests but no violence. They were nowhere close to adequate for the violence on January 6. Davis said a bipartisan, bicameral commission to understand what had happened would be the best approach.

The next day, January 12, Rodney Davis formally introduced the commission legislation, a bill to establish a "National Commission on the Domestic Terrorist Attack Upon the United States Capitol."

Peter Meijer, a freshman member from Michigan, raised concerns about the continued claims that the election had been stolen. He said many of our voters still believed this had been a landslide victory for Trump. He asked how we could get the truth out and begin rebuilding trust. Kevin McCarthy agreed with Meijer. He said we all needed to work toward a smooth transition, and we all had an obligation to educate the American public as well. I certainly agreed with that. Millions of Americans still believed Trump's lies.

The call grew tense when Lauren Boebert spoke up to say she'd seen videos of police officers moving bike racks and letting the mob in. She also alleged that DC Mayor Muriel Bowser had refused to send help when the Capitol Police needed it.

McCarthy intervened to correct Boebert. He explained that the police had moved the bike racks away as a tactical maneuver when the mob started using them as weapons. Rodney Davis also spoke up to say

Boebert was wrong about the Metropolitan Police: Not only did they respond to the urgent requests for help at the Capitol, their arrival on the scene prevented a far worse disaster that day.

Republican Jaime Herrera Beutler confronted Boebert next: "Is it true that you were live-tweeting from the floor our location to people on the outside as we were being attacked, Lauren?" By then, we all knew Boebert had provided updates, including announcing when Speaker Pelosi was evacuated from the House floor. "Don't ask us about security," Herrera Beutler said, "if you're telling the attackers where we are."

The possibility that members of Congress, including some on this call, had been coordinating with the violent mob was reverberating through the conference. Nancy Mace of South Carolina said she'd had to walk by "a crime scene where a young woman was shot" to vote on objections being led by "QAnon conspiracy theorists." She wanted to know if the bipartisan commission we had been discussing would be investigating not only the president but also members like Boebert who seemed to be in league with the rioters.

A number of members also asked whether you could impeach someone who was out of office. Kevin assured them it could be done. What he wanted, he said, was a bipartisan commission to conduct an investigation and gather more facts before we had to vote on impeachment.

We had a few days of clarity where most of the House Republican Conference was ready to either impeach or censure Donald Trump—to condemn him and his actions. And most Republicans recognized that a detailed investigation was necessary.

This moment wouldn't last.

18.   IMPEACHMENT

I was in touch with Senate GOP Leader Mitch McConnell throughout this period. He was as clear and direct in private as he had been in his remarks on the Senate floor on January 6: Donald Trump had committed impeachable offenses. McConnell believed the House should act. I thought it was likely he would support conviction.

On January 11, a story had run in the *New York Times* suggesting that McConnell was contemplating voting to convict Trump if the House impeached him. McConnell did not correct the story. That was intentional: "I like where I am," he told me as the House impeachment debate got underway.

It had been clear to me since January 6 that Donald Trump had to be impeached. I saw no choice. I had heard all the rationalizations for voting against impeachment. I had heard members say they were looking for a reason to vote no on impeachment and instead censure him. This seemed wrong to me. When a president behaves the way Donald Trump behaved, and refuses to accept the peaceful transfer of power, he poses a risk that America cannot bear. Donald Trump had not just made a momentary mistake; he had worked for multiple months to find a way to overturn the results of a lawful election.

The impeachment vote was scheduled for Wednesday, January 13. I planned to issue a statement on the night of January 12 explaining my decision to vote to impeach. I wanted to be able to capture—especially for my colleagues and for the voters in Wyoming—why I was doing this. I was an elected member of House Republican leadership, reelected by acclamation some eight weeks earlier, and I would be voting to impeach a president who was a member of my party. I needed to explain why.

I knew that what I was about to do would likely have negative political consequences for me in Wyoming. But there was no question what my oath required.

On Tuesday, January 12, the first Republican member of Congress to announce support for the impeachment of Donald Trump was John Katko of New York. Katko, the ranking member of the House Homeland Security Committee, was a former federal prosecutor. In his statement, he explained that he was approaching "the question of impeachment by reviewing the facts at hand." Then Katko proceeded to describe what we knew about what happened:

> Last week, the U.S. Capitol was attacked by a mob intent on dis-
> rupting a Joint Session of Congress and preventing certification of
> the Electoral College results.
>
> Consequently, the US Capitol Police were overrun. Insurrec-
> tionists stormed and vandalized the US Capitol, assaulting those
> who stood in their way and leaving five Americans dead...
>
> It cannot be ignored that President Trump encouraged this
> insurrection—both on social media ahead of January 6th, and in
> his speech that day. By deliberately promoting baseless theories
> suggesting the election was somehow stolen, the president cre-
> ated a combustible environment of misinformation, disenfran-
> chisement, and division. When this manifested in violent acts on
> January 6th, he refused to promptly and forcefully call it off, put-
> ting countless lives in danger.
>
> We take oaths to defend the Constitution because at times,
> it needs to be defended. Without the peaceful transfer of power
> and the acknowledgment of election results, we can't sustain our
> political system.

Katko was demonstrating exactly the kind of approach we should be able to expect from officials in positions of public trust when faced with issues of grave constitutional importance. A short while later, just after 5:30 p.m. on Monday, January 12, I sent this statement to my colleagues:

> On January 6, 2021, a violent mob attacked the United States Capitol to obstruct the process of our democracy and stop the counting of presidential electoral votes. This insurrection caused injury, death, and destruction in the most sacred space in our Republic.
>
> Much more will become clear in coming days and weeks, but what we know now is enough. The President of the United States summoned this mob, assembled the mob, and lit the flame of this attack. Everything that followed was his doing. None of this would have happened without the President. The President could have immediately and forcefully intervened to stop the violence. He did not. There has never been a greater betrayal by a President of the United States of his office and his oath to the Constitution.
>
> I will vote to impeach the President.

Later that evening, I ran into Jamie Raskin of Maryland in the Capitol Building. "Your statement is one of the most powerful things I have ever read," he said. "Thank you."

I received an outpouring of similar messages from Democrats and Republicans across the country. Some I knew and some I didn't. One Republican who had served on the Hill and at the Pentagon said, "You fulfilled the ancient charge from the Bible: 'Be strong and have courage.'" Another Republican staffer said, "You represent the reason my parents left everything to come to this country. Thank you." A retired four-star general told me he was "very proud of the courage and clarity" of my statement. A prominent conservative legal analyst texted me to say, "You are doing the honorable, constitutional, American thing. That's what matters."

Early the next morning, President George W. Bush sent me this note:

Liz, Courage is in short supply these days. Thank you for yours.
You showed strong leadership and I'm not surprised. Lead on. 43.

———

Kevin McCarthy's chief counsel, Machalagh Carr, forwarded an article to me that had been published in the conservative *National Review*. Entitled "Impeach, Convict, Remove," it began: "And, if there isn't time, impeach and convict anyway." The author, Kevin D. Williamson, thought impeachment would have been justified even before the January 6 attack, based on Trump's pre-1/6 efforts to overturn the election, including Trump's call to Georgia Secretary of State Brad Raffensperger on January 2. He wrote, "If that's not an impeachment-worthy offense, nothing is." Along with the article, Machalagh sent a text: "Sending you strength today."

The House Republican Steering Committee convened that morning in the Ways and Means Committee Room, the same room where we had spent multiple hours during the attack. The steering committee is responsible for making committee assignments for all Republicans in the House. On the morning of January 13, we were selecting ranking members for some of the key committees.

Steve Womack of Arkansas asked for time at the beginning of the meeting to play audio of some of the most incendiary sections of Mo Brooks' January 6 speech on the Ellipse. Womack believed that Brooks should be removed from committees for his comments threatening other members. Steve Scalise had likewise raised this prospect on our leadership call a few days before. Yet now Kevin McCarthy deferred. He said this meeting wasn't the place to discuss it, because we were only selecting ranking committee members. He said it would be discussed at the next steering meeting when we were populating committees. Kevin never brought it up again.

During the meeting, I got a message from Matt Pottinger, Donald Trump's former deputy national security advisor, who had resigned on

January 6. He had thanked me the night before when my impeachment statement went out. Now he was asking if there was anything he could do to help convince others that impeachment was the right response. He was offering to make calls to any members still on the fence.

Matt had the same view I did: Donald Trump's impeachable conduct did not relate solely to the Ellipse speech. It involved a number of steps aimed at overturning the election, both before and on January 6. I gave Matt a few colleagues' names, and he followed through.

————

Although Kevin McCarthy voted against impeachment, his remarks during the debate on January 13, 2021, made it clear that Trump was culpable: "The president bears responsibility for Wednesday's attack on Congress by mob rioters. He should have immediately denounced the mob when he saw what was unfolding." Kevin also said something that everyone who was present on January 6 already knew: "Some say the riots were caused by Antifa. There's absolutely no evidence of that, and conservatives should be the first to say so."

Kevin argued that censuring Donald Trump was the better course. The Republican censure resolution enumerated Trump's impeachable offenses clearly, which made it difficult to conclude that censure was a sufficient response. Chip Roy of Texas, a member of the House Freedom Caucus, acknowledged the dilemma this posed as he contemplated language for such a resolution. Chip texted me on January 10, reflecting on the list of Trump's actions: "Every time I think through this...I have trouble figuring out how that list is not impeachable conduct, and thus demanding of impeachment." Despite ultimately voting against impeachment, Roy said this in his remarks on the House floor on January 13:

> The President of the United States deserves universal condemnation for what was clearly, in my opinion, impeachable conduct: pressuring the vice president to violate his oath to the Constitution to count the electors. His open and public pressure courageously rejected by the vice president purposely seeded the false

belief among the president's supporters, including those assembled on January 6, that there was a legal path for the president to stay in power. It was foreseeable and reckless to sow such a false belief that could lead to violence and rioting by loyal supporters whipped into a frenzy.

It was clear that Trump's plan, had he succeeded, could have jeopardized the fundamental structure of our republic. Impeachment was absolutely required. Censure was not nearly enough. This kind of conduct must have severe and immediate consequences.

Before the impeachment vote, some were estimating that a couple of dozen Republicans might vote to impeach. That was a reasonable estimate. And had it not been for concerns about security and threats that they would be "primaried"—that is, defeated by a Trump loyalist in their next Republican primary race—we might have seen many more. I knew of a number of Republican members who shied away from a *yes* vote very late in the day. A couple of weeks later, in one of our House Republican Conference meetings, a prominent member who had not voted to impeach suggested that a "few dozen" more Republicans were struggling with the issue and were ready to vote to impeach. In the end, 10 Republicans did.

———

The 10 of us came from different parts of the country and different wings of the Republican Party. We were on opposite sides of some of the other major policy issues of our day. But we all recognized what our duty required. I was honored to serve alongside these colleagues—some of the most honorable public servants I've ever known.

Peter Meijer, a veteran who had served in Iraq, had been in Congress for 10 days when he had to make the courageous decision to vote to impeach. A few days after that, he was providing advice to other impeachers about how they could acquire body armor. Meijer lost his primary in 2022 to an election-denier opponent—whom the Democrats had backed in an effort to flip the seat. When he was asked if he had any regrets about his vote to impeach, Meijer said, "Not one. I would rather lose office with my character intact than stay reelected having made sacrifices of the soul."

Tom Rice, a tax attorney from South Carolina, was a member of the House Freedom Caucus, and his impeachment vote caught people by surprise. Steve Scalise called him as he was leaving the House floor, trying to pressure him to go back and change his vote. Tom refused. When asked to explain his vote during a debate in 2022, Tom's answer was clear and patriotic: "Democracy is a fragile thing, and the one thing we have to protect us from tyranny is our Constitution. Our Constitution has to be protected at all costs."

Jaime Herrera Beutler was a leader in Congress and a young mother who often brought her kids to work with her in the Capitol. Before the vote on impeachment, Jaime spent hours asking detailed questions and seeking information, including about what Donald Trump was doing during the attack. She was relentless in her search for the truth, and issued a comprehensive statement to her constituents, outlining what she had learned about Trump's conduct during those critical hours. Many others had heard the same things Jaime did. They lacked her courage and patriotism. They stayed silent.

Adam Kinzinger never wavered in his commitment to put country over party in recognizing the danger Donald Trump posed. He issued some of the most prescient warnings throughout this dangerous period, including telling the Republican Conference in a call in late December that people who kept making false claims about the election being stolen were going to incite violence. In response, Kevin McCarthy abruptly said, "Operator, next question please." Adam was the only other Republican to serve on the January 6th Select Committee.

Dan Newhouse and I served together on the Rules Committee during my first term. He was a quiet and thoughtful member who was dedicated to serving his constituents and doing the right thing. In his remarks on the floor of the House announcing that he would vote to impeach, he made clear the decision had been a painful one. But he knew that "turning a blind eye to this brutal assault on our republic is not an option."

Fred Upton understood perhaps better than anyone what the political

cost of his impeachment vote would be. He'd been in Congress the longest and had chaired the powerful House Committee on Energy and
Commerce, but his experience also informed his recognition of the danger Trump posed. The 10 of us gathered for memorable dinners at Fred
and Amey Upton's house, including one the night before the first effort to
oust me from leadership. Fred's seasoned advice and good humor were
indispensable as we navigated these difficult months.

John Katko was a former federal prosecutor and the ranking member
on the Homeland Security Committee. Standing near the back of the
House chamber one evening in the days after our impeachment vote,
Katko and I were watching other members of Congress filing in and out
to vote. He turned to me and said, "No job can ever be more important
than our oath to the Constitution."

David Valadao, whose California congressional district borders Kevin
McCarthy's, disagreed with the timing of the vote and the process the
Democrats followed. Unlike other members, however, he refused to use
those concerns as a politically expedient excuse to vote against impeachment. Valadao said, "I have to go with my gut and vote my conscience" to
impeach Donald Trump for conduct that was "unAmerican, abhorrent,
and absolutely an impeachable offense." He and Dan Newhouse were the
only two Republicans who voted to impeach Trump who returned to
serve in the 118th Congress.

Anthony Gonzalez's grandparents escaped from Castro's Cuba in
1959. He kept their photograph on the wall of his office in the Rayburn
House Office Building. No one understood the value and fragility of freedom better than he did. While most of our colleagues were working to
find an excuse to vote against impeachment, Gonzalez refused to look
away from the truth: "I probably could have found a reason to vote no,"
he said, "but I would never be able to defend it to my kids in 20 years
when they ask me about it."

My vote to impeach Donald Trump is occasionally portrayed as if I
were standing alone in opposition to my party. I wasn't. Nine other
Republicans stood with me, all for essentially the same reasons. For the
next few years, we became known both within the Republican

Conference and in the press as "the impeachers." If there had been a vote on January 13, 2021 for censure and condemnation of Donald Trump, my bet is that we would easily have had more than half the conference, including all of the Republican leadership team. And had the impeachment vote been by secret ballot, it would have been overwhelmingly in favor of impeachment.

———

The United States House of Representatives impeached Donald Trump shortly after 4:30 p.m. on January 13, 2021.

Minutes later, Senate Leader Mitch McConnell sent a letter to Republicans in the Senate saying he had not decided whether he would vote to convict. He said he intended to listen to the legal arguments at the Senate trial. However, his letter also indicated there would be no trial until after Trump left office.

The Senate was out of session. Calling them back for an emergency session would require the agreement of both Democratic Leader Chuck Schumer and Republican Leader Mitch McConnell. McConnell would not agree. I had communicated my view to McConnell that the Senate should move forward immediately, but many others seemed to be pushing for a delay. Some Democrats believed that an impeachment trial would overshadow Biden's first days in office. Still others pointed to the need to get the new president's key Cabinet officials confirmed. Ultimately, the article of impeachment was not transmitted to the Senate until January 25.

I suspect that some in Washington believed impeaching Donald Trump was enough. They thought that, after all that had happened, he would no longer be a force in American politics. This was wishful thinking—and a serious miscalculation.

19.   TRUMP LIED. PEOPLE DIED.

THE FRONT PAGE OF THE *New York Times* on the day after the impeachment vote was dominated by a photo of members of the National Guard who had been deployed to defend the Capitol. They were resting on the ground floor of the Capitol under a bust of George Washington, their weapons leaning up against the walls and around the statue's base. It reminded me of drawings I'd seen of Union soldiers stationed in the House chamber during the Civil War. As I looked at the picture, I thought about what it would take to pull our country back from this moment of crisis.

Trump's lies about the election had led to the violent assault on the Capitol. People had died. His ongoing attacks against the integrity of our elections were undermining our democracy, and could lead to still more violence. We had to find a way to defeat these fake stolen-election claims that had captured so much of the Republican Party. People had to hear the truth. The power and reach of Fox News, especially among conservative audiences, made it the obvious place to begin if we were going to refute Trump's lies. I thought Fox management might now realize how dangerous Trump was. As I sat looking at the newspaper photo on my desk, I picked up the phone and called Paul Ryan.

Ryan had been Speaker of the House during my first term in office, and he was now serving on the board of Fox Corporation, parent of the Fox News Channel. I had known Paul for many years, and I respected both his judgment and his commitment to substance and conservative principles. We had spoken several times in the prior weeks, and I knew he was deeply troubled by all that was happening. I asked for his help.

We talked about having Fox put together a one-hour show, or perhaps a series of shows, to debunk the election lies. The show could track the outcomes of the election-related lawsuits and examine the allegations one by one — focusing on objective details and the truth. This would be an important step in starting to reverse the damage that Donald Trump's election lies had done over the past several months.

I did not see how the Republican Party, or our country, could move forward without first rejecting the stolen-election fraud and embracing the truth. Paul agreed it was important and promised to see what he could do. Later that afternoon, he called back to say he had talked to Fox management. They liked the idea and planned to start working on it.

Several months later, I heard the show had been in the final stages of production when it was shut down. Someone at Fox had apparently decided not to finish it. The show never aired.

Compare this episode with the way Fox later handled a three-part series called *Patriot Purge,* which ultimately *did* air on its streaming service. Narrated by Tucker Carlson, *Patriot Purge* seemed to be a purposeful effort at misinformation. It made false and incendiary claims suggesting that federal agents had incited the January 6 attack in order to entrap American citizens.

Press reports indicated there had been widespread opposition within the news staff at Fox to Tucker Carlson's series because of its false and dangerous claims. Yet Fox News's leadership decided to air it anyway. Lies about the January 6 attack were apparently acceptable programming; the truth about the election was not.

When *Patriot Purge* ran despite the internal objections, two respected conservatives — Fox News contributors Steve Hayes and Jonah Goldberg — resigned in protest. Fox was willing to run a show spreading incendiary and false conspiracy theories, but it never ran the program debunking Trump's election lies.

————

As President Joe Biden and Vice President Kamala Harris were sworn in to office on January 20, and as the Senate prepared for the impeachment trial, House Republicans had a fresh opportunity to chart a path toward the future. I had been describing this path to my colleagues and in press interviews: Where we could find bipartisan agreement, we would. Where we opposed policies that the new administration was putting in place, we would advocate for the conservative substance and ideals we believed in for the nation. We would reject insurrection, embrace the truth and the Constitution, and look toward the future.

This road map wasn't complicated. It was common sense. It was the course any responsible political party led by serious people would have followed. It was the course that Americans guided by principle and patriotism would have chosen.

But it's not the course Kevin McCarthy took.

On January 25, as the article of impeachment was being transmitted to the Senate, McCarthy appeared on Fox News claiming the impeachment had been "purely political" and "a farce." In comments that directly contradicted Kevin's prior remarks condemning Trump in our conference calls and on the House floor, he now suggested the impeachment was baseless. He went on to say he didn't think we needed National Guard troops at the Capitol, and he mocked the additional security measures that he had been advocating just a few weeks earlier.

We had become accustomed to the whiplash Kevin's unprincipled leadership was causing, but this was schizophrenic. When one member confronted Kevin directly about the interview and asked why he was changing his view on Trump's January 6 conduct, Kevin claimed he hadn't changed it at all—which, as the member described it, was "total bullshit."

McCarthy's motive became clear a few days later when, on January 28, he visited Donald Trump at his Mar-a-Lago resort in Palm Beach, Florida. Three weeks after the attack on the US Capitol, the Republican Leader of the House of Representatives was prostrating himself before the man responsible for January 6.

20. TRUMP'S NOT EATING

WHEN I FIRST SAW THE photo of Kevin McCarthy standing next to Donald Trump at Mar-a-Lago on January 28, grins on both men's faces, I thought it was fake. Not a month had passed since Kevin was running through the hallways of the Capitol to escape Trump's violent mob and calling members of Trump's family, with fear in his voice, begging them to get Trump to call off the riot.

Not even Kevin McCarthy could be this craven, I thought.

I was wrong.

Republican members were angry and disgusted as they tried to comprehend what McCarthy had done. Some mocked him, circulating the Trump/McCarthy photo along with the clip from the movie *Jerry Maguire* where Tom Cruise tells Renée Zellweger, "You...complete...me."

During the visit, McCarthy had sent out a fundraising text directing people to contribute to a website called Trumps-majority.com. Just over two weeks earlier, Kevin had told us he knew Trump was responsible for the attack, and that the president should resign from office. Now he was at Mar-a-Lago, rehabilitating Trump's image and raising money to elect a "Trump majority" in Congress. One member summed it up to me this way: "So, McCarthy falls at the feet of the man who storms the Capitol..."

I went to see Kevin when he got back to DC:

"Mar-a-Lago? What the hell, Kevin?"

He tried to downplay the whole thing. He said he had been in Florida anyway when Trump's staff called him.

"They're really worried," he said. "Trump's not eating, so they asked me to come see him."

"What? You went to Mar-a-Lago because Trump's not eating?"

"Yeah, he's really depressed."

I was still trying to process this unexpected rationale when Kevin added, "He keeps trying to talk to me about January 6th and I tell him we can't. We're under oath."

Kevin said "We're under oath" in the present tense, as though he had already been sworn in as a witness. I assumed one of Kevin's lawyers had warned him not to talk to Trump about January 6, because they thought Trump might be in serious legal jeopardy. Apparently, Kevin was trying to say back to me what he'd been told by his lawyers.

The truth was pretty simple. Kevin McCarthy went to Mar-a-Lago because his ability to raise money had dried up after January 6 when nearly every major corporate donor announced it would stop making campaign contributions to Republicans who had voted to object to the Electoral College votes. Kevin's strength in our conference was derived largely from his fundraising ability. He was not a policy expert or a natural leader. And now his strength was gone.

Kevin needed money. Trump had lists of small-dollar donors. But Kevin would have to go beg Trump for them. And in order to use those lists, Kevin would have to help Donald Trump cover up the stain of his assault on our democracy.

It was a price Kevin McCarthy was willing to pay.

The irony was that House Republicans never had to be in this position in the first place. Things would have been very different if McCarthy had done the right thing from the beginning. Instead he humored Trump, went on national television to claim the election had been stolen, signed Mike Johnson's amicus brief, and encouraged members to object to electoral votes—even after the violent attack.

Every time Kevin McCarthy had faced a decision of consequence, he had done the wrong thing. Now Donald Trump was the only one left who would help him.

I thought of what Kevin's mentor, former Republican Congressman

Bill Thomas, had said after January 6. Thomas, a legend in the United States House of Representatives, had represented Kevin's district for 28 years. After January 6, he was not shy about criticizing Kevin: Thomas called McCarthy a "hypocrite." "You never know what's inside [him] really," Thomas said later.

> Kevin basically is whatever you want him to be. He lies. He'll change the lie if necessary. How can anyone trust his word?

The same day Kevin visited Trump at Mar-a-Lago, we all got another reminder of the clear and present threat of political violence. Police arrested a man parked in his truck near the Capitol with a firearm, ammunition, and Stop the Steal materials. Also in his possession: lists of names and contact information for members of Congress.

21. REMOVELIZ.COM

AROUND THE TIME OF KEVIN McCarthy's Mar-a-Lago pilgrimage, members of the Freedom Caucus began circulating a petition to recall me from my leadership position for having voted to impeach Donald Trump.

Anonymous sources were leaking to the press that they had collected close to 120 signatures, which would have been a majority of Republicans in Congress. Although I had been working to move House Republicans back to a more normal mode of operations, we were about to fight yet another very public battle about Trump within the Republican Conference. This was obviously originating from Trump, and after visiting Mar-a-Lago, Kevin wasn't willing to shut it down. He scheduled a conference meeting for Wednesday, February 3, where House Republicans would debate whether I should be removed from leadership.

That morning I met with McCarthy and a number of other members in Kevin's office. Among them was Patrick McHenry of North Carolina, who had previously been chief deputy whip. I liked and respected Patrick, but I knew he would be following Kevin's direction. They suggested that I should issue some kind of apology, either before or during the conference meeting later that day.

I said I wasn't going to apologize for my impeachment vote.

"Well, maybe you could apologize for your statement?" They meant my statement on January 12 announcing that I would vote to impeach and saying that Donald Trump "lit the flame of this attack." I wasn't going to do that, either.

Could you show some kind of contrition for *anything*? they wanted to know. A few days earlier, McCarthy had admonished me that I needed to "change my tone." This was feeling more like middle school than the US Congress.

"How about this?" McHenry suggested. "You didn't mean to put members in a tough position in their districts, did you?"

"No," I said. "That was not my intent."

"Okay, how about that? Can you say that?"

It was clearly going to be a long night.

"How's your whip count?" they asked. They wanted to know if I had a sense of what the vote would ultimately be on my removal.

"Good," I said, without telling them our numbers. If it came to a vote, I was confident we would prevail.

Conference rules provided a number of procedural options we could use to avoid a vote if the Freedom Caucus formally offered their motion to remove me. These included things like referring the motion to the steering committee. None of those alternatives appealed to me. I didn't want this to linger, and I certainly didn't want it to be something anyone had hanging over me. I wanted an up or down vote. Freedom Caucus members were saying I feared a vote because so many members supported the removal resolution. I wanted to call their bluff.

———

Before the House Republican Conference met on February 3, McCarthy, Scalise, and I attended the memorial service in the Capitol Rotunda for Officer Brian Sicknick, who died from injuries he sustained while defending the Capitol. President Joe Biden, Vice President Kamala Harris, Secretary of Defense Lloyd Austin, and most of the nation's other senior leaders were in attendance. After the service, we gathered with Officer Sicknick's family in the Rayburn Room near the House floor. Despite this tragic reminder of the violence of January 6, some House Republicans were already working to whitewash what had happened.

Shortly after 4:00 p.m., House Republicans convened in the auditorium of the Capitol Visitor Center. Dan Bishop of North Carolina stood to offer what he called *a resolution of no confidence in the chair.* Despite the claims of at least 120 signatures that Freedom Caucus sources had been making, it turned out that Bishop's was the only signature they submitted. Their claim had been a deliberate lie, apparently to intimidate me into resigning.

McCarthy suggested that the conference could first just have a discussion about the issues Bishop was raising. After that, Bishop could offer his resolution if he still felt the need to do so. After some back-and-forth, Bishop agreed to that. McCarthy and Scalise then made opening comments urging unity. McCarthy said he wanted to keep our leadership team together. Everyone stressed that we should leave the auditorium unified, no matter the session's outcome.

When it was my turn for opening remarks, I talked about how much I loved the institution of the House of Representatives. A year earlier, I'd had an opportunity to run for the Senate; instead I'd chosen to stay in the House, because I believed it was a special place where we could have serious and substantive debates about the policies that mattered most to our nation. Now, however, I was deeply troubled by what was happening inside the Republican Party.

I talked about what we had all seen on January 6, when a mob of people—some wearing the insignia of neo-Nazis and white supremacists—had attacked our Capitol. "We cannot become the party of QAnon," I said. "We cannot become the party of Holocaust denial. We cannot become the party of white supremacy. That can never be us. We are the party of Abraham Lincoln and of Ronald Reagan. We believe above all else in fidelity to the Constitution."

I had talked to many of my colleagues over the previous weeks, and we obviously had come to different conclusions on impeachment. But we owed each other honesty and clarity. I said I would not apologize for my impeachment vote, and I would not apologize for my statement explaining the vote.

I knew this conference meeting—like all our meetings and calls—would likely be leaked to the press as it was happening. Journalists would be reporting what was said in real time. I didn't want anyone to claim I had given ground or issued an apology.

And I wanted to convey the import of the issues we were dealing with. History was watching us. I had once read a lecture given by historian David McCullough about the US Capitol. He talked about the statue of Clio, muse of history, that stands over the door in Statuary Hall. I reminded my colleagues of what she stood for and why she was there. Clio is depicted riding in the chariot of time, making notes in the book in her hand, as a reminder that what we do in the Capitol Building is written in the pages of history. I said I hoped we could come out of this meeting unified in our commitment to conduct ourselves in a manner worthy of our history and worthy of the mantle of Abraham Lincoln.

Microphones stood in the aisles on each side of the auditorium and members lined up to speak as we opened the floor for debate. The criticisms ran mostly along predictable lines, with Freedom Caucus members assailing my lack of loyalty to Donald Trump. But there were some surprises, too. Andy Biggs, one of nine representatives from Arizona, said my statement announcing that I would vote to impeach Trump had resulted in 3,600 Arizona Republicans leaving the party in the last three weeks. I was pretty sure we had lost those 3,600 voters because of what Donald Trump did, not because of my statement confirming that his conduct was impeachable.

Biggs and Georgia's Andrew Clyde each used some of their speaking time to read directly from my statement, evidently to demonstrate how offensive it was to them. I stood at the podium, watching Clyde say, "The President of the United States summoned this mob, assembled this mob, and lit the flame of this attack." Biggs read aloud: "There has never been a greater betrayal by a president of the United States of his office and his oath to the Constitution." Hearing my words come out of their mouths added to the surreal nature of the entire proceeding.

Other members said they were upset that my impeachment vote had caused them trouble at home. They thought I should have provided them cover for their votes against impeachment. Jeff Van Drew of New Jersey, who had been a Republican for even less time than Donald Trump, said my vote had made it hard for him to explain to people in his swing district why he hadn't voted to impeach. I had heard this same complaint a few weeks earlier from an angry Elise Stefanik of New York. She told me that, because of my vote to impeach, people were writing letters to the editors of her local papers criticizing her and asking why she hadn't taken the same "principled" stand I had. That seemed less my problem than hers. Many of us who had known Elise since before she abandoned all principle were curious about how she had lost her sense of right and wrong.

A number of the men who spoke in favor of removing me said they didn't like my *tone*. I wasn't *contrite enough*, nor had I *learned my lesson*. Ralph Norman of South Carolina kept repeating that his problem with me was my *attitude*: "You've just got such a defiant attitude!" John Rutherford of Florida said I was *just too recalcitrant* and hadn't learned from my mistakes. Then he accused me of not "riding for the brand."

I'm sure Rutherford thought he was being clever quoting a cowboy phrase to lecture me about loyalty. "John," I reminded him, "our 'brand' is the US Constitution."

A couple of my male colleagues were so enraged by my unwillingness to apologize that they got themselves really worked up and seemed on the verge of tears as they lectured me. I tried to follow what the most emotional members were saying, but it wasn't always easy. Mike Kelly of Pennsylvania, for example, seemed angry because I had released a statement *before* I voted. In an effort to describe how upset he was, he said, "It's like you're playing in the biggest game of your life and you look up and see your girlfriend sitting on the opponent's side!"

These were grown men. This was 2021. I was standing at the podium at the front of the auditorium thinking, You've got to me kidding me. Other female members started yelling, "She's not your girlfriend!"

"Yeah," I said, "I'm not your girlfriend."

———

·Halfway through the meeting we took a break when votes were called on the House floor. When we reconvened in the auditorium a short time later, Tom Rice, one of the 10 Republicans who had voted to impeach Donald Trump, rose to speak:

Guys, I think we're confused. Liz's statement did not cause the problems we face. It didn't cause the thousands of registered

Republicans in Arizona, or South Carolina, or Georgia to move over. What caused that was the president throwing a two-month temper tantrum after the election on November third, which culminated in a ransacking of the Capitol and the death of one, maybe three, Capitol Police officers. The president sat in the White House surrounded by Secret Service, tweeting that Mike Pence was a coward, and watching TV, and couldn't be bothered to answer calls for help.

There's a poll out today that says the president has lost 20 points since December. In December, 65 percent of registered Republicans wanted him to run for president again. Today [that's] 45 percent. And yet Kevin went to Mar-a-Lago this weekend, shook his hand, took a picture, and set up Trumps-majority.com. Personally, I find that offensive.

"Trump's-majority" was the name of the group on the fundraising message Kevin sent out while he was at Mar-a-Lago. Some of my colleagues had been very angry about the solicitation, concluding that Kevin had sold them out. Less than three weeks after calling for Trump to be censured and condemned, Kevin McCarthy had obviously done a deal with Trump. And now McCarthy was calling the House Republicans "Trump's majority." The message, they concluded, was that "Trump owns us." It seemed that Trump had gotten Kevin to admit to the world that he—and indeed our entire conference—was once again subservient to Trump.

Up until that moment in the discussion, this meeting had been cost-free for Kevin McCarthy. I was the one standing at the podium, taking the incoming fire while he sat on the stage and watched. But now Tom Rice had identified a significant issue. In concept, the House Republican Conference could have moved away from Trump and returned to the normal way a conservative party operates. But not if our leadership remained dependent on Trump for fundraising. Both things could not happen at the same time.

At that point, Kevin intervened. His response was convoluted: He denied the charge that Tom was making, said he was working hard to raise money, and said he'd visited Mar-a-Lago because he would go to lunch with anyone, even Joe Biden. He said he had lots of fundraising entities, then tried to distance himself from Trumps-majority.com by denying that the timing of the message had anything to do with his visit to Trump. His explanation of his visit to Mar-a-Lago was quite different from what he'd told me earlier. Apparently, Trump didn't have some secret eating disorder after all.

While Kevin was claiming to be *working for us all,* Rice pointed out what the official Republican digital-fundraising organization, WinRed, was in fact doing: "There's a website up on WinRed right now called RemoveLiz.com. They're using WinRed to raise money to take her out." We all knew that Kevin could control exactly what WinRed was doing.

That stopped the discussion. Kevin did not offer any further response.

A bit later in our meeting, Republican Don Bacon took the microphone. Don is a retired Air Force general and an honorable man. He urged us to stop the "circular firing squad." Only 10 Republicans may have voted in favor of impeachment, he pointed out, yet "dozens and dozens more struggled with it."

Then Bacon went even further:

Thank God we had a good vice president that did the right thing...we would have had a Constitutional crisis unlike [any] we've seen since the Civil War. So this was serious...

Secondly, the election was decided at 14 December, when the states certified. There was no way on 6 January we were going to turn that around. Why did we go down this path? This was never going to work. We fed false hopes to millions of people. And that's what we saw on the sixth of January. I appreciate the fact that Liz spoke up and tried to forewarn us before the 6th.

"She spoke up and warned us, and we needed that leadership," Don concluded. "The president needed to stop what he did as 6 January approached and concede gracefully and we wouldn't have been in this position."

As the meeting neared the four-hour mark, I wanted to call the vote. I think McCarthy would have preferred to let people air their grievances and then avoid an actual vote. I suppose he thought that was best for him. I wanted an up or down vote so the outcome would be clear and unambiguous.

Shortly before 7:30 p.m., I texted McCarthy that we should call the vote. He said okay. Right before the vote began, Virginia Foxx of North Carolina, who supported Trump, made a motion to keep the results secret. It was apparent that she was now scared how the vote would turn out, and I was sure she was doing Kevin's bidding. Thankfully, conference rules did not permit us to keep the results secret. The outcome would be read aloud for all to hear.

I turned the gavel over to Tom Cole so he could preside over the vote. He read the resolution:

It is hereby resolved that Elizabeth Lynne Cheney has lost the confidence of the majority of the members of the House Republican Conference needed to continue as the chair of the House Republican Conference, and it is hereby resolved that Elizabeth Lynne Cheney is removed as the chair of the House Republican Conference.

Members filed up to tables at the front of the auditorium to cast their votes. While we awaited the final tally, Jenniffer González-Colón of Puerto Rico gave me a hug and handed me a rosary. She said she and her staff had been praying that I would prevail. It meant a lot to me.

Mike Turner from Ohio joined us and summed up the meeting this way: "Well, I just got to spend four hours listening to a bunch of men tell a woman that she wasn't taking their feelings into account."

Going into the meeting, our whip count was 142 to 56 in my favor. Caroline Boothe, who did a tremendous job handling all member services for the House Republican Conference, had been in charge of our vote-counting operation. Caroline's professionalism and responsiveness in working with the Republican members and their staffs undoubtedly contributed to my margin of victory. I suspect that McCarthy and other members of leadership thought I would lose the vote. While the meeting was underway, members of Kevin's staff had made a point of telling my staffers that we were bound to lose: "You guys don't have the votes — you know that, right?"

The final vote was 145 opposed to the removal motion and 61 in favor. I had won without even a hint of the type of apology that Kevin McCarthy was pressuring me to give.

We had defeated this first effort to oust me from leadership. But it seemed clear, particularly from Kevin's exchange with Tom Rice, where the House Republican leader was ultimately headed.

22.   THEY STARED DOWN AT
THEIR DESKS

By the time the Senate impeachment trial of Donald Trump began in February 2021, I was growing concerned that Mitch McConnell had lost his earlier resolve. As McConnell and I had conferred throughout the impeachment proceedings in the House, he had been firm in his view that Trump should be impeached. He had said publicly that the decision to vote to convict Donald Trump in the Senate trial would be a vote of conscience. But then McConnell voted in favor of a procedural motion introduced by his fellow Kentucky senator, Rand Paul, claiming the trial was unconstitutional because Trump was no longer president. The motion failed, but McConnell's support of it signaled that his position was shifting. If members of the Senate thought there was a legal issue with trying Trump once he was out of office, the trial should not have been delayed.

I hoped that every senator would listen to all the evidence presented and make a fair judgment. I didn't think any senator should publicly say they had already made up their mind about the underlying facts before actually hearing the evidence.

The trial opened with a devastating video of the attack. I couldn't imagine how anyone could watch that video and then continue to downplay or excuse what Donald Trump had done. Maybe this would help begin to show people the truth.

I sent a link to the video to one of my longtime donors in Wyoming who had embraced Donald Trump's lies. Before January 6, she had urged me to object to the electoral votes, and we had exchanged messages during the objection debate. At one point, I had sent her a link to a January 1 tweet from Lin Wood, an attorney working on Trump's behalf. Wood had called for the execution of Vice President Mike Pence by firing squad. She acknowledged it was crazy—then went back to urging me to object to electors.

I thought maybe this video of the violent attack would help her begin to see the truth. "I'm sure you guys are watching," I said, "but in case you haven't seen it—this is worth taking 14 minutes to watch."

Her response to me began with this:

Liz, We are not watching the democrat political theater. We believe Trump won the election, (I have first-hand knowledge of what happened in Michigan and have spoken [with] an expert involved in the forensic audit of Dominion), that the impeachment is unconstitutional, and that he did NOT incite the pre-planned attack on the Capitol . . .

This was sad. She had fallen for all the nonsense. I was direct in my reply:

I'm sorry, but you've been misled. Not only did President Trump lie about the election, he provoked the mob attack, and once it was underway, he failed to take action to stop the mob and instead tweeted out that Vice President Pence is a coward, while the mob hunted him and his family through the halls of the Capitol. We almost lost our republic that day. You should watch the video footage.

Jamie Raskin, the lead House impeachment manager, told me later that, during the trial, certain senators in the chamber had stared down at their desks as the video of the violent attack played.

As the trial wound down, the Senate had to consider whether the impeachment managers could call witnesses. One of the witnesses they were contemplating calling was a Republican member of the House of Representatives, Jaime Herrera Beutler, who had voted to impeach Trump.

Jaime had been diligent in considering her impeachment vote. She had taken careful notes, for example, of Kevin McCarthy's description of a call he had with Donald Trump during the violence on January 6. McCarthy had described this call many times in meetings with other House Republicans. Dozens had heard him tell the story of being evacuated from his office as the rioters were breaking in, including some of the details of the call. Jaime described what happened in several interviews:

> And he [Kevin McCarthy] said [to President Trump], "You have got to get on TV. You've got to get on Twitter. You've got to call these people off." You know what the President said to him?
>
> This is as it's happening. He said, "Well, Kevin, these aren't my people. You know, these are Antifa." And Kevin responded and said, "No, they're your people. They literally just came through my office windows and my staff are running for cover. I mean they're running for their lives. You need to call them off." And the President's response to Kevin to me was chilling. He said, "Well, Kevin, I guess they're just more upset about the election, you know, theft than you are."

The details of this call were one of many pieces of evidence of Donald Trump's *intent*—evidence showing that Trump knew about the violence but did not, for multiple hours, take the actions required to instruct his supporters to stand down and evacuate the Capitol.

The Senate initially voted 55 to 45 on February 13 in favor of calling Jaime Herrera Beutler as a witness to describe the details of the McCarthy-Trump call. But the potential to call more live witnesses kicked off negotiations among key players—including the impeachment managers, Senate leadership, and Trump's defense counsel. Senators on both sides of the aisle seemed hesitant to add the multiple additional days to the trial that live witnesses would require. We know today, because of the Select Committee hearings, that if witnesses—including Republican witnesses from Donald Trump's White House—had been called during the Senate impeachment trial, it would have been clear that the facts were even more damning than we knew them to be at the time. Conviction might well have become even more likely.

Ultimately, House impeachment managers agreed to enter into the record a statement issued by Herrera Beutler in which she detailed the contents of the McCarthy-Trump call. She never wavered in her commitment to the truth. And Herrera Beutler called on others who knew the truth to come forward as well, saying:

> To the patriots who were standing next to the former president as these conversations were happening, or even to the former vice president: If you have something to add here, now would be the time.

Even though the information available at the time was skeletal compared with the mountain of material the January 6th Select Committee ultimately compiled, it was sufficient to convince 57 United States senators—including seven Republicans—to vote to convict Donald Trump. The 57-to-43 vote fell short of the two-thirds majority needed to convict. But it was the largest bipartisan vote in history for the conviction of a president on an impeachment charge.

Ten more Republican votes would have been needed to convict. There were at least 10 more Republicans who had publicly condemned Trump's conduct but voted *against* conviction because Trump was already out of office when the trial took place. Another 16 Republicans made no mention of Trump in their statements, but said they were voting to acquit because they had concluded that the US Senate lacks the authority to convict a former president. Only a handful of Republican senators seemed to argue that Trump's conduct did not actually warrant conviction.

I don't know if Mitch McConnell would have voted to convict Trump if more House Republicans had voted to impeach him. Maybe he always hoped that impeachment alone would be enough to end Trump's political career. Either way, Leader McConnell, who had made a career out of savvy political calculation and behind-the-scenes maneuvering, got this one wrong. Again, if the Senate believed it had a jurisdictional hurdle that could not be overcome, it should have found a way to conduct the trial before Donald Trump left office.

I had known Mitch McConnell for more than 20 years, and I respected him. A little over a year earlier, he had tried to recruit me to run for the Senate when Mike Enzi announced his retirement. Few could match McConnell's mastery of the tactics of political leadership. But I thought he had made a number of serious mistakes in this case, including 1) not agreeing to call the Senate back into session for the impeachment trial and 2) not voting to convict.

McConnell's closing remarks at the trial were well written and powerful. But they did nothing to fix the problem we all faced:

> Whatever our ex-president claims he thought might happen that day, whatever reaction he says he meant to produce, by that afternoon, he was watching the same live television as the rest of the world. A mob was assaulting the Capitol in his name. These criminals were carrying his banners, hanging his flags, and screaming their loyalty to him. It was obvious that only President Trump could end this. Former aides publicly begged him to do so. Loyal allies frantically called the administration. But the president did not act swiftly. He did not do his job. He didn't take steps so federal law could be faithfully executed, and order restored. Instead, according to public reports, he watched television happily as the chaos unfolded. He kept pressing his scheme to overturn the election. Even after it was clear to any reasonable observer that Vice President Pence was in serious danger, even as the mob carrying Trump banners was beating cops and breaching perimeters, the president sent a further tweet attacking his vice president....
>
> We have a criminal justice system in this country. We have civil litigation. And former presidents are not immune from being held accountable by either one.

McConnell had been telling me that he expected Trump to fade away. I already knew that would not happen.

23. THIS ISN'T THEIR PARTY ANYMORE

FOLLOWING OUR HOUSE REPUBLICAN CONFERENCE meetings each week, we usually held a press conference to brief the media and take questions. Sometimes we would use the House television studio. Often we would just set up a microphone in the hallway outside the auditorium in the Capitol Visitor Center, and the reporters covering Capitol Hill would gather around. As conference chair, I would open the briefings, then turn the floor over to other members of leadership to make remarks. McCarthy would speak last and then stay at the microphone to field questions.

On February 24, 2021, McCarthy, Steve Scalise, and I lined up to brief the press, along with Jason Smith, ranking Republican on the Budget Committee. The main topic of discussion was the Covid/stimulus bill the Democrats were pushing through Congress. I talked about the gap we were seeing between President Joe Biden's calls for compassion and unity, and his policies, especially his energy policies, which risked doing real damage to communities across the West. At the end of my remarks, I noted that February 24 was the 30th anniversary of the beginning of the ground war in Operation Desert Storm. I asked that everyone take a minute to remember the brave Americans who had fought in Desert Shield and Desert Storm.

The press conference proceeded uneventfully. I stood next to Scalise and Smith as we listened to McCarthy describe the wasteful spending in the Democrats' Covid bill. Then Kevin took questions.

The final question of the press conference was: "Leader McCarthy, do you and the leadership, especially Congresswoman Cheney, believe President Trump should be speaking at CPAC [the Conservative Political Action Committee] this weekend?"

McCarthy answered, "Yes, he should."

I had addressed CPAC multiple times in the past, but I thought the organization had since veered off course, was poorly managed, and was no longer true to its "conservative" name.

After McCarthy answered, the reporter wanted to know what I thought. "Congresswoman Cheney?"

"That's up to CPAC," I said. "I've been clear in my views about President Trump and the extent to which, following January 6, I don't believe he should be playing a role in the future of the party or the country."

There was a moment of awkward silence. Then Kevin said, "On that high note, thank you all very much," and brought the questioning to an end. The video of the end of the press conference shows me walking off in one direction while pretty much everyone else walks off in the other. It would be the last time Kevin McCarthy and I appeared together at a press conference.

We were scheduled to hold a leadership meeting in McCarthy's conference room shortly after the press event. Kevin asked to see me in his office first.

"You're killing me, Liz," he said when I walked in. It was clear that Kevin was under significant pressure from Trump, and public criticism of the former president by anyone in the party could simply not be tolerated.

I hadn't planned on having a public disagreement at a leadership press conference, I told him, but I was asked a direct question and I answered it. My answer shouldn't have come as a surprise to anyone who had been paying attention.

Far more than a policy dispute was at issue here.

"Kevin," I said, "this is about the Constitution. Think of what Trump did. Think how appalled *any* of our previous Republican leaders would be about this. How would Reagan have reacted to this? How would Bush have reacted? Think of my dad."

A large portrait of Ronald Reagan hangs in Kevin McCarthy's office. But he apparently no longer believed in the conservatism of our 40th president.

"This isn't their party anymore," Kevin said.

He wasn't wrong. The GOP was becoming an anti-Constitution party. And too many of our leaders were willing to accept that.

24. BUT WHAT IF HE IS OUR ONLY HOPE?

ONE OF MY RESPONSIBILITIES AS conference chair was to plan the annual retreat we held for all Republican members. I wasn't a fan of retreats—they seemed like a waste of time and money. I preferred sessions like the one Paul Ryan organized during my first year in Congress. All the Republicans had gone to an auditorium at Fort Myer, a military base a few miles from the Capitol, for a daylong series of briefings on the Republican tax plan. Nerdy, yes—but also substantive, useful, and efficient.

Kevin McCarthy had a different approach. He loved big retreats where the conference would spend days at a luxury hotel someplace. I think he imagined himself giving a TED talk as his communications staff filmed him telling members things like "I always say the thing is let's keep our heads while everybody else is getting emotional and get the right people on the bus, and the others." Kevin tended to inject the phrase *and others* or *and the others* at the end of his sentences. I never understood who *the others* were, but Kevin talked about them all the time.

One year as we got ready for the retreat, McCarthy told us he had a great idea for encouraging member participation in small-group breakout sessions. He wanted the GOP Conference to buy basketball-size plushy cubes, each with a microphone inside. The cubes, covered in something like blue shag carpet, resembled one of those stuffed prizes you win at a county fair. During breakout sessions, the idea was that whoever was speaking would hold the cube. When they finished, they were supposed to throw the cube to the next speaker.

As I listened to Kevin explain the concept, I tried to imagine exactly how it would work in the breakout session I was responsible for. The topic was: "US National Security and the Threat from China." Were we really going to ask our outside expert on US defense spending to give his presentation while holding a giant blue plushy cube? And when he got done, were we going to tell him to throw it across the room to our supply-chain expert?

The cube microphones were expensive. *What if someone missed?* (Not unlikely in this crowd.) *How many were we going to break?* We made a command decision in my China session to forgo the carpet-cube game in favor of more traditional handheld microphones.

In addition to the annual retreat for all Republican members of the House, we had a leadership retreat each year attended by the elected leaders, along with the ranking members of each committee and assorted additional members and staff. When we convened for our leadership retreat in Florida in March 2021, tensions within the conference were simmering.

In the two months since the Capitol attack, rather than looking toward the future, the party was increasingly being sucked into Trump's cesspool of election lies and threats. Following Kevin's lead, other Republican members of Congress had started making the pilgrimage to visit Trump at Mar-a-Lago or in New York and then posting photos of their visits online. My staff began taping these photos on the back of a door in our office. They called it the "Door of Disgrace." A place of honor was reserved for one member who apparently hadn't been able to get in to see Trump but had posted pictures of himself outside Donald Trump's building and in Donald Trump's lobby.

It didn't take long for the topic of Trump to come up at our March 2021 leadership retreat. McCarthy claimed that Trump had been a positive force for Republicans in the 2020 election, and that he would continue to be critical to our success moving forward. This was so unmoored from reality that I assumed Kevin was worried someone in the room would report any negative comments back to Trump. In fact, Republican House members had significantly outperformed Trump in key districts because many Republicans and independents simply would not vote for Trump.

When we had a presentation on recent polling results, I asked about Trump's favorability numbers among independent voters. I didn't get a direct answer. Any discussion of Trump that could be perceived as negative in any way was clearly to be avoided. Only praise could be offered.

The discussion turned to social media and big tech. In the aftermath of January 6, Trump had been kicked off multiple social-media platforms. Certain others who had amplified Trump's false claims were also deplatformed in the wake of the violence. Questions about how tech companies such as Facebook and Twitter moderated their content and made their decisions to deplatform certain users had generated a good deal of interest, especially among House Republicans.

McCarthy and Devin Nunes, the ranking Republican on the House Intelligence Committee, led this part of the program. Shortly after our retreat, Nunes left Congress to run Donald Trump's newly launched Truth Social platform. As McCarthy discussed conservative speech being silenced online, he seemed to be mostly reciting boilerplate talking points. But then he claimed that the online platform Parler had been shut down simply because it was conservative.

In reality, Apple, Google, and Amazon had said they suspended Parler's accounts on January 9 and 10 because users of the site were calling for violence, including political assassinations, and Parler had failed to moderate or remove such posts.

According to court records, prior to January 6, Parler had failed to remove posts on its platform, including the following:

- "This cu** [United States Secretary of Transportation Elaine Chao] should be ... hung for betraying their country."
- "Hang this mofo [Georgia Secretary of State Brad Raffensperger] today."
- "We are coming with our list we know where you live we know who you are and we are coming for you and it starts on the 6th civil war ... Lol if you will think it's a joke ... Enjoy your last few days you have."
- "We need to act like our forefathers did Kill [Black and Jewish people] all Leave no victims or survivors."

- "After the firing squads are done with the politicians the teachers are next"
- "Shoot the police that protect these shitbag senators right in the head then make the senator grovel a bit before capping they ass."
- "We are going to fight in a civil War on Jan. 20th, Form MILITIAS now and acquire targets."
- "White people need to ignite their racial identity and rain down suffering and death like a hurricane upon zionists."

Members of the Proud Boys used Parler in the weeks leading up to the attack to coordinate their plans and call for violence. On November 27, 2020, Zachary Rehl, head of the Philadelphia chapter of the Proud Boys, posted, "Hopefully the firing squads are for the traitors that are trying to steal the election..." Proud Boys leader Enrique Tarrio used Parler to instruct his members to "turn out in record numbers" on January 6, 2021, but to conceal who they were: "We will not be wearing our traditional black and yellow. We will be incognito and we will spread across downtown DC in smaller teams." On New Year's Day 2020, Tarrio posted, "Let's bring this new year with one word in mind: revolt." Later he called for a "New Years [sic] Revolution." These posts would later be introduced in the trial in which four Proud Boys, including Tarrio and Rehl, were convicted of seditious conspiracy, or conspiring to overthrow the government of the United States. Tarrio was ultimately sentenced to 22 years in prison.

Although the Proud Boys trial would not conclude until more than two years later, it was no secret in real time what Parler was doing. There had been significant press coverage in the days after January 6 about the content that Parler was hosting. In our conference meeting on January 11, Adam Kinzinger warned that anyone defending Parler needed to be aware of what was actually posted on the platform—including calls for the assassination of members of Congress.

Now, two months after the attack, I was listening to the leader of the House Republicans spread the lie that Parler was shut down simply because it was conservative. The impact of this lie was especially toxic. It wasn't lost on those who had been posting racist, anti-Semitic, hate-filled calls for violence on Parler that Trump and his Republican supporters were defending them. The lie also fed the anger of Trump supporters who believed they were being silenced because of their political beliefs. I thought back to Kevin's concern after January 6; he told us he was receiving FBI briefings about the serious threats of violence against members of Congress. At the time, he had admonished all House Republicans not to fan the flames of this potential political violence. Now he was doing it himself. I left the retreat shortly afterward.

———

The conservative policies and principles that had once defined what it meant to be a Republican were being replaced by complete allegiance to one man—who wasn't actually a conservative. One of the clearest manifestations of this was the lack of any platform for the Republican Party in 2020. In place of the extensive policy document that each party normally adopts every four years, the Republican Party adopted a resolution that simply affirmed, "The Republican Party has and will continue to enthusiastically support the President's America-first agenda."

I talked to Condoleezza Rice in the spring of 2021. I had served as deputy assistant secretary of state for the Near East when Condi was secretary of state, and I'd known her since she served on the National Security Council staff during George H. W. Bush's administration. She was an expert on the Soviet Union and a student of history. We discussed the cult of personality that had captured our party. This was something America had never experienced before. I asked Condi if she could think of any historic examples of countries successfully throwing off cults of personality. "Not without great violence and upheaval," she said.

———

In mid-March of 2021, Fox News host Brian Kilmeade called me. I had been a guest on his radio show and on *Fox and Friends* many times, especially to discuss national security issues.

Kilmeade said he was calling to ask if I would consider sitting down for a meeting with former President Trump. It was an odd request.

"No thanks," I said. "Not interested."

Kilmeade pressed the issue:

The two of you need to bury the hatchet, he said, and a meeting would help do that.

I told Kilmeade that Trump and I weren't having some kind of policy disagreement or political debate. I wasn't going to capitulate: "Trump tried to overturn an election. He went to war with the rule of law. He violated his oath to the Constitution."

Kilmeade didn't dispute any of that.

"I know," he said. "But what if he is our only hope to beat Kamala?"

I was surprised Kilmeade was so direct. Were we really going to torch the Constitution to beat the Democrats? Trump had done things we could not ignore. He had shown he was too dangerous to play a role in our politics. I wasn't willing to give him a second chance to do it all again.

––––––

I wasn't the only Republican during this period speaking out about the dangerous turn our party was taking. But over the course of the spring, the leadership of the Republican National Committee (RNC), and most of the Republican leaders in Congress, cast their lots with Trump. On April 10, the RNC held a dinner at Mar-a-Lago for its major donors. Trump was the keynote speaker. In his remarks, Trump repeated his lies yet again about the 2020 election and lashed out repeatedly at those Republicans, including Vice President Pence and Georgia Governor Kemp, who had declined to go along with his efforts to overturn the election. He reportedly called Senate Republican Leader McConnell "a dumb son of a bitch" for refusing to object to the electoral votes. Trump also attacked McConnell's wife, former Secretary of Labor Elaine Chao, mocking her for resigning because of January 6.

When I appeared on *Face the Nation* the next morning, moderator Margaret Brennan asked me about the former president's remarks, noting that Trump was, among other things, expressing pride about the size of the crowd on January 6. She wanted to know if I thought he was really the best messenger for the party. This was about far more than party messaging. I said that what Trump was doing was dangerous:

> The former president is using the same language that he knows provoked violence on January 6th. As a party, we need to be focused on the future. We need to be focused on embracing the Constitution, not embracing insurrection. I think it is very important for people to realize that a fundamental part of the Constitution, and of who we are as Americans, is the rule of law. . . . If you attack the judicial process and you attack the rule of law, you aren't defending the Constitution; you're at war with the Constitution.

A few days later, in an interview on Fox News, Neil Cavuto asked me if I would support Trump if he were the Republican nominee in 2024. "I would not," I said. My views had not changed over the months since January 6.

By contrast, Kevin McCarthy's position had undergone a drastic shift from the views he had shared with House Republicans — and in public — immediately after the attack. In the days after January 6, McCarthy had said that Trump bore responsibility, and he told us he believed Trump should resign. He said, among other things, "I've had it with this guy. What he did is unacceptable. Nobody can defend that, and nobody *should* defend it."

By April 2021, however, McCarthy *was* defending Trump's actions. When McCarthy appeared on *Fox News Sunday* on April 25, host Chris Wallace asked him about Representative Jaime Herrera Beutler's account of the call Kevin had with Trump while the violence was underway. McCarthy wouldn't comment on the details Herrera Beutler described — details many members had heard Kevin recount months earlier. Instead, Kevin tried to recant: "What he ended the call with saying, with telling me, he'll put something out to make sure to stop this, and that's what he did. He put a video out later." When Wallace pointed out that it was "quite a lot later and it was a pretty weak video," McCarthy doubled down on his defense of Trump: "I engaged in the idea of making sure we could stop what was going on inside the Capitol at that moment in time and the president said he would help." This was impossible to reconcile with Kevin's earlier public statements.

Less than four months since the Capitol was attacked, McCarthy was not even pretending he had any self-respect anymore. Two reporters who had interviewed both McCarthy and Trump during this period wrote this: When Trump took to calling McCarthy a "pussy," McCarthy "responded not by defying the former president but by more or less setting out to prove him right."

That sounded accurate to me.

25. THAT WE LOVE OUR COUNTRY MORE

As April turned to May, it became clear that we were headed for another showdown among House Republicans. In the days leading up to the unsuccessful February 2021 effort to remove me from leadership, I had spent time calling colleagues and lining up votes. I had prevailed in overwhelming fashion. In February, it had still been possible to envision the Republican Party looking to a post-Trump future, rejecting insurrection, and embracing the Constitution and the truth.

By May, that had changed dramatically.

In 1995, my mother, Lynne Cheney, wrote a book titled *Telling the Truth*. She talked about the importance of teaching history and highlighted the dangers of political correctness in our educational institutions and elsewhere. At the time, *political correctness* was the term for what many today call *wokeness*. But my mother was not handling the issue in the divisive way people address wokeness today. She was tackling it historically and analytically, including by comparing political correctness with the orthodoxies found in societies that are not free.

I recalled a passage about Vaclav Havel, the writer and democratic reformer who later became president of what was then Czechoslovakia. Havel told the story of a Czech greengrocer who, during the years of Soviet domination, decided not to display a sign bearing the Communist Party's slogan in his shop window. That small act of dissension from the state orthodoxy had the potential to shatter everything, so the state could not accept it. The greengrocer would have to be punished.

I kept thinking about this story as I reflected on what was happening in the Republican Party—and, in particular, within the House Republican Conference. House Republicans could not accept it when I answered questions truthfully, when I refused to repeat Trump's party line about the 2020 election, or January 6. Dissent was no longer permitted.

I knew from my time overseas, a free society that abandons the truth—that abandons the rule of law—cannot remain free.

———

To remain in House Republican leadership, I would have to abandon the truth and embrace Trump's ongoing efforts to unravel our democracy. That wasn't a price I was willing to pay.

I contemplated resigning. I talked to several trusted colleagues about it. I also sought my father's counsel.

Ultimately, I decided against quitting. If the Republican Party was going to kick me out of leadership because I refused to lie about Trump, the country needed to see what they were doing. I was not going to make things easier for them by quietly stepping out of the way as they marched down the dangerous anti-constitutional path they were on.

The second conference meeting to remove me from leadership was scheduled for Wednesday, May 12, 2021. I planned to speak to open the meeting, but I knew those comments would be reported in whatever snippets were texted to the press by attendees at the meeting. The issues we were confronting were too important for that. I decided to make a speech on the floor of the US House the night before, to lay out publicly exactly what was happening and where things were headed.

Securing floor time for this speech would not be easy. I knew the Republicans wouldn't give it to me, and I didn't want to ask the Democrats. I would have to find a member of Congress willing to yield some reserved time to me in the evening—the only part of the day when speaking slots extend beyond two or three minutes. We would normally check with staff in the Leader's office to find out who had time reserved. That wasn't an option here. If the Leader's office figured out I was looking for time to speak, they would likely have worked hard to prevent it, including pressuring members not to yield me time.

My chief of staff, Kara Ahern, checked around quietly, and came back with good news: "Guess what—Ken Buck has time reserved on Tuesday night. You won't believe what the topic is: cancel culture." It was perfect.

Ken is a member of the Freedom Caucus, and a good friend. I called and asked him if he could yield some of his time to me on May 11. He agreed right away.

While I worked on my floor remarks, I thought about how to convey the danger we were facing—and the consequences for our nation, and the world, if American democracy was allowed to unravel. I thought about my parents and all they had done to teach my sister and me to love this country and learn her history.

As a little girl, I had walked the hallowed grounds of Antietam, Gettysburg, and Bull Run with my dad, learning about the sacrifices so many had made for our freedom. I remember holding his hand the first time I ever set foot inside the US Capitol. I couldn't have been much older than five or six. He stood beside me years later when I first took the oath of office as a member of Congress, filling the seat he had held as Wyoming's representative. I watched my dad serve in the highest offices in our country for nearly 50 years. From him, I learned what it means to have the courage of your convictions.

My mother is an author and a scholar of American history. She was my first teacher about the Constitution. Together, we visited Independence Hall in Philadelphia and walked the Freedom Trail in Boston. She took us to see John Adams' home in Quincy, Massachusetts, Thomas Jefferson's Monticello, and James Madison's Montpelier. I'll never forget standing in Madison's study with my mother and my daughters, looking at ink stains in the floorboards dating from the period when Madison was drafting the Bill of Rights in that very room.

It was my mother who first read me these words from Abraham Lincoln's 1861 Inaugural address:

The mystic chords of memory, stretching from every battlefield and patriot grave to every living heart and hearthstone all over this broad land, will yet swell the chorus of the Union, when again touched, as surely they will be, by the better angels of our nature.

There is no more beautiful description of what binds us together as Americans. It is my mother's voice I still hear when I read these words today.

My understanding of the blessing of American freedom, instilled by my parents, had been deepened by the years I spent working in countries around the world where people were striving to be free. Before I was elected to Congress, I worked for the State Department and the US Agency for International Development. After the Berlin Wall came down in 1989, I began working in countries across Eastern Europe to help newly free nations establish the institutions of democracy and the rule of law. I had also worked on projects to provide aid to Chinese students in the aftermath of the Tiananmen Square massacre. After the collapse of the Soviet Union, I worked on American assistance programs in Russia, as well as in Ukraine and other nations that had once been part of the USSR. I worked for the State Department in countries across the Middle East on programs to empower women, establish the rule of law, and promote economic and political reforms. I worked for the International Republican Institute on initiatives to promote democracy in Africa.

I have seen firsthand how powerful—and how fragile—freedom can be.

I wanted to convey the urgency of the moment, the threat we were facing, and the solemn obligation we had to put duty above partisanship. And I wanted to talk about the cost of silence. From Republicans across Wyoming and around the country since January 6, I had often heard some version of: If what Trump did is so dangerous, why aren't more Republican leaders saying so?

Some of my colleagues thought they could just be silent and Donald Trump would simply fade away. Mitch McConnell believed this, but I knew it to be false. It was wishful thinking. Instead, their silence was emboldening Trump and giving life to his lies.

When I walked out onto the House floor on the night of Tuesday, May 11, some of the Republicans who had spoken earlier during Buck's reserved time were still hanging around. When they saw me, they scattered. Buck stepped up to the mic and yielded me time.

"Madam Speaker," I began, "I rise tonight to discuss freedom and our Constitutional duty to protect it." I talked about Boris Nemtsov, whom I'd met in Nizhny Novgorod, Russia, in 1992, when he was first fighting to bring democracy and economic reforms to post-Soviet Russia. His decades-long struggle to secure freedom for his people ended when Putin's thugs shot him on a Moscow street in 2015. I talked about a Cuban immigrant who escaped Castro's totalitarian regime; a young man who grew up behind the Iron Curtain in the Baltics and became his country's minister of defense; and a dissident who spent years in a Soviet gulag. All these people told me it was the miracle of America captured in the words of Ronald Reagan that had inspired them to seek freedom. And I talked about watching Pope John Paul II, who had helped defeat communism in Poland, take my father's hand and tell him, "God bless America."

"God *has* blessed America," I said, "but our freedom survives only if we protect it, if we honor our oath—taken before God in this chamber— to support and defend the Constitution, if we recognize threats to freedom when they arise."

I described the threat confronting us—one we have never faced before, a former president who provoked a violent attack on the Capitol in order to overturn an election. His aggressive effort to spread the lie that the 2020 presidential election had been stolen risked inciting further violence and undermining our democratic process. His lie was also feeding the propaganda of our enemies—that American democracy is a failure.

A man who was willing to do those things can never be trusted with power again.

I pledged that I would not sit back in silence while others led our party down a path that abandoned the rule of law and joined the former president's crusade to undermine our democracy. Every one of us who has sworn an oath to the Constitution has a duty to prevent the unraveling of our democracy.

The week before my speech, I received a message from a Gold Star father whose son had been killed in Afghanistan. "Standing up for the truth," he told me, "honors all who gave all."

The stories in my remarks were personal, but they described the universal truth about the value and cost of our freedom. I hoped they also conveyed the gravity of what was happening in my party and what it meant for the country.

In 2015, my father and I had coauthored a book called *Exceptional: Why the World Needs a Powerful America.* It celebrated America's unique role in the world. I believed in my country's noble purpose, and I was proud of her history, a history that was possible only because of the men and women who had sacrificed so much to keep us free. Too many of my colleagues seemed to be willing to squander this priceless gift, including by looking the other way while others dismantled it. I wanted to remind them what was at stake:

> We must all strive to be worthy of the sacrifice of those who have died for our freedom. They are the patriots Katharine Lee Bates described in the words of "America the Beautiful": *O beautiful for heroes proved in liberating strife, who more than self their country loved and mercy more than life.*
>
> Ultimately, this is at the heart of what our oath requires — that we love our country more. That we love her so much we will stand above politics to defend her, and that we will do everything in our power to protect our Constitution and our freedom.

26. THE INESCAPABLE FORCE OF FREEDOM

THE MORNING AFTER MY FLOOR speech, our conference meeting convened at 9:00 a.m. in the Capitol Visitor Center auditorium. It was a single-purpose meeting, and it lasted only 15 minutes. When the meeting began, I was still the Republican Conference chair, so I held the gavel, and called the meeting to order. I told my colleagues that we were going to vote on a resolution, and that I was going to take a moment of personal privilege to address the conference first.

I didn't need to describe what the resolution was. By that point, everyone knew.

Normally at the beginning of one of these meetings, I would recognize another member to offer our opening prayer. On May 12, however, I chose to deliver the prayer myself, as part of my final remarks to the conference:

> I have tremendous affection and admiration for many of you, most of you, in this room. I know that we all came to Washington to do important work for the nation. History has chosen every single one of us, and history has put us all here together at this moment of challenge for the country.
>
> Our nation needs this Republican Party as a strong party based on truth so that we can shape the future. To do that, we must be true to our principles and to the Constitution. We cannot let the former president drag us backward and make us complicit in his efforts to unravel our democracy.

Down that path lies our destruction—and potentially the destruction of our country. If you want leaders who will enable and spread his destructive lies, I am not your person. You have plenty of others to choose from, and that will be their legacy. But I promise you this: After today, I will be leading the fight to restore our party and our nation to conservative principles, to defeating socialism, to defending our republic, and to making the Republican Party worthy once again of the mantle of Abraham Lincoln.

Please join me in prayer. "Dear God, fill us with a love of freedom and a reverence for all your gifts. Help us to understand the gravity of this moment. Help us to remember that democratic systems can fray and suddenly unravel and when they do, they are gone forever. Help us to speak the truth and remember the words of John 8:32: 'Ye shall know the truth and the truth shall set you free.' May our world see the power of faith, may our nation know the strength of selfless service. And may our enemies continue to taste the inescapable force of freedom."

The last lines of my prayer that morning were borrowed from a blessing I'd heard many years ago at a dinner I attended for one of the elite units of special operators in our military. The chaplain was from Wyoming, and I have never forgotten what he said. By divine providence, the "inescapable force of freedom" had so far survived in our nation. That is what had made us exceptional in all of human history.

When I finished, Tom Cole, the ranking Republican on the House Rules Committee, took over. He recognized North Carolina's Virginia Foxx, who introduced the resolution to oust me. When she was done, Kevin McCarthy spoke. Then Cole put the question to a voice vote.

As soon as Cole said, "In the opinion of the chair, the *ayes* have it and the resolution is adopted," I stood up and walked off the stage, then up the long center aisle of the auditorium past my conference colleagues. Many were looking down at their hands. Members of the House Republican Conference staff, who had been running logistics for the meeting—the

My great-great-grandfather Samuel Fletcher Cheney served in the 21st Ohio Volunteer Infantry during all four years of the Civil War. In 1893, the regimental historian wrote that the men of the 21st had "a just appreciation of the value and advantage of free government, and the necessity of defending and maintaining it, and they enlisted prepared to accept all the necessary labors, fatigues, exposures, dangers, and even death for the unity of our Nation, and the perpetuity of our institutions."

The Casper Police Department in the 1950s. My grandmother, Edna Vincent, was the only woman.

At Camp David with President Gerald Ford in 1975. President Ford was a man of character and honor. (David Hume Kennerly)

At the White House in 1982 with President and Mrs. Reagan and my father, Dick Cheney, who was then the congressman from Wyoming. The first vote I ever cast was for Ronald Reagan for president in 1984. (Official White House Photo)

Election Night 2000 at the governor's mansion in Austin, Texas, with my parents, Dick and Lynne Cheney, former President and Mrs. George H. W. Bush, Texas Governor George W. and Laura Bush, and Florida Governor Jeb Bush. (David Hume Kennerly)

My sister Mary and me at Cheney for Congress campaign headquarters in Casper, Wyoming, in 1978. We were obviously dedicated and enthusiastic volunteers.

Our family on the front steps of our house on Beech Street in Casper, Wyoming, during my dad's first campaign. (David Hume Kennerly)

With my dad and members of the Wyoming delegation at the 1984 Republican National Convention in Dallas. It was my first convention, and I loved every minute of it. Republicans nominated Ronald Reagan for his second term that year. (Marty LaVor)

With our daughter Kate
the day I graduated from
the University of Chicago
Law School, in 1996.

Campaigning at a "W Stands for Women" event in 2004 with President Bush's mother, Barbara; his sister, Doro; and his daughters, Jenna and Barbara, along with Secretary of Labor Elaine Chao and Secretary of the Interior Gale Norton. (David Hume Kennerly)

In Laramie, Wyoming, in May 2016, debating my nine primary opponents during my first campaign for the US House of Representatives. (Kara Ahern)

Watching returns come in on Election Night 2016 in Casper, Wyoming, with Phil and our children, Kate, Elizabeth, Grace, Philip, and Richard, and my mother, Lynne Cheney. (David Bohrer)

The day I first took the oath of office as a member of Congress, with Phil and our five children, my parents, and Speaker Paul Ryan. (House Creative Services)

Keeper of the Mace Joyce Hamlett on January 6, 2021, at 11:49 a.m. Joyce and I rode the elevator together on our way to the House chamber for the start of the joint session. A few hours later, Joyce would carry the mace out of the chamber to protect it from Trump's violent mob.

As the violent mob attempted to invade the House chamber, Capitol Police officers and members of Congress barricaded the chamber doors. (AP Images/J. Scott Applewhite)

Shortly after 9:00 p.m. on January 6 in the US Capitol Rotunda, thanking those who had fought to defend us and our constitutional republic that day. (Kara Ahern)

With Vice President Pence in Statuary Hall just after midnight on January 7, 2021. I thanked Vice President Pence for what he had done for our nation on January 6 by abiding by his oath and refusing to yield to Donald Trump's pressure. (Kara Ahern)

The memorial service for Officer Brian Sicknick on February 3, 2021. After coming under violent attack while he fought to defend the West Front of the Capitol on January 6, Officer Sicknick died the next day. I promised his mother, Gladys, that we would never forget what he did to defend our democracy. (Brendan Smialowski-Pool/Getty Images)

With Officer Sicknick's parents, Gladys and Charles, and his brothers, Ken and Craig, at our June 9, 2021, Select Committee hearing. (House Creative Services)

Outside the Capitol Visitor Center auditorium on May 12, 2021, moments after my House Republican colleagues removed me as chair of the Republican conference. (David Hume Kennerly)

In House Speaker Nancy Pelosi's conference room on July 1, 2021, during the first meeting of the House Select Committee to Investigate the January 6th Attack. (Office of the Speaker)

With Chairman Bennie Thompson in Statuary Hall on the one-year anniversary of the attack. Bennie was explaining that we had found common ground in the defense of our Constitution, but he promised, in his good-humored way, that when the Committee work was done, "Liz and I will go to our corners and resume" our political disagreements. (David Hume Kennerly)

With my husband, Phil, in our home office in June 2022. (Elizabeth Perry)

With members of the Select Committee before our first hearing on July 27, 2021. (Kent Nishimura/Los Angeles Times via Getty Images)

With Representative Zoe Lofgren in the Committee conference room during a break in one of our hearings. Zoe's judgment and dedication to pursuing the facts were indispensable to the Committee's work. (House Creative Services)

Phil and our daughter Elizabeth watching video of the January 6 attack at the June 9, 2022, Select Committee hearing. (House Creative Services)

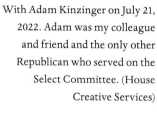

Swearing in witnesses at our July 21, 2022, Select Committee hearing. (Kara Ahern)

With Adam Kinzinger on July 21, 2022. Adam was my colleague and friend and the only other Republican who served on the Select Committee. (House Creative Services)

Capitol Police Officer Caroline Edwards testifying on June 9, 2022, about the bloody violence she confronted defending the Capitol on January 6. (Bill Clark/CQ Roll Call via AP Images)

Arizona Speaker of the House Rusty Bowers, Georgia Secretary of State Brad Raffensperger, and Georgia elections official Gabriel Sterling testifying at the June 21, 2022, Select Committee hearing. (AP Photo/J. Scott Applewhite)

Shaye Moss and her mother, Ruby Freeman, election workers in Georgia, testifying at the June 21, 2022, Select Committee hearing about the terrifying threats they faced because of lies Donald Trump and Rudy Giuliani told about them. (Kevin Dietsch/Getty Images)

Former Acting Attorney General Jeff Rosen, Acting Deputy Attorney General Richard Donoghue, and former Assistant Attorney General Steve Engel testifying at the Select Committee's June 23, 2022, hearing. (AP Photo/Jacquelyn Martin)

J. Michael Luttig, former federal judge on the US Court of Appeals for the Fourth Circuit, and Greg Jacob, former counsel to Vice President Mike Pence, arriving to testify at the June 16, 2022, Select Committee hearing. (Drew Angerer/Getty Images)

Cassidy Hutchinson arriving for her testimony on June 28, 2022. (Demetrius Freeman/The Washington Post via Getty Images)

Former Deputy National Security Adviser Matthew Pottinger and former Deputy Press Secretary Sarah Matthews testifying at the Select Committee hearing, July 21, 2022. (AP Photo/ Patrick Semansky)

At my desk in the Cannon House Office Building on June 15, 2022. (Kara Ahern)

At an Honor Ceremony on the Wind River Reservation in Wyoming on July 16, 2022, with Northern Arapaho Tribal leaders, including Lee Spoonhunter and Jordan Dresser. (Adam Amick)

Speaking to protestors in Rock Springs, Wyoming, in May 2021. They were protesting outside one of our campaign events with signs that read LIZ CHENEY IS A TRAITOR. I invited them inside for a conversation. (Kara Ahern)

At the Mead Ranch in Jackson, Wyoming, on August 16, 2022. After I conceded my race, I pledged, "The primary is over, but now the real work begins." (Patrick T. Fallon/AFP via Getty Images)

My mother and father and our dear friend Toni Thomson at the Mead Ranch on August 16, 2022. (Kara Ahern)

With Will Henderson, my special assistant, and members of my Capitol Police detail on January 2, 2023, my last night in office. I will forever be grateful for all they did. (Kara Ahern)

I was privileged to work with a staff of incredibly talented and dedicated people who understood the importance of protecting our democracy and fighting for the truth. Right: On May 12, 2021, they sent me this photo a few hours after I was removed as chair of the House Republican Conference. (Ashley Jordan)

Below: On primary election night in Jackson, Wyoming, August 16, 2022. (Caroline Jones)

timers, the lights, the AV system — stood and followed me out. These young Republican staffers knew that walking out with me would ensure they wouldn't continue to be employed by whoever followed me as Conference chair. They did it anyway, and I was proud to stand with them.

I learned later that one of my colleagues, a member of the Freedom Caucus, asked to be recognized after I left. He said he didn't agree with me on some things, but he thought the conference should thank me for the job I'd done. Garret Graves, a representative from Louisiana, texted me a few minutes later: "You just got a standing O. Seriously."

27. A PERSONAL FAVOR

IN THE WAKE OF EVERY significant crisis in our recent history, bipartisan commissions have been established to uncover what happened and make recommendations to prevent similar crises in the future. This was true after the attack on Pearl Harbor, the Kennedy assassination, and the 9/11 attacks.

There was near unanimity in the weeks after January 6 that we needed to do the same thing. Indeed, back on January 12, 30 of my colleagues — including several members of the Freedom Caucus — had cosponsored a bill to form just such a commission. The fundamental model was the same framework we had seen work after 9/11: A group of prominent Americans from both political parties would be appointed to determine what had caused January 6.

At the time, of course, House Minority Leader Kevin McCarthy had supported the establishment of such a commission in both his public and private remarks. So, too, had Democratic Speaker of the House Nancy Pelosi. So did a number of Senate Republicans — including South Carolina's Lindsey Graham, who said on *Fox News Sunday:* "We need a 9/11 Commission to find out what happened and make sure it never happens again."

McCarthy assigned a senior Republican, John Katko, to negotiate the terms of an independent commission with Democratic Congressman Bennie Thompson, who chaired the House Committee on Homeland Security. As those negotiations made headway, Pelosi agreed to each of Katko and McCarthy's demands for the commission:

She agreed that the panel would be evenly split between Republicans and Democrats.

She agreed that subpoena power would be shared.

Having gotten everything he asked for, Kevin then abruptly withdrew his support for the Thompson-Katko bill. Pelosi and others said it best at the time: Kevin McCarthy would not accept yes for an answer.

On May 19, the independent-commission bill came up for a vote in the House. It was the same in substance as the bill proposed in January by Republicans with Kevin McCarthy's support. But McCarthy was now urging members to vote against it. For obvious reasons, Trump did not want an investigation into January 6, so McCarthy could not support it. Thirty-five Republicans defied Kevin's direction and joined with Democrats to pass the bill by a margin of 252 to 175. It wasn't even close. The bill now moved to the Senate.

McCarthy met with Republican senators that day and urged them to vote against the commission bill.

As the Senate was deliberating, I called Senator Susan Collins, a Republican from Maine, to figure out the state of play. She was working to convince fellow Republican senators to back the legislation. Mitch McConnell was urging Republicans to vote against the bill, she said. He had called her and asked her for "a personal favor"—not to support the bill. Collins supported it anyway, along with five other Republican senators. The bill needed 60 votes to pass, however, and the final tally was 54 to 35. Eleven senators— nine Republicans and two Democrats—simply did not show up for the vote.

I was disappointed when I learned that McConnell had been lobbying against the creation of this bipartisan commission. I couldn't imagine what he was thinking. I didn't bother calling him to ask. Still, it rankled: How could he portray the commission's defeat as "a personal favor"?

A year later, Mitch McConnell would speak approvingly of what the House Select Committee on January 6 was accomplishing. I appreciated it, and I had long respected Mitch, but I never stopped wondering why he had opposed the creation of a 9/11-style bipartisan commission to investigate what had happened.

28. THE POWER OF PROPAGANDA

EVER SINCE JANUARY 6, I had been visiting with and hearing from people in Wyoming about what I was doing. Initially, on January 17, 34 Wyoming lawyers—including retired judges and Wyoming supreme court justices and three former governors, led by former chief justice of the Wyoming supreme court Marilyn Kite—wrote an op-ed titled "The Rule of Law Matters." They expressed their shock at the events of January 6 and described the courage of individuals around the country who had "stood up to do their constitutional duties" under tremendous pressure. Describing the danger of President Trump's attempts to overturn the election, they wrote:

> We are proud of Rep. Cheney's courage. In the face of calls to law-
> lessness from high places, she adhered to her solemn oath to pro-
> tect and defend the Constitution...all Wyomingites should
> applaud her understanding of her duties and her willingness to
> perform them, irrespective of the personal or political cost she
> might pay.

It meant a great deal to me that the signatories, many of the most respected jurists in our state, recognized the peril of the moment and were willing to step up publicly and say so. They republished the letter in July 2022 with additional signatories and a link to a report debunking Donald Trump's stolen-election lies. Titled "Lost Not Stolen," the report had been issued earlier in 2022 by prominent conservative lawyers and legal scholars, including several retired federal judges, senators, and a former solicitor general who served in the Bush administration.

For months, my office was inundated with calls, emails, and letters about January 6. Some were supportive, others less so. The young staffers who answered calls from angry citizens—many not even Wyoming constituents—earned their pay every day. They also demonstrated tremendous professionalism and patience in the face of some vile attacks. They calmly provided details to rebut some of the claims we heard repeatedly, but certain callers would not listen to reason.

There were messages of gratitude, too. Among the many incoming messages, one of my favorites was a handwritten note from a Wyoming voter: "Liz: Never liked you much, but I'm starting to."

Most of the county-level Republican Party organizations across the state passed resolutions censuring me. The language of all the censure resolutions was the same, and falsely blamed Antifa for January 6. Later in the year, a number of these same county parties passed resolutions saying they "no longer recognized me as a Republican." I responded that I no longer recognized them, either—they certainly didn't represent the Republican Party of Ronald Reagan I had grown up in.

I was greeted by protestors at some of my events back home. We arrived at a coffee shop in Rock Springs in May 2021, for example, to find a group standing on the sidewalk with signs reading LIZ CHENEY IS A TRAITOR. I walked over to them and invited them to come inside so we could have a discussion. The invitation surprised them. (I'm sure my Capitol Police detail was surprised, too, but they never said a word.)

One man and his wife seemed to be leading the group. It quickly became clear that the man had been in Washington for January 6.

"I was in the Capitol on January 6th," he said.

His wife hurriedly patted his arm: "No, you mean you were *near* the Capitol."

They sat down inside, placing their LIZ CHENEY IS A TRAITOR sign carefully at their feet. I stood and explained how our legal system works, how the courts had ruled, why Mike Pence lacked the authority to undo an election. The husband interrupted to stress that he opposed Biden's policies. I agreed with him on that. But, I said, we can't abandon our constitutional duties simply because we oppose Joe Biden's policies. We went round and round on this. It was as if they believed we in Washington could seize power based on what they had been reading on the internet and watching on cable news.

It was an entirely civil discussion. But the notion that I was bound by our constitutional system, and by the rule of law, was simply not sinking in.

A woman nearby interrupted politely to thank me for what I was doing and saying. Others applauded. But the husband could not be persuaded. He was repeating back to me, almost verbatim, what Donald Trump had been saying in his social-media posts and on certain cable outlets at the time.

—————

That particular encounter may have been civil, but many others were not. The Capitol Police officers with me in Rock Springs were well aware of the death threats that members of Congress had been receiving; they were vigilant and prepared to intervene as needed. A number of members of my detail had themselves fought to defend the Capitol on January 6. They showed unwavering professionalism as they stood by on more than one occasion listening to one of my constituents claim it hadn't been a violent day. The Capitol Police deserve our unending gratitude.

Some of the constituent meetings I had been convening every year in Wyoming now became difficult to arrange, much less to conduct safely. Any widespread public notice about an upcoming appearance increased the security threat. My congressional office received death threats on a regular basis, and the Capitol Police became concerned about my safety.

Some of the people who were completely duped by Donald Trump surprised me. One woman I had known my whole life — and considered one of my mother's best friends — fell for the lies hook, line, and sinker. On January 6, my mother had texted her: "Liz is in the House Chamber where the mob is trying to push down the doors! And Trump encouraged this!"

Her friend responded several hours later. She said she hoped I was safe. Then she said: "I heard that as with BLM demonstrations, ANTIFA has moved in. Truly frightening. When will they be declared a terrorist organization?"

My mother explained that it was not Antifa and then said:

What troubles me so deeply is that the president invited this mob to a "wild time" on January 6, egged them on at his rally, and offered to lead them down Pennsylvania Avenue, his purpose being to delay the certification that ends his presidency. I am grateful that he has now committed to a peaceful transfer of power.

Again, the truth didn't matter.

Growing up in a political family, you tend to learn early on that some people who act like your friends are not genuinely friends but opportunists — sometimes people with money, seeking to get close to those who hold office. This woman and her husband turned out to be people I had completely misjudged.

She and my mother had gone to Wyoming Girls State together in the 1950s. I thought I could trust her, that she had the character to listen and to understand what was happening. I told her how the courts had ruled. I gave her the facts — what Bill Barr was saying, what the Constitution required.

When Dallin Oaks, president of the Mormon Church, to which she belonged, made remarks about our duty to the Constitution, I sent them to her. President Oaks' remarkable statement included the lines: "We are to be governed by law and not by individuals, and our loyalty is to the Constitution and its principles and processes, not to any office holder." But nothing could break the spell that QAnon had cast over her. She threw away a friendship of over 60 years with my mother and my family for nothing.

I also found that many of those in Wyoming who were the most upset or angry were unaware of the violence on January 6. They believed the day to have been almost entirely peaceful. They read *The Epoch Times*, a "news" website that presents extremely slanted reporting in the guise of a straightforward media outlet. They believed what they saw on their social-media feeds. They watched almost exclusively Fox News or Newsmax or OAN. As a result, they were completely unaware of what had actually happened. More than a few believed that I should be pressing for Joe Biden's removal from office and Donald Trump's reinstallation as president.

In the 2020 election, Donald Trump had carried Wyoming by a wider margin than in any other state. I also received about the same percentage of the vote in 2020, winning both my primary and general-election races by more than 40 points. But now, many voters viewed me as a traitor.

The leader of the state's Republican Party is reportedly an Oath Keeper. He appeared on Steve Bannon's podcast shortly after the impeachment vote and suggested that Wyoming was very interested in the possibility of secession. After photographs appeared of him in the crowd outside the Capitol Building on January 6, he admitted that he had indeed been there.

Sometimes after I talked through the facts of the 2020 election — including how the courts ruled and what the judges said — people I met with were willing to reconsider their embrace of Trump's lies. Others remained defiant and angry. It can be tough to learn that you've been fooled, tricked by those you trusted. That you let yourself be deceived. The natural reaction is denial, and a refusal to listen to anything to the contrary.

Over time, it became clear that some of the threats against me followed a pattern. When Tucker Carlson of Fox News aired unfounded attacks on me, for example, threats followed almost immediately. This often happens to members of Congress after Tucker's show, the Capitol Police informed me. After we received threats that referred to our children, Phil contacted one of his former Justice Department colleagues who worked in Fox's Office of General Counsel. That person responded politely, and promised to address the issue. But nothing seemed to change.

———

Some of my Republican colleagues and allies, echoing Mitch McConnell, believed that Donald Trump would simply fade away, and that we could safely ignore him. I think they underestimated the power of his propaganda, what he is capable of doing, and what he accomplished between the 2020 election and January 6. I often thought that people who dismissed Trump's political influence, or counted on him to fade away, had not talked to Trump supporters in towns like Casper, Cheyenne, or Cody. They certainly hadn't talked to the dozens of Republican members of Congress who persisted in supporting Trump's stolen-election claims *even after the January 6 violence.*

What Donald Trump accomplished was this: Despite mountains of hard evidence to the contrary, he persuaded tens of millions of Americans—some 40 to 50 million in all—that their nation had been stolen from them by election fraud. And Donald Trump convinced some of them to believe it absolutely. As if it were a tenet of faith. For millions, their minds may never change on this.

I often think of those hundreds of January 6 rioters who have been convicted or pled guilty—men and women who sacrificed their freedom and their futures for an outright lie. Some now recognize that they wasted years of their lives for a falsehood. But for others, not even a jail sentence has diminished their support for Donald Trump.

Today Donald Trump poses a threat that many in Washington simply fail to grasp. He can move Americans to action based on total dishonesty. I can tell you from my time working to support democracy overseas that the power to rally a mob must never be underestimated. Nor should the fear that a mob can instill in people of reason.

A person with that kind of power—to intimidate and threaten and motivate others to carry out violent acts—does not just slowly fade into the background.

He must be defeated.

A number of those who led the January 6 attack on the Capitol took pains to hide their identities from the many cameras present. But others in the mob took no precautions to disguise themselves, because they had been absolutely convinced that they were engaged in a patriotic mission to, in Trump's words, *take back their country.* They regarded themselves as heroes. They boasted about it, even after assaulting police officers.

No matter how difficult my conversations became within the House Republican Conference and across Wyoming, those exchanges clarified that it was vitally important we uncover everything that happened on January 6 and share it with the American people. Millions of Americans were drowning in ridiculous lies. They had no idea what actually happened—why it was wrong, why it was so destructive for our country. There had to be an investigation.

29.   SELECT COMMITTEE

ONCE THE INDEPENDENT-COMMISSION BILL FAILED, only one option remained: The House of Representatives would have to act alone, without the US Senate.

On June 30, the House voted to create a select committee to investigate the attack on the US Capitol. The family of Officer Sicknick was in the gallery, along with Officers Dunn and Fanone, and several family members of other police officers who had protected us that day. I went to the gallery to see them just after the committee vote passed. I had been in touch with them in the months since January 6, including when 21 of my fellow Republicans voted against a bill awarding the Congressional Gold Medal to police officers who defended the Capitol, and the families of these police officers wanted to know why. There was no honorable answer to that question. I couldn't explain it, but I pledged I would make sure history recorded the courage and patriotism of all the officers who fought that day.

This group of family members and police officers had been determined to ensure the attack would be investigated. They had arranged meetings with key members of the House and Senate, and, along with former Republican Congresswoman Barbara Comstock, they had visited each personally to ask that a bipartisan commission be established. Although that had failed, I was proud that the House of Representatives had acted, and that there would be an investigation.

As I walked out of the gallery, Jeremy Adler, my communications director, was standing there. "I have some bad news," he said. "Former Secretary of Defense Donald Rumsfeld has just died."

We found some chairs in a nearby hallway on the third floor of the Capitol and sat down to work on a statement. I leaned my head back against the wall and closed my eyes. I had known Don Rumsfeld nearly my entire life. He and his wife, Joyce, were among my parents' oldest friends. The last time I had talked to him was on New Year's Eve of 2020, when my dad called to read him the draft letter from the former secretaries of defense warning against the use of the military in any election dispute.

How much worse might January 6 have been, I wondered, *had they not issued that unprecedented public warning?* In the coming months, the January 6th Select Committee would begin to uncover the answer to that question.

PART IV

No Half Measures

SUMMER 2021 TO SPRING 2022

30. A DIFFERENT WORLD

ON THE MORNING OF JULY 1, 2021, Terri McCullough, Speaker Nancy Pelosi's chief of staff, called my chief of staff, Kara Ahern, to say the Speaker would like to call me. I was with my father at his doctor's appointment when the Speaker reached me. I stepped into an empty office to take the call.

"Hello, Liz?"

"Hi, Madam Speaker."

"Please, call me Nancy," she said. She began by thanking me for my patriotism—something she would do many times over the coming months. This was my third term in Congress, but I hardly knew Nancy Pelosi. We stood at opposite ends of the political spectrum, with very sharp policy differences.

She started by expressing her condolences for Secretary Rumsfeld's death. She knew Rumsfeld and my father had been close. I thanked her. She said quickly that, of course, she was not making any sort of a political statement, just speaking personally.

I smiled, thinking, "Oh, yes, there's one of those policy differences."

Speaker Pelosi moved on to the purpose of her call. The previous day, the House of Representatives had approved legislation establishing "The Select Committee to Investigate the January 6th Attack on the U.S. Capitol." She told me she wanted the committee to begin work right away and had asked Congressman Bennie Thompson of Mississippi to be its chairman. She walked through the list of the other members she intended to ask to join the committee, then asked if I'd be willing to serve as well. I'd be honored to do so, I told her.

We discussed plans for a press conference the Speaker planned to hold at the Capitol shortly to announce the members of the January 6th Committee. Because I was with my father, I wouldn't be able to reach the Capitol in time for the announcement. But I told her I would be there a few hours later for a January 6th Committee meeting in her office.

After I finished the call, I walked back into the room next door, where my dad was waiting.

"Well?" he said.

"The Speaker asked me to join the Select Committee, and I said yes."

"I'm proud of you," he said.

My dad understood what was at stake. He knew how dangerous it would be for the country if the Republicans whitewashed what had happened, or succeeded in blocking an investigation into the events of January 6. He believed that serving on the Committee was the right thing—the *only* thing—to do.

He also understood what a momentous step this was for me to take. My dad had represented Wyoming in the House of Representatives from 1979 to 1989 before leaving Congress to become secretary of defense in the administration of President George H. W. Bush. He had been the House Republican Conference chair 32 years before I was elected to the same leadership post. He had also briefly served as House Republican Whip.

Deeply familiar with the inner workings of the House of Representatives, he knew that the House is an institution run entirely along party lines. It was likely unprecedented for a Republican member to accept a committee assignment from a Democratic Speaker. But he fully supported it now. My dad was disgusted and deeply troubled by the conduct of our fellow Republicans.

———

I was not certain how the House Republican leaders would react to my decision to accept a position from Speaker Pelosi on the January 6th Committee. Would they strip me of my seat on the House Armed Services Committee? Would they kick me out of the Republican Conference altogether? I was willing to take those risks. I had lost confidence in the House Republican leaders months ago.

I knew that my decision to join the January 6th Committee, especially as one of Speaker Pelosi's appointees, would have negative political repercussions for me in Wyoming. But I also knew it was the right thing to do. I would work to explain it to my constituents and accept the consequences if they voted me out in 2022. The ramifications for the country of failing to investigate January 6 mattered much more than any congressional seat.

Speaker Pelosi's decision to appoint me to the Committee was not without political risk for her, either. We didn't know each other. Her call that morning was the longest conversation we'd ever had. I had been a vocal advocate for Republican positions in our country's policy and political debates for years. Since 2018, I had overseen messaging for the House Republicans — including during the 2020 election cycle, when we gained far more seats than expected. We had deep policy differences with the House Democrats, and I had defended our positions robustly.

Later, I would learn that when the Speaker was deciding whether to appoint me, her staff pulled together a list of the 10 worst things I had ever said about her. Speaker Pelosi took one look at the list, handed it back to her staffer, and asked: "Why are you wasting my time with things that don't matter?"

We may have disagreed on pretty much everything else, but Nancy Pelosi and I saw eye to eye on the one thing that mattered more than any other: the defense of our Constitution and the preservation of our republic.

———

A few hours after Pelosi and I first spoke, I walked into the conference room in the Speaker's suite in the Capitol for the first meeting of the January 6th Select Committee. Gathered around the table were my seven Democratic colleagues on the Committee: Bennie Thompson, Pete Aguilar, Zoe Lofgren, Elaine Luria, Stephanie Murphy, Jamie Raskin, and Adam Schiff. Jamie and I had been elected the same year, and I knew Stephanie and Elaine from our work together on the Armed Services Committee. Over the next 18 months, I would get to know each member of this committee very well. Speaker Pelosi also introduced me to two members of her staff who would be invaluable to our committee's work: Terri McCullough, her chief of staff, who had placed that morning's call, and Jamie Fleet, the staff director of the House Administration Committee.

The Speaker thanked us all for agreeing to serve on the Committee. She then turned the floor over to Chairman Thompson, who briefed us on preliminary plans for hiring staff and beginning to schedule our work. As the meeting neared its end, we discussed a statement we might make to members of the press gathered outside the Speaker's office. Jamie Raskin took out a pen and began making notes as Speaker Pelosi spoke: "Of course, it's entirely up to you how you all handle this, but if it were me, I would prioritize the Committee's commitment to operating in a nonpartisan fashion and following the facts wherever they lead..."

Two things struck me as I watched Jamie Raskin make notes.

First, I had sat in leadership meetings with Kevin McCarthy for more than two years, and not once had I seen him outline the substance of a press statement, or anything else, to anyone. In our Republican meetings, it was the other way around: Kevin relied on notes prepared by the staff in even the smallest gatherings. He called on staffers to explain anything that required any level of detail.

Second, I couldn't shake the feeling of being a visitor from another planet. It's hard to overstate the extent to which Democrats and Republicans inhabit different worlds in Congress. Our parties meet separately and organize separately, from the broad division of House members into a Republican Conference and a Democratic Caucus to the structure of every committee, most staff positions, and even social clubs — the Capitol Hill Club for Republicans, the National Democratic Club for Democrats.

This is not to say that bipartisanship doesn't exist; it does. And many personal friendships cross party lines, too. But in a legislative body such as the House of Representatives, the majority and minority parties are typically working toward different goals and objectives, trying to thwart the other's plans at every step.

I had the sense that everyone in the conference room that morning knew this committee had to be different. The normal rules could not apply. We had to put partisanship aside, and there was no margin for error. We had to succeed in our work because the stakes for the country were so high.

At the heart of all of this would be my working relationship with Nancy Pelosi. She did not try to micromanage the work of the January 6th Committee, but she was there whenever we needed her. And over the next 18 months, every time I went to her with a concern, a proposed approach, or a request that she intervene with Democrats to help guide things in the right direction, she backed me up. Every time. A relationship that had been unimaginable just a few months earlier would now become indispensable.

In short, this was a whole new world.

————

By the time Nancy Pelosi called me, I had already given considerable thought to the Select Committee's mandate. I knew the investigation had to be fact-based, and I knew it had to be probing. It had to accomplish what the 9/11 Commission had accomplished: presenting a fair and comprehensive set of facts for the historical record. I also recognized the immense hurdles that could prevent a congressional investigation of January 6 from achieving its purposes.

My husband, Phil, and I had been talking about these issues at length. He, too, had firsthand experience with congressional investigations, including as a Republican Senate Counsel to the 1997 Thompson Committee investigating campaign finance abuses; as a Bush administration general counsel; as a high-ranking Justice Department official; and as a lawyer in private practice.

We began by making a list of all the things that could go wrong.

First, it was highly likely that the Select Committee investigation would simply run out of time. At that point Democrats held a narrow majority in the House, and Republicans were favored to regain control in the 2022 midterm elections. We knew they would shut the investigation down. We had to plan to complete our work by the end of 2022—just 18 months away.

The Committee would need to assemble a staff very quickly, with lawyers skilled at direct and cross-examination—that is, lawyers with courtroom experience, who knew how to handle witnesses. We anticipated that former President Trump and others would try to block the Committee from obtaining the documents we needed. This meant the Committee would have to litigate through a barrage of objections, including on executive privilege, to obtain critical documents and testimony. We expected that the investigation's executive-privilege fights would land in the Supreme Court—which they ultimately did.

This, of course, created a serious timing challenge: Litigating a conventional case through federal district court, up through appeal, and then to the Supreme Court can easily take three or four years. We didn't have anything close to that kind of time. We would have to win our cases, obtain the documents, pressure or compel witnesses to appear, and then question them about those documents all in a matter of months. And all before most of the public hearings could begin in 2022.

We also worried about the Committee's ability to obtain forthright testimony. Without detailed documents, it can be very challenging to question a witness who may truthfully or untruthfully say they don't recall, or give answers carefully scripted by their lawyers. We would have to obtain White House records from the National Archives, which was sure to trigger an executive-privilege claim by Trump. Lawyers representing witnesses would understand what an uphill battle the Committee was fighting, and would try to run out the clock. To prepare their witnesses to evade our questioning, some of these lawyers would likely communicate with each other about exactly what the Committee knew and did not know.

The best solution to this problem? Find those witnesses who, as a matter of principle, would not conceal, downplay, or lie about the facts.

We knew a number of the senior people in the Trump White House and across the Trump administration. Some had worked in previous Republican administrations or campaigns. I had gotten to know others—people like Matt Pottinger, the deputy national security advisor—while I was in Congress. Matt had resigned on January 6. I knew he would put his duty to country ahead of any other considerations. I was acquainted with Ivanka Trump and her husband, Jared Kushner. I expected neither one to be fully candid. I knew former Chief of Staff Mark Meadows because we had served together in the House. I believed Mark would do everything possible to conceal what had actually happened.

Phil knew a number of the lawyers in the Trump administration, including White House Counsel Pat Cipollone and his deputy, Pat Philbin; Mike Pence's counsel, Greg Jacob; Acting Attorney General Jeff Rosen; and Labor Secretary Gene Scalia. He thought each of them would be reluctant to testify, and would likely assert applicable privileges—but would ultimately tell the truth.

————

Above all, we faced one unavoidable historical truth: Most congressional investigations fail. This is partly because of the traditional format, which allocates each member of a committee five minutes to question witnesses. This makes it very difficult to piece together the type of witness exam that uncovers the truth. To present a comprehensive account, the January 6th Committee would need to operate much differently than any congressional investigation in recent memory. We would need to lay out the evidence the way a skilled trial lawyer would: making complex topics readily digestible, with no partisan grandstanding or exaggeration.

If the January 6 investigation weren't managed well and conducted in a nonpartisan manner, we would not be able to uncover and convey the facts about what had happened. I thought back to the 2019 impeachment hearings relating to Donald Trump's alleged efforts to get President Volodymyr Zelenskyy of Ukraine to help Trump defeat Joe Biden in the upcoming presidential election. I couldn't understand why the Democrats had decided not to subpoena Donald Trump's former national security advisor, John Bolton. As the impeachment committee discussed the possibility of securing Bolton's testimony, Bolton had threatened to file a case in federal district court seeking a ruling on whether he could be compelled to testify in response to a House subpoena. In response to his threat, the Democrats simply decided to halt their efforts to seek his testimony. Without it, I didn't believe the 2019 impeachment hearings had presented enough evidence for a yes vote.

With all that in mind, I knew there could be no half measures if the January 6th Committee was going to succeed: We would need a firm commitment to litigate immediately and aggressively over executive-privilege claims and any other key issues. We would need to enforce our subpoenas and seek criminal contempt whenever appropriate. We needed to be serious and nonpartisan.

And we could not back down.

31. McCARTHY WITHDRAWS HIS NOMINEES

THE RESOLUTION ESTABLISHING THE SELECT Committee envisioned that Speaker Nancy Pelosi would nominate eight members and Leader Kevin McCarthy would nominate five, subject to the Speaker's approval. This arrangement for appointing members had been used by prior select committees, including the Select Committee to Investigate the Preparation for and Response to Hurricane Katrina. At the beginning of September, Chairman Thompson asked me to serve as the January 6th Committee's vice chair, and I agreed.

While he was considering which Republicans he would appoint to the January 6th Committee, Kevin McCarthy traveled to Bedminster, New Jersey, to meet with Donald Trump. Four days later, on July 19, 2021, McCarthy announced his five nominees to the Select Committee: Congressmen Kelly Armstrong, Jim Banks, Rodney Davis, Jim Jordan, and Troy Nehls. I knew all of these men, and I knew that each of them had strongly supported Donald Trump. Three of them, in my view, were not objectionable.

Rodney Davis was the ranking Republican on the House Administration Committee. In that capacity, he had been involved in security briefings leading up to January 6 and had taken the lead in briefing our conference in the aftermath. Rodney was a serious member of Congress who got along well with colleagues on both sides of the aisle. He had also been the lead sponsor of a bill, introduced on January 12, 2021, to create an independent commission to investigate "the Domestic Terrorist Attack upon the United States Capitol." No matter what he had said since in Donald Trump's favor, he had been willing to be forthright at the outset. I believed Representative Davis would at least listen to the Republican witnesses we hoped to call.

I also thought that Kelly Armstrong would operate in good faith. Kelly is an attorney. He represents North Dakota, a state with a small population, only one House representative, and many issues in common with Wyoming. We had worked together frequently. He agreed early on with the position I laid out in my 21-page memo — that objections to electoral slates were inappropriate. I trusted that Kelly would be a responsible member of the Committee.

I was less certain about Troy Nehls. He had just been elected, and I didn't know him well. But he had said this on January 6:

I was proud to stand shoulder to shoulder with Capitol police barricading [the] entrance to our sacred House chamber, while trying to calm the situation [and] talking to protestors. What I'm witnessing is a disgrace. We're better than this. Violence is NEVER the answer. Law and order!

I thought if Davis or Armstrong, and maybe even Nehls, sat across the table listening to Republican witnesses from the Trump administration and the Trump campaign who told them the truth, these men might ultimately be guided by conscience. None of them had attended the December 21, 2020, White House meeting where President Trump's plan for overturning the election was discussed with at least 11 members of the House.

I would have welcomed the participation of many of my Republican colleagues on the Committee. I believed the vast majority of them would have considered the evidence and testimony and followed the facts.

Jim Jordan was an entirely different matter. A leader of the Freedom Caucus, he was certain to follow Donald Trump's direction. Jordan had attended the December 21 White House planning meeting for January 6. He had also talked directly to Donald Trump and Mark Meadows on January 6 — including during the violent attack.

We knew at the time that Trump was relying on members of the Freedom Caucus for crucial support for his January 6 plans. Jordan was, at the very least, a material fact witness—and perhaps an important focus of our investigation. I recalled Jordan's view—expressed some eight months earlier on a House Republican call, just after the election—that rules and lawsuits do not matter, and that "the only thing that matters is winning." I did not think he should serve on the Committee when he might well become a focus of our investigation. He had a serious conflict of interest.

Indeed, when the Committee later issued Jordan a subpoena, we asked for his testimony on multiple topics, including "communications with President Trump on January 6th" and "any discussions involving the possibility of presidential pardons for individuals involved in any aspect of January 6th or the planning for January 6th." Although Jordan had said publicly that he had nothing to hide, and that he would be happy to speak with the Committee, he declined to do so: He refused to comply with a congressional subpoena.

Jim Banks, too, posed an issue. Jim was a congressional classmate of mine, and in the years before January 6 I had regarded him as a friend. We served on the Armed Services Committee together, and I supported him when he ran to be chairman of the Republican Study Committee. But as with Elise Stefanik, something in Jim seemed to have snapped. His previous commitment to substance and policy had been replaced by a desire to please Donald Trump at any cost. On January 5, Banks issued a statement welcoming those Trump supporters who were coming for January 6. And now, in comments after McCarthy announced Banks' appointment to the January 6th Committee, Banks made clear that he did not intend to operate in good faith. Instead, he would attempt to blame the Capitol Police, Nancy Pelosi, and the Biden administration (which did not yet exist on January 6) for the invasion of the Capitol.

In a statement announcing his appointment to the January 6th Committee, Banks claimed that Speaker Pelosi had "created this committee solely to malign conservatives and to justify the Left's authoritarian agenda." He made it clear that he had no interest in the truth, and that he would not be objective. For Jim Banks, it was purely political.

After calling me to discuss Kevin's five nominees, Speaker Pelosi accepted the appointments of Davis, Armstrong, and Nehls. Citing concerns about the "integrity of the Committee," she also announced her decision that neither Jordan nor Banks could serve, and asked McCarthy to name two Republican replacements.

Jordan and Banks, said Pelosi, had "made statements and took actions that just made it ridiculous to put them on such a committee seeking the truth."

I agreed with the Speaker's decision. Shortly after it was announced — on the afternoon of July 21 — I spoke to reporters about it on the steps of the US Capitol. I wanted to cut through the increasingly partisan Republican spin and remind people of the truth: In order to placate Trump, McCarthy was doing everything he could to prevent an honest investigation into the attack on January 6. I said this:

> The American people deserve to know what happened. The people who did this must be held accountable. There must be an investigation that is nonpartisan, that is sober, that is serious, that gets to the facts — wherever they may lead. And at every opportunity, the Minority Leader has attempted to prevent the American people from understanding what happened, to block this investigation.

I stressed that efforts to thwart the investigation would not be successful. As I said on July 1, "The Committee is going to do a very thorough and fair and nonpartisan job at getting to the truth."

Rather than selecting two Republican alternatives, however, Kevin McCarthy decided to withdraw all five of his nominees. For the next year and a half, he would argue that the Select Committee was irretrievably partisan because Pelosi had rejected his nominees. He suggested repeatedly that she had rejected all of his nominees, which of course was not true: McCarthy had *chosen* to withdraw *all* five nominees. It was a political tactic. He could easily have replaced Jordan and Banks.

About a year later—on June 19, 2022, after we had begun to present our evidence in a series of televised hearings—Trump would criticize McCarthy over this:

> Unfortunately, a bad decision was made. This committee—it was a bad decision not to have representation on this committee. That was a very, very foolish decision.

Following Kevin's decision to withdraw all his nominees, Speaker Pelosi asked me whether I thought she should offer one of the vacant slots to Republican Adam Kinzinger from Illinois. I knew and respected Adam and thought he would make an excellent addition to the Committee. He had taken principled stands early on as we were debating the Electoral College objections. In the wake of the January 6 attacks, he never wavered in his determination to speak the truth. Speaker Pelosi extended the invitation, and Adam joined the Committee.

In the months that followed, many potential witnesses would attempt to resist Committee subpoenas by making the spurious argument that Pelosi had rejected all of McCarthy's nominees, and that the Committee was therefore improperly constituted. Multiple courts ultimately addressed these arguments, and every one of them ruled in the Committee's favor.

Jim Banks announced that he would lead a Republican effort to conduct a January 6 investigation of their own. The effort never amounted to much. Banks did, however, send letters requesting documents to a handful of federal agencies, falsely representing in his signature block that he was the "Ranking Member" of the Select Committee. This was, of course, false. I knew that Banks was desperate for attention, but I was shocked that he would claim to be the ranking member of a committee to which he had not even been appointed.

———

Shortly after joining the January 6th Committee, I set out to recruit capable lawyers who would work for me throughout the investigation.

Joe Maher, the principal deputy general counsel at the Department of Homeland Security, had been appointed by Phil to that position nearly 15 years earlier. Joe is a very skilled lawyer; a University of Chicago Law School graduate, he clerked for well-known conservative Judge E. Grady Jolly in the Fifth Circuit, and he had worked for Gene Scalia when Gene was solicitor at the Department of Labor. Joe is incisive, with a deep understanding of the constitutional principles at issue in the Committee's work. His appointment to the Committee staff was supported by five prior general counsels of Homeland Security — from both Republican and Democratic administrations. As my senior counsel, Joe Maher was indispensable from the day he started until the day our investigation concluded.

We also persuaded another extremely talented lawyer, John Wood, to come on board. A graduate of Harvard Law School, John had clerked in the Fourth Circuit for a prominent conservative judge, Michael Luttig, as well as for Supreme Court Justice Clarence Thomas. John had served as the US Attorney for the Western District of Missouri, and in several other high-ranking positions at the Department of Justice. He had been Phil's principal deputy in the associate attorney general's office at DOJ, and later at the White House Office of Management and Budget. Like Joe Maher, John was critical to many aspects of our investigation, notably the conduct of key witness exams, the litigation to secure John Eastman's emails, and the formulation of the Committee's criminal referrals.

Not long after John committed to join the Committee staff, Joe, John, Phil, and I met at our house. We were joined by our daughter Elizabeth, who served as an unpaid research assistant and would go on to law school the next fall. Sitting around the dining-room table, we began to formulate a game plan — and priorities for the next steps in our investigation.

When I joined the Select Committee, I knew I would be asking some of the incredibly talented members of my staff to take on additional assignments. At the top of that list was my chief of staff, Kara Ahern. I had first gotten to know Kara when she worked on the Bush-Cheney 2004 campaign. When my dad was vice president, she was his political director in the White House. She had run my campaigns for Congress and worked in leadership positions in multiple presidential campaigns. Kara had been my chief of staff since I was elected to Congress in 2016, and when I became conference chair, she ran the operations of the House conference as well. Kara is savvy, smart, incredibly talented, and totally trustworthy. She has tremendous judgment and a great sense of humor. And although she has occupied some of the most senior staff positions on Capitol Hill and in political operations at the White House, she is always willing to roll up her sleeves to get things done — focused on the mission without any ego. Kara continued to oversee all the operations of my congressional office and became an indispensable asset for the Select Committee's work, too.

I also asked my communications director, Jeremy Adler, to take on expanded responsibilities. He effectively and impressively handled every new challenge, as I knew he would. Jeremy had been communications director for Speaker Paul Ryan's political operation before he came to work for me. Jeremy also expertly managed all communications messaging and strategy for House Republicans when I was conference chair. And I'm pretty sure that — given the volume of work he produced, strategies he developed, and press matters he dealt with — he never slept. His communications skills and expertise became crucial to the work of the Select Committee.

Another member of my staff who played a key role in all I did was Will Henderson. Will graduated from Texas Christian University in 2017 and joined my staff in 2018, handling constituent correspondence. It was clear immediately that Will could take on additional responsibilities, and he quickly moved up. When I ran for conference chair, we recruited Will to oversee our vote-counting process — keeping track on large charts in my office of pledges of support from each Republican member of the House. From then on, Will's judgment, capability, and tremendous work ethic made him an essential member of our team.

Michael "Sully" Sullivan also provided crucial support for the Select Committee's work. Sully initially came to work for me in 2019. His capacity for research, analysis, and rapid response is second to none. He processed huge amounts of information in compressed periods of time and is tireless. His contributions, especially as the Committee completed its report, were very important.

Early in 2022, I also persuaded Tom Joscelyn to join the Committee staff. I had first met Tom 20 years earlier, when we were both working on national security policy issues. In the aftermath of 9/11, Tom had taught himself Arabic and become one of the world's experts on al-Qaeda terror- ist networks. He has an encyclopedic memory—and a dedication to facts and detail—that I knew we needed. Tom came on board to help super- vise work on the Committee's report. Chapter 8 of that report is Tom's superb analysis of the attack, which shed new light on the planning and tactical operations of groups such as the Oath Keepers and the Proud Boys.

Although it should be obvious to any objective person that my staff could not remotely be described as "liberal Democrats," Trump's allies in Congress nevertheless tried to characterize the investigation as a partisan effort, run entirely by Democrats. It wasn't.

I worked day in and day out with a long list of exceptionally capable lawyers and staff appointed by Chairman Thompson, a number of whom were experienced prosecutors. I never asked them what their political affiliations might be. Their dedication and hard work—especially in their skilled questioning of many of our witnesses—were ultimately critical to the Committee's success. David Buckley served as staff director and ensured that all aspects of the Committee's work operated efficiently and in a manner that enabled us to fulfill our mandate and complete our work on time. As chief counsel, Kristin Amerling helped to manage a complex set of issues related to litigation, subpoenas, and our interactions with fed- eral agencies. Tim Heaphy, who had served as US Attorney for the Western District of Virginia, joined us as chief investigative counsel and managed a skilled team of dedicated investigators. Tim Mulvey brought years of experience in communications and press operations to the Select Committee. He oversaw important aspects of our hearings and other pre- sentations to the American people.

Dozens of additional people made very significant contributions. A number of members of our staff had spent years as Assistant US Attorneys, in other prosecutorial roles, or in criminal-defense practices. We also benefited greatly from the work of a number of skilled younger lawyers just launching their careers. I came to know and trust a great many of them.

In the months ahead, we would need every one of these talented individuals to overcome the roadblocks and evasions that many witnesses threw in our way.

32.   I WAS ELECTROCUTED AGAIN AND AGAIN AND AGAIN

As the January 6th Committee was still staffing up, we held our initial hearing. Our witnesses were four members of the Capitol and Metropolitan Police Departments. Nearly seven months had passed since January 6, and Chairman Thompson wanted to begin our investigation by reminding everyone of that day's intense — and inexcusable — violence.

I regarded this initial hearing as an opportunity to frame exactly what we were about to spend the next 18 months doing, and to give people a sense of why it mattered:

> We must know what happened here at the Capitol. We must also know what happened every minute of that day in the White House — every phone call, every conversation, every meeting leading up to, during, and after the attack. Honorable men and women have an obligation to step forward. If those responsible are not held accountable and if Congress does not act responsibly, this will remain a cancer on our Constitutional republic, undermining the peaceful transfer of power at the heart of our democratic system. We will face the threat of more violence in the months to come — and another January 6th every four years.

I wanted to describe exactly why I had joined the January 6th Committee, despite the certainty of dramatically negative political consequences for me:

The question for every one of us who serves in Congress, for every elected official across this great nation—indeed, for every American—is this: Will we adhere to the rule of law? Will we respect the rulings of our courts? Will we preserve the peaceful transition of power? Or will we be so blinded by partisanship that we throw away the miracle of America? Do we hate our political adversaries more than we love our country and revere our Constitution? I pray that that is not the case. I pray that we all remember, *Our children are watching.* As we carry out this solemn and sacred duty entrusted to us, our children will know who stood for truth, and they will inherit the nation we hand to them—a republic, if we can keep it.

As this inaugural hearing moved to the witnesses and the evidence, we played a collection of verbatim audio and video clips from several of the violent rioters:

"Okay, guys, apparently the tip of the spear has entered the Capitol Building."

"Can I speak to Pelosi? We're coming, bitch. Oh, Mike Pence—we're coming for you too, f'ing traitor."

"They've got a gallows set up outside the Capitol Building. It's time to start f'ing using them."

"Start making a list. Put all those names down, and we start hunting them down one by one."

Then Sergeant Aquilino Gonell and Officers Michael Fanone, Daniel Hodges, and Harry Dunn, wearing their dress uniforms, shared compelling accounts of how they had been accosted, attacked, and injured. It is well worth remembering what each of these men told us. Dragged from the police line in the Capitol's West Entrance and savagely beaten by Trump supporters, Officer Fanone sustained multiple very serious injuries. Here's how he recounted that traumatic experience:

I can remember looking around and being shocked by the sheer number of people fighting us. As my body camera shows, there were thousands and thousands of people determined to get past us by any means necessary.

At some point during the fighting, I was dragged from the line of officers and into the crowd. I heard someone scream, "I got one!" As I was swarmed by a violent mob, they ripped off my badge, they grabbed and stripped me of my radio, they seized ammunition that was secured to my body. They began to beat me with their fists and what felt like hard metal objects. At one point I came face-to-face with an attacker who repeatedly lunged for me and attempted to remove my firearm. I heard chanting from some in the crowd: "Get his gun!" and "Kill him with his own gun!"

...I was electrocuted again and again and again with a Taser...

At the hospital, doctors told me that I had suffered a heart attack. I was later diagnosed with a concussion, a traumatic brain injury, and post-traumatic stress disorder.

Officer Hodges had been defending one of the doorways on the West Front as the mob surged forward. Here is some of what he told us:

The acrid sting of CS gas, or tear gas, and OC spray, which is Mace, hung in the air as the terrorists threw our own CS gas canisters back at us, and sprayed us with their own OC spray, which they either bought themselves, or stole from us. Later I learned, at least one of them was spraying us in the face with wasp spray.

Eventually there was a surge in the crowd. The fence buckled and broke apart, and we were unable to hold the line. A chaotic melee ensued. Terrorists pushed through the line and engaged us in hand-to-hand combat. Several attempted to knock me over and steal my baton. One latched onto my face, and got his thumb in my right eye, attempting to gouge it out. I cried out in pain and managed to shake him off before any permanent damage was done.

The mob of terrorists were coordinating their efforts now, shouting "Heave ho!" as they synchronized pushing their weight forward, crushing me further against the metal doorframe. The man in front of me grabbed my baton...and in my current state I was unable to retain my weapon. He bashed me in the head and face with it, rupturing my lip and adding additional injury to my skull.

Sergeant Aquilino Gonell gave similarly harrowing testimony:

The rioters shouted that I—an army veteran and police officer—should be executed.

"We'll get our guns, we outnumber you," they said.

The physical violence we experienced was horrific and devastating. My fellow officers and I were punched, kicked, shoved, sprayed with chemical irritants, and even blinded with eye-damaging lasers by a violent mob who apparently saw us law enforcement—ironically dedicated to protecting them as US citizens—as an impediment to their attempted insurrection.

The mob brought weapons to try to accomplish their insurrectionist objectives. They used them against us. These weapons included hammers, rebars, knives, batons, and police shields taken by force, as well as bear spray and pepper spray....

I could feel myself losing oxygen, and recall thinking to myself, *This is how I'm going to die, defending this entrance.*

The testimony of these men reminded us that only a percentage of the crowd outside the Capitol had managed to gain entry to the building. Thousands of angry and armed rioters on the West Terrace had tried to break through, fighting with officers who successfully—but at a high cost—held their ground and defended the entrances. Had the officers not held the line, many thousands more rioters would have entered the Capitol, bearing the weapons many carried. The situation could have been far worse.

Officer Dunn recalled struggling to process what he was seeing:

I was stunned by what I saw, and what seemed like a sea of people; Capitol Police officers and Metropolitan Police officers were engaged in desperate hand-to-hand fighting with rioters across the West Lawn. Until then, I had never seen anyone physically assault the Capitol Police or MPD, let alone witness mass assaults being perpetrated on law-enforcement officers. I witnessed the rioters using all kinds of weapons against officers, including flagpoles, metal bike racks that they had torn apart, and various kinds of projectiles. Officers were being bloodied in the fighting. Many were screaming and many were blinded, coughing from chemical irritants being sprayed in their faces.

Officer Dunn recounted racial slurs being hurled at him by the rioters as he fought to defend the United States Capitol Building. Images from that day had shown members of the mob that invaded the Capitol wearing anti-Semitic and neo-Nazi insignia.

Another chilling part of Officer Dunn's testimony drove home the sheer enormity of our task. As the riot began, he had received a social-media post, forwarded by text, suggesting that Trump supporters had an organized plan to surround and invade the Capitol by day—and then return later with firearms:

It said, "Trump has given us marching orders" and to "keep your guns hidden." It urged people to "bring your trauma kits and gas masks," to "link up early in the day in 6- to 12-man teams." It indicated there would be "time to arm up."

We ultimately learned that members of the Oath Keepers, who have since been convicted of seditious conspiracy, did indeed have a plan to "arm up" that evening. But at the time of our initial July 2021 hearing, our information about the preplanning by the many militia groups present, and the links among those groups, was largely skeletal. We had a very long way to go, and a short time to get there.

The next day, I ran into a group of students from Miami University of Ohio outside the Capitol Building, talking with Jamie Raskin. It was a typical Washington summer evening: hot and humid, with the sky a hazy pink as the sun began to set. Jamie told the students it was my birthday, and they responded with a memorable rendition of "Happy Birthday." They also had insightful and informed questions about January 6 and the work of the Committee.

As the conversation wound down and the group started to leave, one of the students, a young woman, came over to talk to me. I remember what she said as we stood together on the steps of the Capitol: "I don't know if I agree with you on any policy issues," she told me, "but I want to be part of fighting for our Constitution with you."

It was a sentiment I would hear over and over in the coming months, especially from young women. I was moved to tears more than once by these young Americans who seemed to understand—often better than people many years older—what was at stake and what it will take to save our republic.

33. HIDEAWAY

FORMER SENATOR MIKE ENZI OF Wyoming had retired from office at the end of 2020. Mike was an honorable and good man, an outstanding senator, and a dear friend. Wyoming's congressional delegation is small, so Senators Enzi, Barrasso, and I worked together often. We usually appeared at the same events across our state. I especially loved seeing Mike and his wife, Diana, surrounded by their grandkids, as we rode in county-fair parades every summer.

Mike was the only CPA in the Senate, and I valued his wisdom, experience, and guidance—particularly as we dealt with budget issues every year. He had a dry sense of humor and loved to fish, like my dad. After Mike retired, he still followed what was happening in Congress, and he knew the backlash I was facing in Wyoming. Occasionally he would send me texts urging me to be courageous. He was a man of deep faith and I especially treasured the prayers and scripture he sent during this time. One morning his message to me was from Psalm 7:6-11: "My shield is God Most high, who saves the upright in heart."

Mike passed away after a cycling accident at the end of July 2021. His memorial service was held in the events center in the Enzis' hometown of Gillette, Wyoming. It was a moving ceremony celebrating Mike's love of family, of Wyoming, and of America. A military flight had been arranged to bring many members of the United States Senate to Wyoming for the service.

I was seated in the front row when the senators filed into the auditorium to take their seats. As they walked past and we greeted each other, more than a few of the Republicans leaned over and quietly said some version of *You're doing great. Thanks for standing up and doing what's right.*

I appreciated the support, but I couldn't help thinking that each of *them* could be speaking out as well.

————

Over the course of the summer, a few key former staffers from the Trump White House had begun quietly reaching out to Adam Kinzinger and to me. One of these was Alyssa Farah Griffin, who had been press secretary to Vice President Pence — as well as director of the White House Office of Strategic Communications — before she resigned from the administration in early December of 2020. She had been direct and public in her condemnation of the events leading up to and during January 6.

Alyssa informed us that Sarah Matthews would be willing to come in to speak with me off the record. Matthews had been the deputy White House press secretary. She resigned on the evening of January 6. We knew that she likely had firsthand information about the events inside the West Wing that day — including while the attack was underway.

A few weeks earlier, Jamie Fleet, the House Administration Committee staff director, had handed me the keys to a small, windowless office tucked into the basement of the Capitol Building. To reach it, you descended a short flight of steps to an unmarked door next to a large set of pipes running the length of the hallway. It was a convenient place to work and to hold meetings — especially with individuals whom the press would no doubt recognize had they come to meet with me in my main office in the Cannon House Office Building. This hideaway is where Alyssa Griffin, Sarah Matthews, and I met one day in early October of 2021.

The world would hear Sarah's testimony a few months later, when she appeared in a public hearing of the January 6th Committee. As I listened to her tell her story in the Capitol basement office that fall day, I was impressed by her strength, composure, and courage.

Later that month I set up another private meeting, this time with former Deputy National Security Advisor Matt Pottinger. I called Matt and asked if he would be willing to speak informally with Committee lawyers

John Wood, Tim Heaphy, and me. When Pottinger agreed, I arranged for the four of us to meet in a room at the Army and Navy Club in Northwest Washington.

As the sun went down outside the windows of the club, Matt walked us through the awful hours of January 6 inside the West Wing. The memories were painful ones. Matt, a Marine, understood the magnitude of Donald Trump's dereliction of duty. He took no pleasure in recounting what had happened.

———

By the fall of 2021, we had further refined our investigative plan. We had comprehensive lists of White House and Trump administration personnel, and a road map as to who might be willing to cooperate and provide information. We had begun issuing subpoenas and pursuing witness testimony.

It was increasingly clear that the sheer volume of information, the number of witnesses involved, and the time constraints under which we were working meant that we needed to accelerate our investigative efforts and materially enlarge our staff. This was one of many times that I turned to Jamie Fleet and Terri McCullough. With the support of Chairman Thompson and Speaker Pelosi, they were able to jump-start the effort to hire more attorneys and secure all the resources we needed. Jamie and Terri were integral to many important elements of the Committee's work, including keeping everyone on the same page, and keeping our staff and members focused on our task.

Late in September of 2021, veteran journalist Lesley Stahl interviewed me on *60 Minutes*. The bulk of the interview covered the January 6th Committee's investigation. I wanted to reinforce the fact that we were conducting a bipartisan and professional process. But she also asked a political question—whether my decision to oppose Trump on and after January 6 had been a calculated political move: "There wasn't a yellow pad with the pros and cons?"

The answer was easy. My decision had not been driven in any way by politics, and I told her so: "No...I watched while the attack was underway—understood very clearly what he did on January 6th, what he failed to do on January 6th. Instead of stopping the attack while it was underway, he was busy calling up senators, trying to get them to delay the [electoral] count. So there was no calculation; I think he's very dangerous."

I had made the decision in the midst of the January 6 attack to vote to impeach Donald Trump. It was the right decision when I made it, and I was still doing what I knew was right, regardless of the impact it might have on my political prospects.

Of course, I knew that my decision to join the Select Committee was directly contrary to the advice any campaign consultant (or even the most casual observer of politics) would have given me. Nobody who knew anything about Wyoming or Republican politics would genuinely believe that voting to impeach Donald Trump or agreeing to serve on the January 6th Committee was helping me politically.

Around this time, campaign consultants who worked for me began to receive threats, including from Kevin McCarthy's political operation, that they would be blackballed by all other Republican campaign entities if they continued to work for me. I was proud of and grateful for the handful who stayed with me, regardless of the McCarthy threat. One consultant told me he had lost business and friends—but at least he could sleep at night.

34. WINNING IN COURT

By October of 2021, what Phil and I anticipated in the early phase of the investigation played out: A number of our initial subpoenas met significant resistance. We were aware of the House Counsel's view at that time — that efforts at civil enforcement of a subpoena could fail, due to an unfavorable DC Circuit Court decision in an unrelated case. Whereas the Senate has clear statutory authority to enforce their subpoenas, the House Counsel cautioned us that the House of Representatives lacked such clear authority. In addition, he warned that pursuing civil enforcement of our subpoenas, even if ultimately successful, could take years.

These were make-or-break moments in our investigation. If we didn't move aggressively, witnesses would conclude that they could defy our requests for interviews and documents. We would not be able to secure the evidence our investigation required.

When Donald Trump's former chief strategist Steve Bannon defied our subpoena, we did not hesitate to act. The Committee immediately took steps to seek a criminal contempt citation against Bannon, who had refused to appear for testimony or turn over any documents to the Committee. Bannon had left his job as a White House adviser back in 2017, but nevertheless he was trying to assert some form of executive privilege or absolute immunity for his interactions with Trump. We already understood that Bannon would be a key witness, not least because of what he had said on January 5:

> All hell is going to break loose tomorrow . . . It's going to be quite extraordinarily different. All I can say is strap in . . . Tomorrow is

game day . . . So many people said, "Man, if I was in [the] Revolution, I would be in Washington." Well, this is your time in history.

This is what I explained on the House floor during the debate on whether Bannon should be held in contempt:

I urge all Americans to watch what Mr. Bannon said on his podcast on January 5th and 6th. . . . He said, "We are coming in right over the target. . . . This is the point of attack we have always wanted."

Mr. Bannon's own public statements make clear he knew what was going to happen before it did, and thus he must have been aware of, and may well have been involved in, the planning of everything that played out on that day. The American people deserve to know what he knew and what he did.

We learned later that Bannon also had information about Trump's plans even before the 2020 election and that Trump had planned in advance—before a single vote was counted—to lie about the election being stolen. In other words, Trump's plan was *premeditated*. Here is Bannon speaking to a group from China:

And what Trump's going to do is just declare victory, right? He's gonna declare victory, but that doesn't mean he's the winner, he's just going to *say* he's a winner. . . . He's gonna declare himself a winner. So when you wake up Wednesday morning, it's going to be a firestorm. Also . . . if Trump is losing by 10:00 or 11:00 at night, it's going to be even crazier, you know, because he's gonna sit right there and say they stole it.

That is exactly what Donald Trump did.

After the Select Committee met on October 19, 2021, and approved the contempt report on Steve Bannon, Chairman Thompson and I testified the next day before the House Rules Committee as part of the formal process for moving a contempt resolution to the full House.

The Rules Committee is one of the oldest committees in the House. The Speaker uses this committee to control what legislation reaches the floor of the House, including which amendments will be allowed and how much time there will be for debate. A total of 13 members of Congress sit on the Rules Committee—nine from the majority and four from the minority. This larger than 2:1 ratio is meant to ensure that the majority and the Speaker can always maintain control.

The committee meets in a small, ornate hearing room on the top floor of the Capitol Building. It often meets late into the night. Unlike in other committees, there is no time limit for debate in Rules. Each committee member may take however long they wish to ask as many questions as they choose.

Paul Ryan appointed me to the Rules Committee during my first year in Congress. I had initially been reluctant to join, because I knew it would be a huge commitment of time—and, frankly, because I didn't fully understand how important the committee is. But Ryan was persuasive, and my time on the committee turned out to be invaluable. There is no better place to learn how the House of Representatives works, to be able to speak on and influence every major piece of legislation, and to gain insights into the personalities, politics, and procedures that characterize the House itself.

I left the Rules Committee in 2018 when I was elected chair of the House Republican Conference. When I walked into the committee's top-floor hearing room with Chairman Thompson on October 20, 2021, to testify about the Bannon contempt resolution, it was my first time back in three years.

We took our seats at the witness table, just a few feet from the members of Congress sitting on the committee dais. When it was my turn to speak, I directed my remarks to my Republican colleagues. I thanked the Republican ranking member, Tom Cole, and said, "We've been through a lot together. We're not just colleagues, we're friends. And I served with a number of you on this committee for two years when we were in the majority. I could not have imagined then that we would meet again like this."

As I continued, I described very frankly what other Republicans were telling me about how they would vote on the Bannon contempt resolution:

> [They] say they just don't want this target on their back, they're just trying to keep their heads down, they don't want to anger Kevin McCarthy, the Minority Leader, who has been especially active in attempting to block the investigation of the events of January 6, despite the fact that he clearly called for such a commission the week after the attack. I ask each one of you to step back from the brink. I urge you to do what you know is right.

I wasn't expecting to sway any of the four Republican votes in the Rules Committee. But I knew what Tom Cole had said a couple of days after January 6—that there were "real grounds" for impeaching Donald Trump—and I wanted to remind them that history was watching:

> As you cast your votes, think about how you will answer when history asks, What did you do when Congress was attacked? When a mob, provoked by a president, tried to use violence to stop us from carrying out our Constitutional duty to count electoral votes? When a mob, provoked by a president, tried to overturn the results of an election? Will you be able to say you did everything possible to ensure Americans got the truth about those events? Or did you look away? Did you make partisan excuses and accept the unacceptable?

When the chairman and I finished our testimony, Jim Jordan and Florida's Matt Gaetz testified in opposition to the contempt resolution. Jordan said repeatedly that the Select Committee should not be investigating the January 6 attack, because the Department of Justice and the FBI already had a criminal investigation underway. Jordan even *praised* the job that the DOJ and the FBI were doing in that investigation.

It bears repeating: At this point in the fall of 2021, Jim Jordan was saying that investigating January 6—including what Donald Trump did on that date—*was the job of the Department of Justice.* Today Jordan calls that same investigation the "weaponization" of the Justice Department.

During Jordan's testimony, Rules Committee Chairman Jim McGovern questioned him about his telephone calls with Donald Trump on January 6. Jordan struggled to furnish a consistent answer. Initially, he simply avoided answering. Then Jordan confirmed that he had talked to Trump on January 6. He said he couldn't remember how many times, but he was sure it was only "after" the attack. Next McGovern read him a news story that quoted Jordan saying he was sure one of the calls took place *while* he was in the Ways and Means Committee Room, the room in which members sheltered during the attack. Jordan deflected, but a few moments later seemed to confirm the story was accurate.

McGovern asked Jordan about notes taken by Acting Deputy Attorney General Richard Donoghue during a December 2020 phone call, during which President Trump had instructed Donoghue to "just say the election was corrupt and leave the rest to me and the Republican congressmen." Elsewhere in the call, the president specifically mentioned Jim Jordan and Pennsylvania Republican representative Scott Perry. So McGovern naturally asked, "Did you discuss with President Trump a coordinated effort to overturn the results of the election?"

Jordan laughed nervously and said he had no idea what McGovern was talking about. Perhaps Jordan could have benefited from the advice of a good criminal lawyer before giving his testimony.

Tom Cole seemed to recognize the hole that Jordan was digging, so he said to Jordan:

> You should not be on trial here for, you know, if somebody wants to talk to you they can, you know, charge you with something, I guess they could do that, or if the Select Committee wants to call you, I guess they could do that. But I think you're here to talk about testimony and your view of the [Bannon] subpoena....

Cole said he wanted to offer Jordan the opportunity to add anything to his comments. Jordan responded, in part, by admitting that he had talked to Trump on January 6 after members had been evacuated from the chamber, and said, "I may have talked to him before. I don't know."

———

On October 21, 2021, the House of Representatives voted to hold Steve Bannon in contempt of Congress. Nine Republicans supported the resolution. Scarcely three weeks later, the Department of Justice indicted Bannon. He was tried during the summer of 2022, convicted, and sentenced to four months in federal prison. As of the fall of 2023, his case was still on appeal.

As our work on the January 6th Committee progressed, I began to receive more and more threats, and security again became an issue. Speaker Pelosi assigned a Capitol Police detail that was with me until our investigation concluded at the end of 2022. These brave men and women demonstrated true professionalism, skill, flexibility, and dedication to duty. There were moments when—especially in Wyoming—a misinformed individual would assert some unfounded claim, such as *January 6 was not really all that violent,* as these law-enforcement officers, some of whom had valiantly fought off assailants that day, stood just a few feet away. They never reacted or showed a trace of anger.

Near the end of my time in Congress, a Capitol Police officer on my detail told me he could be seen in one of the videos we had shown in a Select Committee hearing. In that footage, he is donning tactical gear as Proud Boys advance on the Capitol.

35. THE MEADOWS TEXT MESSAGES

BY THE FALL OF 2021, it was becoming clear that Mark Meadows would likely also refuse to testify. We might need to pursue contempt for him as well. I knew Mark and had worked with him during his time representing North Carolina in Congress, and occasionally after he had gone to work in the White House. I never believed that Mark was suited to the role of White House Chief of Staff. I thought he was in over his head—that he lacked the gravitas and judgment required to do the job well. I doubted that Meadows would ever say no to Donald Trump. My experience with Mark further led me to believe that he would say whatever Trump told him to say about January 6.

The January 6th Committee subpoenaed Meadows, seeking a host of his communications, including text messages and emails related to Trump's efforts to overturn the 2020 election. Mark was represented by George Terwilliger, whom I knew from my early days as a practicing lawyer. George was a senior partner in the law firm that I had joined just out of law school. I was surprised by George's initial letters to the Committee on Mark's behalf. Among other things, they said: "We believe that any documents responsive to that subpoena would not be in Mr. Meadows' personal care, custody or control, but rather would be in the possession of the Archivist of the United States. . . ."

This suggested that Meadows had no relevant material on his personal cell phone—a notion that was highly suspect. I knew Meadows used his personal cell to communicate with members of Congress, for example. He had texted and called me from his private cell repeatedly over the years, including when he was White House Chief of Staff. Knowing George Terwilliger, I was reluctant to believe that he would intentionally try to deceive us. It was much more likely that Meadows was lying to Terwilliger about the communications on his private cell.

Was Mark Meadows really so afraid of Donald Trump that he would lie to his own lawyer?

And, if so, what exactly was he trying to hide?

We were negotiating with Meadows' counsel about exactly what information Meadows would be willing to address in a Select Committee interview. We also continued to request information contained in his private email accounts and cell-phone texts. We were increasingly specific about the contents of his private cell phone, even identifying the personal number I knew Meadows had used. Perhaps unaware that Meadows might be lying (and, in fact, had relevant texts on his cell), Terwilliger committed to us that he *would* provide any contents of Meadows' private phone and email—subject, of course, to privilege claims.

By early December, the Committee began to receive Mark Meadows' private cell-phone text messages and emails. Terwilliger claimed privilege as to many of these messages, asserting they were covered by executive privilege, attorney-client privilege, and what Terwilliger called "marital privilege." Some of those privilege claims seemed overbroad and unjustified. But having committed to provide the Committee with non-privileged material, Terwilliger had little choice but to supply us with thousands of messages that Meadows had exchanged with people outside the Trump administration. These messages went to and from Fox News hosts, members of Congress, members of President Trump's family, and many others. We weren't seeing everything, but we were seeing a great deal.

When I saw the text messages, I knew what would happen: Terwilliger was not going to let Meadows appear for any Committee interview—under any circumstances. No privilege could prevent Meadows from testifying about the text messages he had provided to the Committee, and his testimony would likely be very damaging both to himself and to Donald Trump. The texts would also make it very difficult for Meadows to lie to us.

We predicted that Terwilliger would pull the plug on our negotiations and invent a pretext for Meadows not to testify. This is exactly what Terwilliger did, just one day before our scheduled interview: He argued that he was canceling Meadows' appearance because the January 6th Committee had "issued wide-ranging subpoenas" for Meadows' communications. Terwilliger simultaneously filed a lengthy complaint in a civil suit against the Committee, asking a court to excuse Meadows' failure to comply with the subpoena.

Meadows' refusal to appear and testify about text messages and emails that were not covered by any potential privilege put him clearly in contempt of Congress. We knew that Mark Meadows had pivotal information on Donald Trump's efforts to overturn the election, and the Committee needed his testimony. We also knew that other witnesses would be watching to see if Meadows was able to defy our subpoena. We moved quickly, once again, to bring a contempt resolution to the House floor.

In early December, Mark Meadows had appeared on Sean Hannity's Fox News show to complain that the Committee was pressuring him to testify. Hannity remarked: "Liz Cheney's mission is to align with people who called her father a murderer, war criminal, and crook." Meadows suggested that he was trying to cooperate. But it was already clear that he did not intend to do so. We needed to show that we meant business, and that we would not be cowed or pressured by Sean Hannity, Mark Meadows, or anyone else.

The Committee's public presentations regarding Meadows' contempt needed to be careful and scrupulously factual, with no politics or spin. They needed to plainly lay out the evidence we had to justify our conclusion that Meadows was obligated to testify.

We also needed to explain to the American people exactly why the information was relevant legally, and why we were taking the dramatic step of pursuing testimony from Donald Trump's White House chief of staff. It was important to be clear that the Committee understood the gravity of moving to hold a former White House chief of staff in contempt of Congress.

———

When the Committee convened on December 13 to consider the resolution holding Meadows in contempt, I explained in my opening remarks, "We do not do this lightly, and indeed we had hoped not to take this step at all."

However, Mark Meadows had important information, including about a crucial area of our investigation—what exactly Donald Trump had been doing for 187 minutes while the Capitol was besieged by rioters on January 6. Mark Meadows had sent and received a long series of text messages directly relevant to that topic. The texts left no doubt that those in the White House knew exactly what was happening at the Capitol. I began to read the messages from the dais:

"We are under siege up here at the Capitol."

"They have breached the Capitol."

"Hey, Mark, protestors are literally storming the Capitol. Breaking windows on doors. Rushing in. Is Trump going to say something?"

"There's an armed standoff at the House Chamber door."

"We are all helpless."

Dozens of texts, including from Trump administration officials, pleaded for immediate action by the president:

"POTUS has to come out firmly and tell protestors to dissipate. Someone is going to get killed"

"Mark, he needs to stop this. Now"

"TELL THEM TO GO HOME"

"POTUS needs to calm this s*** down."

Indeed, according to the records, multiple Fox News hosts knew the president needed to act immediately. They texted Mr. Meadows, and he has turned over those texts:

"Hey, Mark, the president needs to tell people in the Capitol to go home. This is hurting all of us. He is destroying his legacy...," Laura Ingraham wrote.

"Please get him on tv. Destroying everything you guys have accomplished," Brian Kilmeade texted.

"Can he make a statement...Ask people to peacefully leave the Capitol," Sean Hannity urged.

As the violence continued, one of the president's sons texted Mr. Meadows:

"He's got to condemn this shit. ASAP. The Capitol Police tweet is not enough," Donald Trump, Jr. texted. Meadows responded, "I'm pushing it hard. I agree."

Still President Trump did not immediately act.

Donald Trump, Jr. texted again and again, urging action by the president: "We need an Oval address. He has to lead now. It's gone too far and gotten out of hand."

But hours passed without the necessary action by the president.

And I explained exactly why all of this was relevant to our investigation:

These non-privileged texts are further evidence of President Trump's supreme dereliction of duty during those 187 minutes. And Mr. Meadows' testimony will bear on another key question before this Committee: Did Donald Trump, through action or inaction, corruptly seek to obstruct or impede Congress's official proceeding to count electoral votes? Mark Meadows' testimony will inform our legislative judgments.

Those texts were not the only reason we were seeking Mark Meadows' testimony. We knew he had firsthand knowledge about matters at the heart of our investigation—matters about which there was no possible executive-privilege claim. For example, Meadows had participated in Donald Trump's call with Georgia Secretary of State Brad Raffensperger on January 2, when Trump had pressured Raffensperger "to find 11,780" votes. Meadows had texted with others on the call while it was underway. We also knew from the texts that Meadows, in the days before January 6, had been working with Congressman Scott Perry to try to replace the leadership of the Department of Justice. No claim of executive privilege could cover that testimony, either.

I ended my remarks in the Committee meeting this way:

> January 6th was without precedent. There has been no stronger case in our nation's history for a congressional investigation into the actions of a former president. This investigation is not like other congressional inquiries. Our Constitution, the structure of our institutions, and the rule of law—which are at the heart of what makes America great—are at stake. We cannot be satisfied with incomplete answers, or half-truths; and we cannot surrender to President Trump's efforts to hide what happened. We will be persistent, professional, and nonpartisan. We must get to the objective truth and ensure that January 6th never happens again.

————

Meadows' texts to and from Fox News hosts brought more scrutiny to what Fox had been broadcasting in the weeks leading up to January 6. Fox News had been particularly active in spreading Donald Trump's intentionally false election-fraud claims. It was important for the public to realize that Fox personalities were simply not leveling with the network's viewers.

Sean Hannity, for example, had privately expressed concerns in advance of January 6. He texted Meadows on January 5: "I'm very worried about the next 48 hours."

Hannity also knew about the plan to pressure Pence to refuse to count electoral votes. He sent Meadows this text on January 5: "Pence pressure. WH counsel will leave."

In the days just after January 6, Hannity regarded Donald Trump as someone who needed to be watched—and managed—very closely. That much was evident from his texts on January 7 to Kayleigh McEnany and his texts on January 10 with Mark Meadows. Of course, Hannity didn't say any of that on the air.

Fox News had changed considerably since the days when I worked there over a decade ago. Back then, Charles Krauthammer was a regular panelist, providing brilliant, insightful, and responsible analysis. Charles had been the conscience of Fox News. The network had never been the same since his passing in 2018.

In 2023, discovery materials from Dominion Voting Systems' defamation suit against Fox appeared to reinforce this point. Court documents including deposition testimony, as well as email and text exchanges, appear to indicate that Fox News hosts and executives knew the election-fraud claims were false, despite what Fox News was broadcasting to its viewers. Sean Hannity, for example, had reportedly testified that he never believed Trump's claims that Dominion machines had stolen the election from Trump: "I didn't believe it for one second." In a text exchange with Tucker Carlson about Sidney Powell and Rudy Giuliani, Laura Ingraham allegedly said, "Sidney is a complete nut. No one will work with her. Ditto with Rudy." Dana Perino reportedly referred to the election-fraud claims as "total bs," "insane," and "nonsense." And Fox Corporation CEO Rupert Murdoch reportedly said in an email about January 6: "wake-up call for Hannity, who has been privately disgusted by Trump for weeks, but was scared to lose viewers." Fox settled the Dominion litigation for $787 million.

The Meadows texts would help illuminate another key question for the Committee, which I asked this way near the end of my remarks: "Did Donald Trump, through action or inaction, corruptly seek to obstruct or impede Congress's official proceeding to count electoral votes?" This was a reference to a specific federal criminal statute, 18 USC §1512(c)(2), which makes it a crime to corruptly obstruct Congress's official proceeding to count electoral votes.

Phil, along with our daughter Elizabeth, had been following the

Justice Department prosecutions of individuals involved in attacking the Capitol. These cases were being heard in the federal courthouse in the District of Columbia. Phil had spent decades litigating cases there and correctly predicted most of the judges' rulings on these charges. His instinct was that §1512(c)(2), along with certain other criminal statutes, might be applied to Trump and others involved in his attempt to overturn the election. We recognized, for example, that Donald Trump and his team had coordinated an effort to create fraudulent electoral-vote certifications in states that Joe Biden had won, to send these false slates to Congress for January 6, and to pressure Vice President Pence to disregard the genuine certifications from those states. We were in the process of evaluating whether §1512(c)(2) could apply to that conduct.

After my remarks, a much more public discussion began about the criminal charges the Department of Justice might consider against Donald Trump and other individuals who had attempted to overturn the election. And in the months that followed, a federal judge concluded that Donald Trump and his adviser, John Eastman, had likely violated §1512(c)(2) and at least one other criminal statute in their many efforts to overturn the election.

36.   PRESIDENTS ARE NOT KINGS

WHILE THE BANNON AND MEADOWS contempt processes were underway, we were simultaneously litigating the case brought by Donald Trump to challenge the January 6th Committee's subpoena to the National Archives. Trump had asked for an injunction, halting the Archives from supplying us with the White House documents our investigation needed. This was an all-hands-on-deck effort for the Committee, and many are owed thanks—including the office of the Counsel for the House of Representatives. We worked together to move the initial stages of this litigation quickly and aggressively. We won in federal district court on November 9, 2021—in a highly expedited process. Judge Tanya Chutkan ruled that former President Trump could not prevent the Committee from accessing the relevant documents. The court's well-written opinion was memorable—and widely quoted for this point: "... Presidents are not kings, and Plaintiff is not President."

Trump appealed the ruling. The appeals process was similarly highly expedited. Oral arguments were held on November 30, 2021, and an exceptionally well-reasoned, 68-page decision was issued just 10 days later. The court concluded that "[t]he January 6th Committee has ... demonstrated a sound factual predicate for requesting these presidential documents specifically. There is a direct linkage between the former President and the events of" January 6th. The court also concluded that our committee would have been entitled to the presidential documents *even if Donald Trump were the sitting President.*

This last point was critical. Despite the fact that President Biden had waived executive privilege with respect to the documents the Committee sought, we suspected that some Supreme Court justices might believe a former president could still assert an executive-privilege claim. But after weighing all the relevant interests, the appellate court had concluded that Donald Trump could not have blocked the Committee's access to these documents *even if* he were still president.

Phil and I believed the Committee had an excellent chance of success in the Supreme Court—that we might get anywhere from five to eight votes, possibly all but that of Justice Clarence Thomas. The House Counsel's office was not as optimistic, suggesting we might not get even four justices. They warned that the Supreme Court might not take any action until June 2022, which would have been a disaster for us, given the Committee's need to obtain the documents, question the witnesses, and begin the hearings by that time.

I witnessed this sort of disconnect with the House Counsel's office a few times during the investigation. We tended to view most judges appointed by Republican presidents—including those nominated by President Trump himself—as fair-minded and principled. We believed they were likely to recognize the importance of the information the Committee needed. The House Counsel's office, by contrast, was far more negative in assessing our chances before judges or justices appointed by a Republican president. Sometimes that office wanted to avoid litigation altogether: At one point they suggested that we should let the Justice Department litigate against Trump alone, without our participation in the briefing at all. That seemed counterproductive. We needed to stand and fight. I knew we would not encourage witnesses to cooperate with our investigation by retreating in the face of our first major challenge.

Throughout all these discussions, Speaker Pelosi supported my position. We did not back down.

Ultimately, the Supreme Court issued its 8-to-1 ruling in our favor on January 19, 2022. As we had foreseen, only Justice Thomas dissented. The Court explained: "Because the Court of Appeals concluded that President

Trump's claims would have failed even if he were the incumbent, his status as former President necessarily made no difference to the Court's decision."

From start to finish, this litigation was astonishingly fast. And this success materially strengthened the Committee's hand.

37.   LEGITIMATE POLITICAL DISCOURSE

ALTHOUGH MOST MEMBERS OF THE January 6th Committee had personally witnessed elements of the attack, we still needed a much more granular understanding of what transpired at the Capitol that day. We needed to see where the breaches had occurred, where police officers had been attacked, where each element of the battle had been fought. And we needed to walk the route the mob had taken through the Capitol hallways.

We knew if we did this during the day, it would become a press event. We therefore made plans to spend several hours late one night at the end of 2021 getting a walk-through and briefing on precisely what had happened in the Capitol, including from officers who fought that day.

On the plaza on the West Front of the Capitol, officers showed us where reinforcements from the Metropolitan Police Department of the District of Columbia had arrived at a crucial moment in the battle.

We walked up the steps inside the Capitol where the mob had threatened Officer Eugene Goodman, who courageously lured them away from the Senate chamber. We stood in the gallery of the United States Senate where members of the mob, carrying zip ties and wearing tactical gear, had been photographed climbing over the seats and jumping down onto the Senate floor. We saw the stairway down which Vice President Pence and his family had been evacuated.

We walked through the hallways and conference rooms in the office suite of the Speaker of the House, where staff had barricaded themselves for hours as the mob rampaged just outside, banging on the doors as they hunted Pence and Pelosi. We spoke to a member of the Speaker's staff who had been blockaded in the room that day.

We stood on the East Front of the Capitol, looking across the plaza at the Supreme Court, its white marble lit up in the dark night, as members of the Capitol Police described the breach of the doors. We walked through the Rotunda and Statuary Hall toward the doors of the House chamber, following the same route the mob had taken on January 6. We heard how the violent rioters had moved down the hallway around the House chamber and violently attacked the doors at the Speaker's lobby, shattering the glass and attempting to break through as House members and staff were being evacuated.

Until you have walked the halls in this way, it is difficult to fully understand how close the violent rioters came to Vice President Pence, and indeed to many of us. Until you have heard it firsthand from the Capitol Police officers involved, it is difficult to understand how profoundly the violence affected them—and how angry these officers are with members of Congress who try to downplay everything that happened.

———

On the one-year anniversary of the attack, there was a small ceremony and a moment of silence on the floor of the House of Representatives. My dad came with me to the Capitol that day. We walked into the House chamber and took two seats in the front row on the Republican side. As we sat down, my dad looked over his shoulder at row after row after row of empty seats. We were the only Republicans there. Shaking his head, he said to me, "It's one thing to hear about what's happening in our party, but to see it, like this, in such stark terms..." His voice trailed off. It was a profoundly sad moment.

A few weeks later, the Republican National Committee (RNC) convened for its winter meeting. They adopted a resolution censuring Adam Kinzinger and me. In a statement referring to the January 6 investigation as "the persecution of ordinary citizens engaged in legitimate political discourse," the RNC accused Kinzinger and me of engaging in "behavior which has been destructive to the institution of the US House of Representatives, the Republican Party, and our republic. . . ."

The resolution reflected a political party that had lost its principles and, frankly, seemed to be led by morons. This was my reply:

> The leaders of the Republican Party have made themselves willing hostages to a man who admits he tried to overturn a presidential election and suggests he would pardon Jan. 6 defendants, some of whom have been charged with seditious conspiracy. I'm a Constitutional conservative, and I do not recognize those in my party who have abandoned the Constitution to embrace Donald Trump. History will be their judge.

RNC Chair Ronna Romney McDaniel immediately found herself having to explain how Republicans could possibly view the events of January 6 as "legitimate political discourse." At one point, McDaniel said her principal concern was the Committee subpoenas that had gone out to 16 Michigan Republicans, all of whom had signed a fake electoral slate falsely certifying President Trump as the election winner. Two years later, Michigan Attorney General Dana Nessel indicted those same 16 individuals for participating in the fraudulent scheme. As the Committee's investigation would show, McDaniel had been involved in helping facilitate President Trump's and John Eastman's fake-electors scheme.

Not too long ago, the Republican Party had been the party of Ronald Reagan. George W. Bush and my father were the last Republican candidates to win the popular vote in any presidential election, and that was *two decades ago,* in 2004. And it was no wonder why.

In the aftermath of January 6, Ronna McDaniel was either unable or unwilling to stand up to Trump. Instead, she apparently agreed to have the party pay Trump's legal bills, and go along with everything else he wanted.

In the choice between the Constitution and Donald Trump, the leaders of the Republican Party were turning away from the Constitution.

38.   TAKING THE 5TH

As we moved toward winter, our teams of investigators were conducting an increasing number of witness interviews. Fairly early on, Democratic Congresswoman Zoe Lofgren and I realized that certain Committee interviews had not been recorded on video, even when conducted over Zoom. We instructed that a video recording must be made of every interview. Both Zoe and I knew we had to consider the reality of our task. Reading the transcripts of witness interviews into the record in a televised hearing was unlikely to be effective. We needed the public to see the witnesses on camera.

This might have been the first time that Zoe and I began to discuss in detail how the investigation should play out. Over the course of the investigation, as our committee discussed and debated important issues, Zoe and I almost always saw eye to eye. Although we likely didn't share many views on politics or public policy, we concurred about the gravity of the matters we were investigating and the responsibility we had to present our work effectively, without spin or partisanship.

In January 2022, our team composed a series of letters, followed by subpoenas, seeking cooperation from key witnesses. These letters explained in detail why their testimony would be relevant. Witnesses were well aware of our recent efforts to pursue criminal contempt against Steve Bannon, Mark Meadows, and others. These letters were intended to demonstrate that we had more than enough information to take the same course again. And we also wanted the Department of Justice to understand the evidence we had already developed. The DOJ had been exceptionally busy prosecuting the rioters, but we had not yet seen any clear indication that the department's investigation was turning to the topics we were covering. Many of our letters served their purposes; several key witnesses cooperated quickly, and we made real progress.

However, some individuals who had direct contact with Donald Trump did everything they could to resist providing testimony. John Eastman, for example, was the Chapman University law professor who had worked with Trump on the plan to overturn the election. Our investigation showed that Eastman himself did not believe Trump's plans to be legally defensible. Indeed, Eastman admitted that the Supreme Court would rule 9 to 0 against Trump if it heard the case.

When Eastman had appeared on Tucker Carlson's Fox News show on December 6, 2021, Carlson suggested that Eastman could simply refuse to comply with the Committee's subpoena: "Obviously," Carlson said, "we can't comply with this...the country does not belong to Bennie Thompson, Nancy Pelosi, and Dick Cheney's daughter." Despite what Tucker said, Eastman came in for an interview on December 9, 2021. But he invoked his 5th Amendment privilege against self-incrimination 100 times, including in response to questions about his direct discussions with Donald Trump.

Jeffrey Clark, the DOJ lawyer who had met with Donald Trump repeatedly, also came in and took the 5th. Like Eastman, Clark invoked the 5th regarding questions about his communications with Donald Trump.

General Mike Flynn, who met and spoke with Trump numerous times in the run-up to January 6—including on December 18 and perhaps afterward—likewise pleaded the 5th regarding *his* direct communications with Donald Trump. Flynn even took the 5th when I asked him if he believed in the peaceful transition of power in the United States.

Political operative and convicted felon Roger Stone, who also apparently had conversations with Trump, also took the 5th in response to questions about those communications. All in all, dozens of witnesses took the 5th in the course of our investigation.

During the attack on January 6, House Republican Leader Kevin McCarthy had talked to Donald Trump, as had Jim Jordan. Both men refused to comply with Committee subpoenas. So did Pennsylvania Congressman Scott Perry, who had talked to Trump repeatedly about the issues we were investigating.

Mark Meadows, Dan Scavino, Steve Bannon, and Peter Navarro had each talked to Donald Trump about January 6, and each of them refused to testify before the January 6th Committee. The House of Representatives voted to hold them in criminal contempt. These four had chosen to risk criminal charges rather than discuss their interactions with Donald Trump.

Testimony obtained by the Committee suggested that Meadows may have contacted both Flynn and Stone at Donald Trump's request on the evening of January 5. Flynn and Stone had both been photographed with certain members of the Oath Keepers or Proud Boys. Of course, members of both the Proud Boys and Oath Keepers were directly involved in the attack on the Capitol on January 6, and a number of the leaders and members of these groups have since been convicted of seditious conspiracy.

We also learned that in the midst of the violence of January 6, members of the Oath Keepers were texting one another about Republican Congressman Ronny Jackson of Texas.

One text said this:

"Ronnie Jackson (TX) office inside Capitol—he needs OK [Oath Keeper] help. Anyone inside?"

Another text read:

"Dr. Ronnie Jackson—on the move. Needs protection. If anyone inside, cover him. He has critical data to protect."

Even Stewart Rhodes—the Oath Keepers leader who would later be sentenced to 18 years in prison for seditious conspiracy—texted about Jackson:

"Give him my cell."

Ronny Jackson had served as physician to President Trump before being elected to Congress in November 2020. He had attended President Trump's January 6 speech at the Ellipse. But when the January 6th Committee asked Jackson to appear for an interview to explain why the Oath Keepers had been talking about him by name during the attack, he refused. Instead, he said publicly that he had no idea how the Oath Keepers would have known him, or why they texted about him.

And yet the texts regarding Representative Ronny Jackson did not simply appear from nowhere. Something triggered the exchanges. As far as I know, the Committee found no similar texts among the Oath Keepers relating to the safety of any other member of Congress. Was someone communicating with the Oath Keepers about Jackson? Who exactly was that person? And finally, what was the "critical data" that Jackson supposedly had "to protect"?

If anyone can get to the bottom of those questions, it will be Special Counsel Jack Smith.

39. THE ILLEGALITY OF THE PLAN WAS OBVIOUS

ALTHOUGH JOHN EASTMAN HAD INVOKED the 5th Amendment and claimed other privileges, the Committee believed it was legally entitled to his emails and other communications. Under what is known as the "crime-fraud exception" to attorney-client privilege, certain of those documents could be available if they provided evidence of what was likely a criminal or fraudulent scheme to overturn the election. We knew that John Eastman had communicated from an email account administered by Chapman University. Chapman had parted ways with Eastman about a week after January 6, announcing that Dr. John Eastman "will retire from Chapman, effective immediately."

John Wood and our investigative team believed that Chapman University might agree to turn over Eastman's email communications in response to a Committee subpoena but that Eastman might then file suit to prevent the college from doing so. We subpoenaed Chapman University, and sure enough, Eastman sued both the Committee and Chapman University in federal district court in California.

Almost at once, we recognized that Eastman's suit could be pivotal. But to receive these supposedly "privileged" emails, we needed to convince the federal court that Eastman and Trump were involved in what was likely a criminal or fraudulent scheme. Phil and I had already been discussing these issues in great detail with Committee lawyers John Wood and Joe Maher, including which potential criminal statutes might apply given the evidence the Committee had already developed. Our team worked closely with the House Counsel's office, which did an excellent job in this case, to compile and present our voluminous evidence to the court and file our briefs in very short order.

With the Committee evidence in hand, Federal Judge David Carter conducted what is known as an *in camera* review of John Eastman's Chapman University emails. We did not know then exactly what was in these emails, but Judge Carter reviewed them all—and reached some stark conclusions.

Judge Carter's decision began with a general description of the evidence: "In the months following the election, numerous credible sources—from the President's inner circle to agency leadership to statisticians—informed President Trump and Dr. Eastman that there was no evidence of election fraud." This, of course, is the same conclusion now found in Special Counsel Jack Smith's August 1, 2023, indictment of Donald Trump.

Judge Carter then turned to Donald Trump's efforts to overturn the election, identifying Trump's effort to install Jeffrey Clark as attorney general; numerous attempts to persuade state officials and legislatures to alter the election results; and a plan, coupled with sustained pressure on Vice President Pence, to ensure that certified slates of electoral votes in several key states would not be counted on January 6.

The decision reached specific conclusions on the crime-fraud exception. First, Judge Carter addressed the same provision of criminal law that I had referenced in support of our contempt resolution for Mark Meadows, 18 USC §1512(c):

> President Trump attempted to obstruct an official proceeding by launching a pressure campaign to convince Vice President Pence to disrupt the Joint Session on January 6...
>
> The illegality of the plan was obvious. Our nation was founded on the peaceful transition of power, epitomized by George Washington laying down his sword to make way for democratic elections. Ignoring this history, President Trump vigorously campaigned for the Vice President to single-handedly determine the results of the 2020 election. As Vice President

Pence stated, "No Vice President in American history has ever asserted such authority."

Every American—and certainly the President of the United States—knows that in a democracy, leaders are elected, not installed. With a plan this "BOLD," President Trump knowingly tried to subvert this fundamental principle.

Based on the evidence, the Court finds it more likely than not that President Trump corruptly attempted to obstruct the Joint Session of Congress on January 6, 2021.

The Committee's briefing had also focused on another section of the criminal code, 18 USC §371, which makes it illegal to conspire to defraud the government through "deceitful or dishonest means" by obstructing the counting of electoral votes. Here were the court's conclusions on that provision:

President Trump and Dr. Eastman participated in numerous overt acts in furtherance of their shared plan. As detailed at length above, President Trump's acts to strong-arm Vice President Pence into following the plan included meeting with and calling the Vice President and berating him in a speech to thousands outside the Capitol. Dr. Eastman joined for one of those meetings, spent hours attempting to convince the Vice President's counsel to support the plan, and gave his own speech at the Ellipse "demanding" the Vice President "stand up" and enact his plan.

Based on the evidence, the Court finds that it is more likely than not that President Trump and Dr. Eastman dishonestly conspired to obstruct the Joint Session of Congress on January 6, 2021.

In specific response to John Eastman's argument that he was operating under a "good-faith legal theory," the court concluded:

Dr. Eastman's views on the Electoral Count Act are not, as he argues, a "good-faith interpretation" of the law; they are a partisan distortion of the democratic process. His plan was driven not by preserving the Constitution, but by winning the 2020 election:

[Dr. Eastman] acknowledged that he didn't think Kamala Harris should have that authority in 2024; he didn't think Al Gore should have had it in 2000; and he acknowledged that no small-government conservative should think that that was the case.

Dr. Eastman also understood the gravity of his plan for democracy—he acknowledged, "[y]ou would just have the same party win continuously if [the] Vice President had the authority to just declare the winner of every State."

The evidence shows that Dr. Eastman was aware that his plan violated the Electoral Count Act. Dr. Eastman likely acted deceitfully and dishonestly each time he pushed an outcome-driven plan that he knew was unsupported by the law.

After laying out all of these specific findings, the court reached a final conclusion:

Dr. Eastman and President Trump launched a campaign to over-turn a democratic election, an action unprecedented in American history. Their campaign was not confined to the ivory tower—it was a coup in search of a legal theory. . . .

If Dr. Eastman and President Trump's plan had worked, it would have permanently ended the peaceful transition of power, undermining American democracy and the Constitution. If the country does not commit to investigating and pursuing account-ability for those responsible, the Court fears January 6 will repeat itself.

As far as I know, this ruling is the first time that any congressional investigation has successfully invoked the crime-fraud exception in federal court.

40. TRUMP THOUGHT PENCE
DESERVED TO BE HANGED

WHILE WE WERE PLEASED WITH the federal court's Eastman ruling, it was difficult to understand why the Justice Department still had not taken any action with respect to Mark Meadows and the criminal contempt resolution against him. By March 2022, we had been waiting three months for the Justice Department to indict Meadows for contempt of Congress. It should have been an easy case: Meadows had produced documents to us, including his text messages. We were entitled to question him about those documents. None of that material could conceivably be privileged.

For months, January 6th Committee staffers had been fielding questions from DOJ lawyers who were compiling a record to support a Meadows indictment. Our committee's investigatory team was convinced that Justice *would* indict Meadows, and that it would happen soon. Indeed, they believed that Justice lawyers had recommended such an indictment up the chain at the department.

Justice had indicted Steve Bannon only a few weeks after our contempt vote, so we were now growing understandably frustrated. Recognizing that time was running out before our upcoming hearings, I concluded that we could no longer wait for the Justice Department to act. We would need to adopt a different approach.

I had publicly cited several key reasons why we needed Meadows' testimony. But we had other reasons I did not mention at the time. Mark Meadows had written a book entitled *The Chief's Chief* that was published in December 2021. It contained a number of intentionally false descriptions about what had happened on January 6. Indeed, the book was so obsequious that it could have been dictated to Meadows by Donald Trump himself. Some on our investigative team even believed *The Chief's Chief* was an attempt to communicate the company line for other witnesses to follow.

Today, the book is famous for another reason. The Justice Department indictment against Donald Trump for obstruction of justice and unlawfully retaining national security documents at his Mar-a-Lago retreat in Florida relies in part on an audiotaped meeting between Trump and the ghostwriters for Meadows' book.

Here is just one example of a deliberate Meadows falsehood from the book. Meadows claimed that Donald Trump had ordered 10,000 National Guard troops to be on standby for January 6. Meadows also suggested publicly that Donald Trump had given an order to deploy those troops. But when asked if that statement was true, Acting Secretary of Defense Chris Miller told the committee under oath: "Not from my perspective. I was never given any direction or order or knew of any plans of that nature. So I was surprised by seeing that publicly."

Pressed again on whether Trump had ordered those 10,000 troops to be ready, the former acting secretary said, "There was no order from the President."

As we later showed in detail during Committee hearings, President Trump *did not want* to ask the violent rioters to leave the Capitol, and he refused for multiple hours to go on the air and instruct them to leave. It seemed absurd to us that Donald Trump would argue that he had dispatched the National Guard to forcibly remove the rioters from the Capitol when for three hours he would not take even the most elementary step of asking the rioters to stand down and leave.

Meadows made numerous other intentionally false claims, including that Donald Trump never intended to travel to the Capitol with the crowd on January 6. Donald Trump, of course, announced his intention during his Ellipse speech that day. Meadows claimed that Trump had told him he was speaking "metaphorically."

Again, not true: Multiple witnesses testified that Trump was adamant about going to the Capitol, and that he got very angry when told he could not go.

In addition to what witnesses disclosed, I had personally received other information that led me to believe Meadows was concealing the facts. For more than seven years after the attacks of September 11, 2001, I had been a Secret Service protectee. I kept in touch with a number of the men and women who had protected our family during that time.

During the course of the January 6 investigation, I had contact with certain of the agents who had been on our details. At one point, it was suggested that our investigation should look closely at what happened when Donald Trump got in the presidential vehicle leaving his Ellipse speech around 1:10 p.m. on January 6. We did. My understanding was that many agents had heard—either through chatter with their colleagues or otherwise—that President Trump was very angry when he was told he could not travel to the Capitol that afternoon, and that something had happened inside the presidential limo. Thus, even before we began questioning White House witnesses, I had reason to believe the statements in Meadows' book were untrue.

Back in December 2021, the day after Meadows had announced he would not attend our scheduled interview, he sued the January 6th Committee in federal district court in the District of Columbia. Meadows' suit raised all sorts of arguments. One of them was that, as a former president's former chief of staff, he was protected from testifying by executive privilege and by a doctrine of *absolute immunity*. Meadows' suit gave us another opportunity: We could file a motion for summary judgment with the court, asking the judge to issue a ruling that Meadows' arguments were wrong on every front. This would remove any legal shield Meadows thought he might have to avoid testifying. After all, we had already litigated and won on Donald Trump's executive-privilege arguments.

This idea was debated with the House Counsel's office. House Counsel had been reluctant since the fall of 2021 to bring any civil case to enforce our subpoenas. If we lost, the argument went, it would create a bad precedent for the House as an institution. I argued that we could not throw in the towel; our investigation was more important than any risk of a bad ruling. Giving up would only show weakness.

At this point in the investigation, the January 6th Committee still had many witnesses to pursue, and I was concerned about any public perception that our resolve was weakening. I could explain litigating and losing about Meadows. I could not explain failing to even try to secure the testimony we needed. Speaker Pelosi supported my view.

I prevailed in the debate, and we filed summary judgment briefs detailing the facts that supported our arguments. We also filed specific evidence from the Committee's interview transcripts related to Mark Meadows' actions on and before January 6.

Some of this evidence came from interviews of Mark Meadows' principal aide in the White House, a woman named Cassidy Hutchinson.

Alyssa Farah Griffin had initially alerted us that Hutchinson could be a key witness. While we did not know this at the time, we learned later that the detailed factual material we had filed in our briefs in the Meadows case had an immediate impact on Cassidy. By that point, Cassidy had sat for only two of the many interviews we would ultimately conduct with her.

Cassidy had worried from the moment she agreed to be represented without charge by a Trump-affiliated lawyer. She sought advice from a Republican member of Congress not on the Select Committee, and he had cautioned Cassidy: "I want you to know that you can't take money like that and expect them to just be working for you and your interests," implying that the Trump lawyers representing her would have Trump's interests in mind. When Cassidy read our brief in the Meadows case, she realized what had happened:

> So I just search my name, and I see that there are citations from my transcript—both of my transcripts. So I'm reading through them. And then I read through them again and again and again . . . and I just kept thinking, "Oh my God, I became someone that I never thought I was going to become."

Shortly after Cassidy Hutchison read this material, she talked to Alyssa Farah Griffin about her situation:

Alyssa, I know you know I had a Trump World attorney. I don't think I have to go into excruciating detail to tell you the situation I'm in right now, but I think that I should go in and elaborate on a few things. I think I need to go in and kind of expand on some things.

Alyssa called me in April 2022. She said she had spoken to Cassidy, and that Cassidy had additional information she wanted to share with the Committee. Alyssa gave me examples of the information. She said that on January 6, Cassidy had heard Meadows and others saying President Trump believed Mike Pence "deserved to be hung" in response to the mob chants of "Hang Mike Pence." And Cassidy had observed Mark Meadows burning documents in the fireplace of his West Wing office on a number of occasions. Alyssa also said that Cassidy was concerned about the Trump-funded lawyer who was representing her.

I shared this information with the Committee counsel who had led Cassidy's initial interviews, and we discussed the right approach to take. Through Alyssa, Cassidy was approaching the Committee directly. Although Congress is not required to recognize attorney-client privilege for any witness, we did not want to obtain testimony addressing the events at the heart of our investigation without a witness's counsel present. I told Alyssa that we would like to speak with Cassidy again, but that we could speak with her about the substance of our investigation only if both the Committee counsel and her own counsel were present. And we wanted her testimony to be on the record. Our Committee counsel called Cassidy's lawyer to set up a new interview.

In the meantime, we discovered that the predictions made by our Committee staff about the Department of Justice were wrong: The Justice Department announced that it would *not* indict Meadows for contempt. We were guessing that senior Justice Department officials felt constrained by the legal concept called *absolute immunity*—the same doctrine that Meadows had asserted to avoid testifying before us in December of 2021. Presidential staff often cite absolute immunity when they negotiate what testimony White House officials can and cannot give before Congress. The concept, however, has been subject to significant debate. We were not aware of any precedent supporting Meadows' claim that a former chief of staff to a former president is categorically immune from giving congressional testimony.

As the Meadows case wore on, US District Court Judge Carl Nichols asked the Department of Justice to file a brief about whether Meadows was entitled to absolute immunity. When the Justice Department brief was filed, we learned that the department was *not* applying absolute immunity to Meadows. Justice had concluded that only the more lenient concept of *qualified immunity* applied. They explained further that the January 6th Committee's need for Meadows' testimony outweighed and therefore overcame any qualified-immunity arguments Meadows might have. In other words, "immunity" could not protect Meadows from testifying before our committee.

So why had the Justice Department refused to indict Mark Meadows for contempt of Congress? We were seeking to ask Meadows about his texts and other materials that could not be subject to any privilege claim. It made very little sense for Justice not to indict — *unless*, some suggested, Meadows had started cooperating with the Justice Department in its own January 6 investigation of President Trump. Had our criminal-contempt referral pushed Meadows into cooperating with the Department of Justice? We did not know. But we did know from Cassidy Hutchinson that Mark Meadows probably had many important pieces of information to share with the department.

The speculation about Meadows was also fueled by the fact that he had abruptly halted his appearances on Sean Hannity's Fox News show. Indeed, he seemed to have dropped from public view entirely. By September 2023, there were press reports that Mark Meadows had now testified before the January 6 grand jury. Meadows' testimony could have been exceptionally helpful to the Select Committee. The public deserved to hear from him. We hoped that the Justice Department had a very good reason for its decision not to indict him for contempt.

41. TO THE BEST OF MY RECOLLECTION, I DON'T RECALL

As OUR INVESTIGATION PROGRESSED AND our skilled Committee staff questioned dozens of additional witnesses, I often joined portions of the questioning. This was especially the case for high-ranking members of the Trump administration. I wanted to pose fundamental questions about the duties of a president and the rulings of our courts. I also wanted to understand each witness's personal interactions with President Donald Trump. The public later saw many of these exchanges in our hearings.

We knew that Attorney General Bill Barr had told Donald Trump forcefully and repeatedly that there was no evidence to substantiate Trump's election-fraud claims. Acting Attorney General Jeff Rosen and his deputy, Rich Donoghue, had also done so repeatedly. As had Trump campaign officials. As had Trump White House staff.

As the interviews accumulated, it became clear that Donald Trump was hearing a consistent drumbeat. A number of his advisers, it appeared, had reached the same set of conclusions independently, without consulting one another. It also appeared that many of these staff members believed the information they were giving Trump would eventually sink in—that he would slowly conclude he must give up and concede the election.

Consider this example, from Attorney General Barr's testimony about a meeting on November 23, 2020:

> [A]s I walked out of the Oval Office, Jared [Kushner] was there with Dan Scavino, who ran the president's social media and who

I thought was a reasonable guy....And I said, "How long is he going to carry on with this 'stolen election' stuff? Where is this going to go?"

And by that time, Meadows had caught up with me and... said, "Look, I think that he's becoming more realistic and knows there's a limit to how far he can take this." And then Jared said, you know, "Yeah, we're working on this—we're working on it."

Although Jared's statement to a concerned Bill Barr tended to suggest that Kushner was pushing his father-in-law to the right outcome, other testimony indicated that Kushner was also assisting Trump's very successful efforts to spread to the public what virtually everyone in the White House knew to be election lies. When we asked Jared if he had played any role in organizing Trump's advertising campaign to disseminate the election lies, he said, "Yeah, I was a creative director—so that's a fair assumption."

I wanted to know why Jared had not done more to stop January 6. Jared told the Committee that he had been busy with pardons in December 2020, and with issues in the Middle East. Donald Trump pardoned Jared Kushner's father, Charles Kushner, on December 23, and Jared appears to have left for the Middle East around January 4.

At one point in my questioning of Jared, he recited one of his favorite quotes about Trump. Jared said, "I forget the journalist, but she said that the media took Trump literally but not seriously, and the voters took him seriously but not literally." I had the impression Jared thought this was clever. But the problem with Jared's quote is this: Tens of millions of American voters actually took Trump's election-fraud allegations literally. They did not see the allegations as some kind of clever parody. And hundreds of Trump supporters have now pled to or been convicted of criminal acts, sacrificing their freedom to achieve what they believed Donald Trump asked them to do. People died and scores of police officers were seriously injured.

Jared's "clever" quote implies that Trump was knowingly playing a cynical game the entire time, intentionally misrepresenting the facts for his own purposes. Of course, there is already substantial additional evidence that Trump was acting intentionally, making false statements to motivate his supporters and to raise money from them.

I had met both Jared Kushner and his wife, Ivanka, several times, but I did not know either of them well. Today they appear to be trying to distance themselves from Donald Trump's January 6 conduct. Perhaps they privately acknowledge that Trump spun completely out of control over the last few months of his administration. They should have done much more to stop him.

————

Before the investigation into the attacks of January 6, I had not been sure exactly what to make of White House Press Secretary Kayleigh McEnany. I had seen her press conference on the morning of January 7. It appeared then that she was distraught and had not slept. I thought at that moment that Kayleigh might be having some real problems trying to deal with what had occurred. The evidence shows that, in the days after January 6, Kayleigh worked to rein in Donald Trump. She cooperated with Sean Hannity and a team of others to try to contain Trump's actions, to isolate him, so he could not again take us off a cliff.

But when Kayleigh came in to testify, she seemed overly coached, evasive, and at times combative. Some of her answers, however, were accurate and careful. For example, when I asked Kayleigh if she agreed that the president was bound to accept the rulings of the courts, she agreed. I asked Ivanka Trump the same thing. She agreed as well.

But we thought Kayleigh McEnany had been carefully coached not to reveal certain key details—including those already furnished to the Committee by her deputy, Sarah Matthews. When I asked Kayleigh about some of those details, she responded this way: "For a senior official or for a press secretary who's in the middle of a crisis, conversations with lower-level staffers might not stand out to me."

We all thought this was a rehearsed answer.

We had evidence that the White House, and President Trump himself, had been alerted to the violence almost immediately after it began. I was therefore surprised that Kayleigh, as the press secretary, was taking the position that she did not immediately know about the violence when many others who interacted with her in the White House did. A couple of times during her interview, Kayleigh's attorney-coaching seemed to lead her to say things like "To the best of my recollection, I don't recall."

Ultimately, I concluded that Kayleigh McEnany was trying very hard to avoid saying anything that might anger Donald Trump. This was the opposite approach from that taken by witnesses such as former White House Counsel Pat Cipollone. As our investigation progressed further and it became ever more apparent that the Committee possessed very detailed information about what had happened in the White House, the strategy of lawyers defending Trump allies began to change. Kayleigh was one of our first senior-level White House witnesses. If she had testified after seeing Pat Cipollone's forthright testimony, I suspect she would have supplied very different answers.

Even so, Kayleigh seemed to acknowledge that Donald Trump should have instructed the rioters to leave the Capitol much earlier in the day. And as the interview wore on, she sometimes dropped the lawyerly answers and expressed her genuine thoughts:

Ms. CHENEY: Do you believe that what happened on January 6th was justified?

Ms. McENANY: Absolutely not. What happened on January 6th was not justified. I condemn violence in every form. I am a Christian. I believe in Jesus Christ. I believe in peace. I love people on the other side of the aisle, whether they're Biden voters, Kamala supporters. That's who I am. I'm a good-natured person. Absolutely it was not justified.

Ultimately, we received highly credible testimony from multiple witnesses with firsthand knowledge on almost all the key issues. All

Americans can comb through the transcripts of our interviews, which we released online, and reach their own judgments.

By late April of 2022, our highly professional Committee staff had pieced together a fair amount of the factual predicate that we would ultimately need for our hearings. But we were still concerned about key gaps in our knowledge — gaps that we now set out to fill.

42.   NOT THE MASTERMIND

IN THE SPRING OF 2022, a handful of staff leaks also became a very significant concern. On April 25, 2022, thousands of Mark Meadows' text messages were leaked to CNN. I believed that one particular staff member,
who announced his departure from the Committee the same day, had
leaked the material. The leak was unethical—and counterproductive for
our investigation.

While I hoped that most of the team—including most of those who
had spent their careers laboring under the strict rules that apply to federal
prosecutors—knew the damage that leaks could cause, we sadly now had
to begin to close the circle of those with access to investigative
information.

We also occasionally had to contend with staff recommendations that
we take investigatory steps that did not seem justified by the evidence
before us. One memorable example related to Supreme Court Justice
Clarence Thomas. A Committee staff member had identified electronic
communications from an email address that included the letters *ctiii,* and
concluded that the communications must have originated from Justice
Clarence Thomas.

The staff member who made that determination, which he later
admitted had been erroneous, did not have any legal training. Otherwise
he would have recognized that no Supreme Court justice could have
drafted the various items in the emails. But he made an incredibly aggressive proposal—to subpoena all of Justice Thomas' private communications in multiple forms of media.

It ultimately turned out that the email address belonged to someone else — a former Republican staffer in North Carolina who felt strongly about election-fraud allegations. When that mistake came to light, some staff members who had been very interested in pursuing Justice Thomas recognized that this could have been a horrendous mistake. It was lucky that we were being careful.

Although our investigation never found communications that genuinely came from Justice Thomas, we did find text messages and other communications from his wife, Ginni. I had known Ginni Thomas for decades. By the time we were investigating January 6, I had not spoken to her for some time. I never thought of Ginni as a leader of any conservative group or movement — she was usually assisting someone else. I thought that others tried to use Ginni's notoriety to gain support for their own causes. I suspected she might have fallen into some role supporting the January 6 effort, but from my knowledge of her, I doubted very much that she was a mastermind of any of it.

Although we had been friendly in the past, Ginni had been attacking my involvement in the January 6th Committee ever since I joined it in July of 2021. In December 2021, she signed a public letter urging that "the House Republican Conference act immediately to remove both Rep. Liz Cheney (R-Wyo.) and Rep. Adam Kinzinger (R-Ill.)...due to their egregious actions as part of the House of Representative's January 6th Select Committee." I was amused when liberals in the press or social media accused me of favoritism toward Ginni. As Phil put it, "I guess they haven't googled what she's been saying about you."

I ignored what Ginni Thomas was saying publicly about me. My view was that Ginni should be treated in the same way as every other witness who had engaged in similar conduct — no better and no worse. After some discussion, the Committee composed a letter to Ginni Thomas with that message, and she ultimately agreed to a recorded interview. The transcript of that interview — conducted by professional staffers, with additional questioning by a number of members, including Adam Schiff, Jamie Raskin, Pete Aguilar, and me — was released by the Committee. Here's a typical exchange:

Ms. CHENEY: And so are you aware that the President and his allies brought legal challenges, which was completely their right to do, but that they lost 61 out of 62 of those legal challenges?

MRS. THOMAS: I still believed that there was fraud and irregularity, as millions of Americans do, Representative Cheney.

I was disappointed that Ginni Thomas had been deceived by the demonstrably untrue election-fraud nonsense. I was even more concerned that she did not seem to respect the rulings of our courts. Ginni, like many others, seemed to believe everything she read and saw in the Trump-friendly media. She was asked on a couple of occasions if she might have had a different view had she known that Donald Trump's advisers were privately telling him his fraud claims were unfounded. At first she replied that it wouldn't have changed her views — that she had believed what she was hearing from friends and seeing on the news. Eventually she just answered, "I don't know."

———

At one point during the investigation, Chairman Bennie Thompson gathered the Committee at the Library of Congress for a daylong planning session. We met in a conference room on one of the top floors, overlooking the Capitol. We spent the day working through our upcoming interviews and discussing next steps for the investigation.

Perhaps the most memorable event from that day is what we did during an afternoon break.

Chairman Thompson led us down two floors to the rare-book reading room, where Library of Congress scholars had brought out some of the most important and meaningful documents in the Library's holdings. We stood together, Republicans and Democrats, looking down at a copy of the Gettysburg Address on yellowing paper, written in pencil by Abraham Lincoln himself. We saw Alexander Hamilton's handwritten notes detailing the flaws of the Articles of Confederation, and a copy of Washington's farewell address warning of the danger of political factions—exactly what we were dealing with now. We saw Thomas Jefferson's copy of the *Manual of Parliamentary Practice,* which to this day still forms the basis for rules and procedures in the House of Representatives.

And we saw a note written by Lincoln on August 23, 1864, when he thought he was likely to lose the upcoming presidential election to General George B. McClellan. If McClellan prevailed, Lincoln believed McClellan would seek an armistice with the Confederacy, essentially recognizing the independence of the Confederate states. Lincoln wrote, in part:

> This morning as for some days past, it seems exceedingly proba-ble that this Administration will not be re-elected. Then it will be my duty to so cooperate with the President-elect, as to save the Union between the election and the inauguration; as he will have secured his election on such grounds that he cannot possibly save it afterwards.

When he finished writing it, Lincoln folded the note, sealed it, and took it into a Cabinet meeting. He asked each member of his Cabinet to sign the outside of the document. The memo was Lincoln's pledge to respect the will of the people and the outcome of the election—and to do everything in his power to help his successor if he lost. The note was also a reminder of how monumentally critical Lincoln's reelection was. Everything depended upon it.

PART V

The Relentless March
of Evidence

MAY TO DECEMBER 2022

43. SEVEN-PART PLAN

THROUGHOUT THE SPRING OF 2022, Phil and I had been considering how to organize the hearings. We knew the significant challenges. What Donald Trump and his allies had done, from Election Day to January 6, was far-flung and detailed and would be difficult to address in any concise fashion. There were dozens of presidential calls and meetings supporting all of Trump's efforts. Indeed, the planning for January 6 appears to have consumed the vast majority of the president's time for several weeks in December of 2020. He was doing almost nothing else. Donald Trump did not do all this on a whim. It was not something planned in one hour, or in one day, or even in one week. It was complicated and detailed.

And, above all else, it was premeditated.

As summer approached, Phil and I created an outline for the upcoming hearings, using large poster paper tacked to the walls of my home office. It was an exercise we had both engaged in many times before, in preparation for trials (Phil) or political and legislative debates (me).

We needed to subdivide our presentations into segments, making the content easily digestible by a television audience tuned in to a series of congressional hearings. And we needed to distill an enormous level of detail into something that could be readily understood. Our solution was to divide the factual material into seven parts — and therefore at least seven hearings. Each would highlight a distinct element of the Trump team's efforts to overturn the 2020 US presidential election:

1) We knew we had to begin with Donald Trump's successful effort to persuade millions of Americans that the election had somehow been

stolen from him. That he was still, for that reason, the rightful president. Thanks to what our investigation had uncovered so far, we knew that Trump had been told repeatedly—by his campaign, by his Justice Department, and by his White House staff—that none of his stolen-election claims were true. This had to be the focus of an early hearing, because those lies were the foundation for everything that followed.

2) We also now knew—again thanks to the work of our investigative staff—how Donald Trump had tried to pressure state legislatures and state officials to flip official certified Biden electoral votes to Trump.

3) Our staff had also uncovered significant evidence showing how the Trump team had created fraudulent Trump electoral slates for states that Biden had won. Both of these efforts—the vote flipping and the slate fabrication—were key elements of the Trump plan.

4) When Trump's plot to convince state legislatures to flip the electoral votes did not work, Trump began looking for a way to make the US Justice Department persuade those legislatures to do so. Trump offered an official named Jeffrey Clark the job of acting attorney general after others at Justice refused to spread Donald Trump's stolen election lies, because Clark was amenable to Trump's schemes. Again, another part of the plan.

5) The Trump team planned each of those steps with the January 6 joint session of Congress in mind. The intent was that Vice President Mike Pence, in his formal role as president of the Senate, would agree on January 6 *not* to count the official Biden electoral votes from multiple states. And Pence would rely on the fraudulent Trump electoral slates as a rationale for doing that.

6) To further support what he planned for Mike Pence, Donald Trump summoned his supporters to Washington on January 6, where he would stage an emotionally charged rally with slogans like TAKE BACK OUR COUNTRY before sending them to the US Capitol. The crowd itself would apply the pressure needed to make all this work. Trump was well aware of the potential for violence by those tens of thousands of people, yet he went ahead with that part of his plan anyway.

7) The ultimate element of Trump's plan took shape as the crowd attacked the Capitol. Donald Trump was trying to delay the electoral

count, but once it became clear that Mike Pence would *not* refuse to count genuine Biden electoral votes, Trump had few options remaining. As the crowd became violent, broke into the Capitol, and halted the joint session, the violent attack and the invasion of the Capitol were the only things stopping the electoral count. And it was at this point that Donald Trump refused to do what everyone knew was absolutely necessary: He refused, for hours, to instruct the rioters to stand down and leave, all while continuing to lobby legislators to stop the count. As a result, more than 140 law-enforcement officers were attacked and injured, and five deaths eventually resulted.

———

So these were the seven principal elements of the Trump plan. We recognized that each hearing would require a careful, fact-based presentation. And each would rely on testimony from Republican officials and Republican witnesses.

I began to work with Jamie Fleet, the House Administration Committee staff director who was helping to facilitate operations of the January 6 Committee, and Terri McCullough, the Speaker's chief of staff, to ensure we could get House Speaker Nancy Pelosi's buy-in for this hearing plan. A number of proposals were being considered, including holding a single hearing or combining all the material into two or three hearings. We knew that what we were doing was unprecedented—and that we had to get it right.

Our lead investigative staff had been assembling their most important evidence. Terri McCullough and Jamie Fleet arranged for them to present this evidence to Select Committee Chairman Bennie Thompson and me in a series of meetings in May. We met in Fleet's office on the third floor of the Capitol Building with the Committee's senior staff—Kristin Amerling, David Buckley, Tim Heaphy, Joe Maher, Tim Mulvey, and Hope Goins, who served as senior counsel to the chairman—to review documents and hear from each of the Committee's lead investigators. They presented segments of testimony from the depositions and interviews they had been conducting; they also provided a summary of the work they had completed to date, plus an assessment of their highest priorities moving forward. I had also spent weeks participating in interviews and combing through transcripts, and I worked with the Committee's digital team to begin compiling video clips of what I thought was the key evidence for each part of Trump's plan and for each of the hearings.

We had spoken at length with a couple of news-programming veterans. One of these individuals recommended that we meet with James Goldston, the former president of ABC News. James came in to interview with Chairman Thompson, then met with me later that day in my hideaway office in the Capitol basement. I was impressed. James was humble, but obviously talented and experienced. He came on board and brought with him a number of individuals with years of experience in network news.

As we began to structure each hearing, I recalled my experience as a Fox News contributor a decade earlier. On several occasions I had been a substitute host for Sean Hannity on his prime-time show. I remembered that those programs were organized in segments called *blocks*. An hour-long show was typically divided into five or six blocks. This structure proved to be an essential way of managing the immense amount of material in each hearing. James Goldston and his team were exceptionally helpful in facilitating that type of presentation. And our outline for each hearing—which took the form of a trial presentation—closely paralleled that structure.

We also relied heavily on Tim Mulvey, the January 6th Committee's talented communications director, to help oversee the staff that pulled all the pieces together. He worked with Chairman Thompson on his remarks and was responsible for all aspects of our relations with the press. There was intense interest in the Committee's work. We needed to ensure we did everything possible to prevent leaks and provide facts so the details and the truth would be accurately covered.

———

In a traditional congressional hearing, each member of a committee is allocated five minutes to ask questions. We knew from the start of our process that approach would not work. All Committee members agreed that the *evidence*—not the members—should be the focus of our hearings. This meant, however, that not every member would make remarks in every hearing.

Over the course of several individual and group meetings, Chairman Thompson—with help from Jamie, Terri, and Speaker Pelosi—secured the agreement of all Committee members for the format we ultimately used: Each hearing would have one or two members assigned to present the evidence; Chairman Thompson and I would each make an opening and closing statement; all members would attend every hearing, even if they were not presenting.

Our first 2022 hearing was scheduled for June 9, 2022. One goal of this hearing was to lay out a comprehensive outline for what was to come. The idea we settled on was that Chairman Thompson would first set the scene, describing the work the Committee had done and the grave nature of the challenges we faced. He would also put this in the context of our nation's history. Then I would present a detailed road map for the hearings to come. Another goal of the first hearing was to remind everyone of the stakes—just how terrible the January 6 attacks had been, and why nothing like that must ever happen again. We would feature previously unseen video of the attack, and testimony from at least one law-enforcement officer explaining in even greater depth the violence of January 6.

———

While we were making those plans, I faced a crossroads of a different sort: I needed to decide whether to register again as a candidate for Congress in Wyoming. The filing deadline was May 27, 2022. I gave significant thought to not running for reelection. I had lost confidence in the House Republican leadership. I was disappointed in many of my colleagues who were also my friends, many of whom told me they agreed with what I said but would not step forward or speak out. I also knew I faced a huge uphill battle in Wyoming, but I had been humbled and grateful for the expressions of support I was receiving across the state.

My work on the January 6th Select Committee was vitally important, but doing it well—ensuring that the investigation and our hearings were a success—demanded an enormous investment of time. It was time I would not be able to spend on the campaign trail in Wyoming.

The easiest course by far would have been simply not filing to run again.

But that didn't feel right.

I had received an outpouring of support from friends and allies across the state—men and women who were eager to help me win reelection because they understood what was at stake. These included some people who had always supported me; others who never had; and still others who had opposed me in previous races but had since become strong advocates. I did not want to abandon any of them.

Withdrawing from the race for my seat in Congress would be seen as declaring defeat in my own election. It might also signal that our investigation had failed—that I was giving up, or that this fight somehow no longer merited the effort. I knew that the Trump team would claim my decision to quit as their victory.

I sought the counsel of an old friend who had spent his career working on programs to promote democracy around the world. Since January 6, we had met privately several times in a town house near Capitol Hill, along with a small group of experts on authoritarianism and the rise of antidemocratic movements. We agreed that the threat posed by Donald Trump might well imperil the existence of American democracy.

My friend asked me, "Does withdrawing from your race make you stronger or weaker in confronting the threat Trump poses?"

I thought for a minute before replying. "It weakens my hand."

"Then you've got your answer," he said.

When I considered the decision from every angle—standing with constituents who had stood with me, doing what was right for Wyoming and for the country, and making sure the January 6th Committee had the best chance to effectively complete its work—the choice was clear. I might well lose my race, I knew, but I wouldn't quit. I filed to run for reelection.

———————

As the first of our 2022 hearings approached, Phil and I drafted my opening statement following the seven-part structure we had created earlier, with clips of evidence. The story needed to be told by Trump administration witnesses and members of the Trump campaign. Donald Trump's own words would convey his intent.

I had shared my opening statement with a handful of people, including Joe Maher, Kara Ahern, and Jamie Fleet. Most Committee members and staffers did not see it until our run-through the evening beforehand. Some members of the staff were concerned about the length and level of detail of my remarks. But I stood firm. I believed we owed the public a clear road map for where we were headed, and that an opening statement beginning to lay out our evidence was essential. Chairman Thompson and Speaker Pelosi agreed.

A day before our hearing, Republican Representative Troy Nehls demonstrated just how craven certain Republican members of Congress had become: "They're going to get the sobbing police officer," Nehls predicted, "or sobbing Democrat or somebody that said how terrible this was and now they are suffering from PTSD."

Congressman Nehls must have been surprised when our hearing opened with clips from numerous senior Republicans who had worked for Trump and were now testifying against him. I hope Nehls was ashamed as he listened to Capitol Police Officer Caroline Edwards describe in detail what she faced while engaged in hand-to-hand combat to defend the Capitol.

———————

Our June 9, 2022, hearing convened at 8:00 p.m. in the Cannon Caucus Room. As we took our seats on the dais, I looked out into the large, historic room. It was packed. Rows of journalists sat at long tables. Members of the Capitol Police and Metropolitan Police who had been wounded in the attack were in attendance. A group of members of Congress who had been trapped in the House gallery on January 6 were also present, as were family members of fallen Capitol Police Officers Brian Sicknick and Howard Liebengood.

Chairman Thompson opened the hearing with a vivid and moving statement about the oath we all take to the Constitution and the duty our oath imposes on us. He quoted from the letter we had seen at the Library of Congress a few months earlier—Lincoln's pledge to do all in his power to support his successor if he was defeated, to uphold the rule of law and guarantee the peaceful transfer of power. And he described Donald Trump's refusal to do the same, instead attempting to overturn the results of a presidential election in order to stay in power.

I began my presentation with the issue I believed was central to everything we were doing: *What exactly was Donald Trump's state of mind? What did he think he could accomplish on January 6?* For this, we used Donald Trump's own words. I began by describing his response to the attack:

> Mr. Chairman, at 6:01 p.m. on January 6th, after he spent hours watching a violent mob besiege, attack, and invade our Capitol, Donald Trump tweeted. But he did not condemn the attack. Instead, he justified it. "These are the things and events that happen," he said, "when a sacred landslide election victory is so unceremoniously and viciously stripped away from great patriots who have been badly and unfairly treated for so long."

This is what Donald Trump said to our nation when the violence was freshest in our minds. Members of multiple law enforcement agencies were still attempting to halt the remaining fighting and clear the Capitol. We needed to convey as accurately as possible, in his own words, the malignant state of mind of our former president. And as he walked from the Oval Office up to the White House residence not long thereafter, he commented only that he was angry with Mike Pence for letting him down. He voiced no regrets about what had already happened, and was still happening, at the Capitol. I explained that the Committee's hearings would show that President Trump knew violence was underway and refused to tell his supporters to leave the Capitol:

As you will see in the hearings to come, President Trump believed his supporters at the Capitol, and I quote, "were doing what they should be doing." This is what he told his staff as they pleaded with him to call off the mob, to instruct his supporters to leave. Over a series of hearings in the coming weeks, you will hear testimony, live and on video, from more than half a dozen former White House staff in the Trump administration, all of whom were in the West Wing of the White House on January 6th. You will hear testimony that "the President did not really want to put anything out" calling off the riot or asking his supporters to leave. You will hear that President Trump was yelling, and "really angry at advisers who told him he needed to be doing something more." Aware of the rioters' chants to "hang Mike Pence," the President responded with this sentiment: "Maybe our supporters have the right idea." Mike Pence "deserves" it.

Then, after describing some of the evidence the public would see that evening, I began to focus on the structure of our presentations over the coming weeks:

Tonight, I am going to describe for you some of what our Committee has learned and highlight initial findings you will see this month in our hearings. As you hear this, all Americans should keep in mind this fact: On the morning of January 6th, President Donald Trump's intention was to remain President of the United States despite the lawful outcome of the 2020 election and in violation of his Constitutional obligation to relinquish power.

Our most immediate task was to show that Donald Trump's own advisers knew *the election had not been stolen.* Everything that had happened was premised on an outright lie. So I presented a series of excerpts from Committee witness testimony — from Donald Trump's campaign and his inner circle of advisers. First, we played Jason Miller, Donald Trump's campaign spokesman, testifying that he told Donald Trump in the days after the 2020 election that he had, in fact, lost. This was followed by clips and descriptions of Trump campaign lawyers saying that the allegations of election fraud were not real; that they could not change the outcome; and that Biden had won. We then played multiple clips of Donald Trump's attorney general, Bill Barr, testifying that he had told Trump almost the exact same thing.

None of this testimony had been seen by the public, and it had an immediate impact. Many Americans had heard that courts had ruled against Donald Trump, but few knew that Trump's own campaign leadership had been telling him he lost.

We also realized this: The Trump campaign did not know exactly what Donald Trump was hearing from the Justice Department, while the Justice Department did not know exactly what Trump was hearing from his campaign. Both entities were, in fact, telling Donald Trump the same thing: His stolen-election claims were bogus. And they were telling him this with specificity about each of the claims he was making.

No rational human being could have heard all this information from multiple close advisers and still genuinely believed that the election was stolen. He lost. He knew it.

Next we played a clip of Donald Trump's daughter Ivanka confessing that she agreed with Attorney General Barr that her father had lost. I followed this with a description of the lawsuits that Donald Trump had lost, and a judicial ruling that Donald Trump's chief election-fraud lawyer, Rudy Giuliani, "communicated demonstrably false and misleading statements to courts, lawmakers, and the public at large."

And Giuliani had lost more than the lawsuits; his license to practice law had been suspended.

The foundation for everything that happened on January 6 was entirely made up. All of Trump's ads and speeches about a stolen election were false.

I walked through the specific evidence the Committee would present about each element of Donald Trump's plan to overturn the 2020 election, explaining how each of the pieces fit together. Then I turned to the aftermath of the attack, including that Donald Trump's White House staff immediately recognized how bad January 6 had been, and worked to isolate him so he could not do further harm in the two weeks before leaving office. I wanted people watching to understand just how dangerous this was:

> When a president fails to take the steps necessary to preserve our union—or worse, causes a Constitutional crisis—we are at a moment of maximum danger for our republic. Some in the White House took responsible steps to try to prevent January 6th. Others egged the president on. Others, who could have acted, refused to do so. In this case, the White House Counsel was so concerned about potentially lawless activity that he threatened to resign, multiple times. That is exceedingly rare and exceedingly serious. It requires immediate attention, especially when the entire team threatens to resign. However, in the Trump White House, it was not exceedingly rare and it was not treated seriously. This is a clip of Jared Kushner, addressing multiple threats by White House Counsel Pat Cipollone and his team of lawyers to resign in the weeks before January 6th.
>
> Q: Jared, are you aware of instances where Pat Cipollone threatened to resign?
>
> A: I kind of, like I said, my interest at that time was on trying to get as many pardons done, and I know that, you know, he was always, him and the team, were always saying, Oh we are going to resign. We are not going to be here if this happens, if that happens. So, I kind of took it up to just be whining, to be honest with you.
>
> *Whining.* There is a reason why people serving in our government take an oath to the Constitution. As our founding fathers recognized, democracy is fragile. People in positions of public trust are duty-bound to defend it—to step forward when action is required.
>
> In our country, we don't swear an oath to an individual, or a political party. We take our oath to defend the United States Constitution. And that oath must mean something. Tonight, I say this

to my Republican colleagues who are defending the indefensible: There will come a day when Donald Trump is gone, but your dishonor will remain.

I also believed that our investigation needed to be clear about its principal purpose—to preserve the foundations of our republic. So I ended this way:

Finally, I ask all of our fellow Americans as you watch our hearings over the coming weeks, please remember what's at stake. Remember the men and women who have fought and died so that we can live under the rule of law, not the rule of men. I ask you to think of the scene in our Capitol Rotunda on the night of January 6th. There, in a sacred space in our Constitutional republic, the place where our presidents lie in state, watched over by statues of Washington and Jefferson, Lincoln and Grant, Eisenhower, Ford, and Reagan, against every wall that night encircling the room, there were SWAT teams—men and women in tactical gear with long guns—deployed inside our Capitol Building.

There in the Rotunda, these brave men and women rested beneath paintings depicting the earliest scenes of our republic, including one painted in 1824 depicting George Washington resigning his commission, voluntarily relinquishing power, handing control of the Continental Army back to Congress. With this noble act, Washington set the indispensable example of the peaceful transfer of power. What President Reagan called "nothing less than a miracle." The sacred obligation to defend this peaceful transfer of power has been honored by every American president—except one.

As Americans, we all have a duty to ensure that what happened on January 6th never happens again, to set aside partisan battles, to stand together to perpetuate and preserve our great republic.

Thank you, Mr. Chairman.

———

When I finished my opening statement, Chairman Thompson introduced a video presentation of the terrible violence of January 6. He cautioned viewers that much of what they were about to see would be very difficult to watch.

And it was.

It was graphic footage of the attack, some from police body cameras, and much that had never been seen before. It reminded viewers of the devastating attack that day and our responsibility to ensure it never happens again. The Committee then recessed for 10 minutes and members gathered in the holding room behind the dais.

After 11 months of intense preparation, the hearings of the United States House Select Committee to Investigate the January 6th Attack on the United States Capitol were finally underway. In the span of just an hour, we had shared more evidence than the public had ever seen. Apart from the Committee members and a handful of staffers, few people had previously seen the full picture of where we were headed, or how we intended to get there. But now they knew, and knew in detail.

Nearly 20 million Americans watched our June 9 hearing live, and it would eventually be streamed by millions more—an audience far bigger than we anticipated. A major purpose of these hearings was to inform the public of the evidence and the truth. We were reaching people.

After a few more minutes, we returned to the hearing room and resumed our work. Chairman Thompson gaveled the Committee back into session to hear the testimony of Capitol Police Officer Caroline Edwards.

44. I WAS SLIPPING IN PEOPLE'S BLOOD

OFFICER CAROLINE EDWARDS, ASSIGNED TO a special unit of the Capitol Police trained to respond to mass demonstrations, was stationed on the west side of the Capitol on January 6 when the mob broke through the perimeter of metal bike racks. She was struck by a Trump rioter and knocked unconscious. After coming to, Officer Edwards did not ask to be evacuated. Instead, she resumed duty immediately on the Capitol steps, and attempted to hold the line on the Lower West Terrace.

She was sprayed in the eyes with a noxious chemical irritant—possibly pepper spray, possibly something else. She was tear-gassed. And yet she continued.

Listen to her describe the scene:

When I fell behind that line and I saw, I can just remember my—my breath catching in my throat, because what I saw was just a war scene. It was something like I'd seen out of the movies. I couldn't believe my eyes. There were officers on the ground. You know, they were bleeding. They were throwing up.

They were—you know, they had—I mean, I saw friends with blood all over their faces. I was slipping in people's blood. You know, I was catching people as they fell. It was carnage. It was chaos. I can't even describe what I saw. Never in my wildest dreams did I think that, as a police officer, as a law-enforcement officer, I would find myself in the middle of a battle. You know, I'm trained to detain, you know, a couple subjects and you know, handle a crowd. But I am not combat trained. That day, it was just hours of hand-to-hand combat, hours of dealing with things that were way beyond what any law-enforcement officer has ever trained for. I just remember — I just remember that moment of stepping behind the line and just seeing the absolute war zone that the West Front had become.

The testimony of Officer Caroline Edwards stirred the same anger and resolve that had motivated me since I sat in the House chamber on January 6. These members of our Capitol Police had sacrificed for each of us, and for the same Constitution we all swore to uphold. My grandmother had been the first female deputy sheriff in Natrona County, Wyoming, and I thought of her. It did not matter to me how these hearings might affect my election prospects or my campaign or my future in politics. This was more important.

My father once described being profoundly moved when he heard President John F. Kennedy speak at the University of Wyoming in September 1963. He recounted hearing President Kennedy urge the students to recognize the importance of service to our nation. In that speech, Kennedy talked about the ancient Greeks and their definition of happiness: "full use of your powers along lines of excellence." In no area of life, the president told the students, would it be more important to "use whatever powers you have, and to use them along more excellent lines," than in service to our country. Later I would learn that Democratic Majority Leader Steny Hoyer had been motivated to run for office by a similar Kennedy speech at the University of Maryland.

No matter what your party, government service should be noble, based on love of country and commitment to principles. But what I saw from my party now was unprincipled.

All those who hold office must make a choice of how they will serve, and what they will try to achieve for their country. Members of Congress have a critical responsibility: They must do their duty, to our Constitution and our country. Officer Caroline Edwards' testimony was a reminder of what was at stake.

We knew we had a huge job ahead of us. One commentator at the time wrote: "Throughout June, the committee has to weave together thousands of hours of testimony, tens of thousands of documents...and make it all coherent, compelling, and as concise as Congress can be. In its first prime-time hearings, the committee did that expertly."

A few days later, Donald Trump Jr. was appearing at a campaign rally for one of my opponents a few miles from our home in Jackson, Wyoming. A Trump supporter had posted my home address online and encouraged people to converge on our house after the rally.

I had to call one of our daughters who was home alone that day and tell her to leave the house immediately. Violence — and, more specifically, the threat of violence against Trump's political opponents — was a reality that threatened our families, too.

45.   A GRAVE DISSERVICE TO
THE COUNTRY

IN THE WEEKS BEFORE THE hearings, I asked our investigative team to help compile a catalog of how the January 6 rioters had described their motivations:

Exactly why did they believe they'd been called upon to "take back our country"?

Why had they come to Washington?

And why had hundreds of them violated the law and sacrificed their freedom?

This inventory built upon work my daughter Elizabeth had done as a research assistant over the months beforehand, compiling statements by defendants in all the ongoing prosecutions. Nearly every defendant— and almost every person who can be found on video explaining their actions on January 6—makes it clear that they were in Washington at Donald Trump's behest to "stop the steal," to halt what Trump had told them was a corrupt conspiracy by Democrats and RINOs (Republicans In Name Only) to rob him of the presidency.

Almost none of the rioters had any inkling of the massive amount of information that Donald Trump had received in private rebutting each of his stolen-election claims. They were, nearly all of them, deceived.

With some exceptions, our preparations for hearings followed a common pattern. The starting point was the initial outline Phil and I had prepared, and my opening statement from our June 9 hearing. We would work to compose a hearing outline, with many specific additional details and further evidence we wanted to address. I would discuss the outlines with Joe Maher, Jamie Fleet, Terri McCullough, James Goldston, and Tim Mulvey. The Committee lawyers who had interviewed the subject witnesses and knew the evidence best, would work very closely with us to identify and verify the material to be presented. They would draft witness questions and ensure that the presentation was accurate and true to the evidence the Committee had gathered. Our committee teams would also expertly develop video presentations on certain topics, such as the fake-elector scheme, to help present a significant volume of evidence in a summary fashion. The Committee members responsible for each hearing would edit their own sections; they were responsible for shaping their opening remarks and deciding what they would ask.

We would then go through multiple rounds of edits. This time-consuming process often involved restructuring portions of the planned hearings to ensure we were presenting the most important evidence fairly and effectively. It was important, so we committed a considerable amount of time to working on these drafts. James Goldston and Tim Mulvey oversaw a team of professionals, including some with many years of experience in television news. They worked with Committee staff and attorneys to produce video compilations and other visual exhibits to help us effectively convey the evidence we were uncovering.

The Committee would then conduct at least one and often several run-throughs, where staff and members would all discuss further edits. Often the Committee lawyers would stand in for witnesses during these practice sessions. Almost all the practice sessions occurred from the dais in the same hearing room where we conducted the actual hearings. At all times, the emphasis was on accuracy. We worked to avoid partisanship and exaggeration.

———

Our second 2022 hearing, on June 13, focused in great detail on *exactly what Donald Trump knew* at the time he was telling Americans that his supposed "landslide" victory had been stolen from him. Zoe Lofgren led this hearing. I had not known Zoe well before our work together on the Committee, but I was aware of her reputation as one of the most effective and respected members of the House of Representatives. She is thoughtful and serious, *and* she operates with zero ego—a rarity in Congress. Throughout our work on the Committee, Zoe was a source of wisdom and good judgment on a range of issues, from legal analysis to helping me understand and navigate the dynamics and relationships inside the House Democratic Caucus.

Our June 13 hearing included extensive testimony from members of Donald Trump's 2020 presidential campaign. In some cases, it seemed as if they had been waiting for months to unburden themselves of what they knew and what they had seen. Zoe presented evidence that Trump's own campaign advisers had told him not long after the election that he had likely lost, and then they *confirmed* that he had indeed lost in the week or so that followed. Efforts to find fraud, overseen by lawyers for the Trump campaign, had uncovered no fraud sufficient to overturn the election in any state. Trump campaign lawyer Alex Cannon told the Committee he had conveyed this to Mark Meadows in mid- to late November 2020; in response, Meadows had said: "So there's no *there* there."

Men and women who had loyally served President Trump knew it was over. And later, even as I was writing this book, yet more details emerged: Two expert analyses, both apparently commissioned by the Trump campaign, reportedly reached this same conclusion. In the nearly three years since January 6, 2021, no genuine evidence has come out that could substantiate Trump's stolen-election claims. It was all a lie.

————

On the morning of our June 13 hearing, we learned that one of our principal witnesses—Donald Trump's campaign manager, Bill Stepien—would be unable to testify. Although Stepien had been in Washington and was prepared to testify, he informed the Committee that his wife had gone into labor. We had already selected video clips from Stepien's prior interview on each point that our questioning planned to address. The staff quickly pivoted from live testimony to recorded video, and the Committee conducted the hearing.

Stepien believed that Trump's allegations of fraud were not "honest or professional." His conviction that Trump's election claims were false placed him squarely amid a large group of Trump campaign officials and Trump administration appointees who had concluded the same thing.

Even though Bill Stepien was unavailable, other witnesses testified live that day. A longtime, well-respected Republican election lawyer, Ben Ginsberg, explained what the scores of lawsuits had concluded— that Trump was wrong. Twenty-two federal judges appointed by Republican presidents, including 10 appointed by President Trump himself, and at least 24 elected or appointed Republican state judges dismissed Trump's claims. As Ginsberg pointed out, dozens of courts had analyzed the underlying factual allegations and ruled against Trump and his allies:

> In all the cases that were brought — I have looked at the more than 60 that include more than 180 counts...the simple fact is that the Trump campaign did not make its case....And in no instance did a court find that the charges of fraud were real.

Former Fox News political editor Chris Stirewalt, one of the leaders of the Fox News Decision Desk responsible for the network's accurate call of Arizona for Joe Biden on Election Night, explained that the "red mirage" happens in every presidential-election cycle: Republicans tend to vote in person in greater numbers on Election Day, whereas Democrats increasingly vote early or absentee, so it is not unusual for states that count their Election Day votes first to show an early Republican lead that diminishes as mail-in votes are counted. "Happens every time," Stirewalt said. But until Donald Trump, who falsely claimed that the red mirage proved the election had been rigged, no presidential candidate had ever lied about it.

In this hearing we also presented evidence from a long list of witnesses who had spoken directly with Trump:

> ACTING DEPUTY ATTORNEY GENERAL RICHARD DONOGHUE: I tried to again put this in perspective and to try to put it in very clear terms to the president. And I said something to the effect of, *Sir, we've done dozens of investigations, hundreds of interviews. The major*

allegations are not supported by the evidence developed. We've looked at Georgia, Pennsylvania, Michigan, and Nevada. We're doing our job. Much of the info you're getting is false.

ATTORNEY GENERAL BILL BARR: I made it clear I did not agree with the idea of saying the election was stolen and putting out this stuff. Which I told the president was bullshit.... I didn't want to be a part of it....

BARR ON DOMINION VOTING SYSTEMS: And I told him that the stuff that his people were shoveling out to the public were bull—was bullshit. I mean that the claims of fraud were bullshit. And you know, he was indignant about that. And I reiterated that they've wasted a whole month on these claims—on the Dominion voting machines, and they were idiotic claims.... And I told them that it was—it was crazy stuff and they were wasting their time on that. And it was doing a great, grave disservice to the country.

ACTING ATTORNEY GENERAL JEFF ROSEN: We know that you are getting bad information that's—that's not correct. It's been demonstrated to be incorrect....

TRUMP CAMPAIGN GENERAL COUNSEL MATT MORGAN: I think I had conversations with probably all of our counsel who were signed up to assist on Election Day as they disengaged with the campaign... The general consensus was that the law firms were not comfortable making the arguments that Rudy Giuliani was making publicly.... I seem to recall that I had a similar conversation with most all of them.

With all that testimony and much more, we reached the unavoidable conclusion: No person of even reasonable intellect who heard this information could believe that Donald Trump had won the election. Before our hearings, only a small part of this detail was available to the general public. Donald Trump's ads, speeches, and social-media posts had relentlessly repeated the same false allegations that these witnesses debunked.

When we ultimately compiled all this information for our final report, I asked staffers on the January 6th Committee to create a detailed chart: It would inform the public exactly when Donald Trump had been told that certain fraud allegations were false, and exactly when Donald Trump had said the opposite in a public forum. That chart—perhaps the most easily understood summary of Trump's fraud—can now be found in the report (see pages 22 to 27). And Special Counsel Jack Smith's August 2023 indictment of Donald Trump has since identified even more evidence of Trump's intentional deceit.

———

Our hearings also disclosed communications from the days leading up to January 6, from Donald Trump's senior campaign adviser, Jason Miller, and other witnesses. The evidence indicated that even Rudy Giuliani's legal team knew, in the days before January 6, that they had *failed to prove* that any alleged fraud had altered the election results in any state, much less in multiple states.

But that did not stop Donald Trump and a number of his allies, including those in Congress, from proceeding with their plan to overturn the election on January 6.

It is important to compare the Trump team's knowledge at the time with what Donald Trump, Rudy Giuliani, and John Eastman said at the president's January 6 Ellipse rally before tens of thousands of angry supporters whom Trump was directing to march to the Capitol. Their speeches continued to fraudulently claim that Dominion Voting Systems machines had corrupted the election. Rudy Giuliani urged "trial by combat," while Donald Trump said this: "When you catch somebody in a fraud, you're allowed to go by very different rules."

Donald Trump has frequently returned to this notion—that his election-fraud allegations justified unconstitutional and illegal acts: "A Massive Fraud of this type and magnitude allows for the termination of all rules, regulations, and articles, even those found in the Constitution."

———

The day after our June 13 hearing, columnist Max Boot, who admitted he had been skeptical that the Committee's hearings would provide any new information, wrote an editorial suggesting we were accomplishing at least part of what we'd been striving to do since the prior summer:

> The committee's hearings are exceeding expectations, because it is not behaving like a typical congressional committee. There is no grandstanding and no preening. There are no petty partisan squabbles. There is not even the disjointedness that normally occurs when a bunch of politicians are each given five minutes to question each witness. There is only the relentless march of evidence, all of it deeply incriminating to a certain former president who keeps insisting that he was robbed of his rightful election victory.

46.   TANTAMOUNT TO A REVOLUTION

LIKE SO MUCH OF THE story of January 6, the story of President Trump pressuring Mike Pence to violate the law and his oath to the Constitution tells us exactly who Donald Trump is. The Committee's June 16, 2022, hearing, led by Democratic Congressman Pete Aguilar, covered all the elements of Trump's pressure campaign against his own vice president.

Under our Constitution, the vice president is a member of both the executive branch *and* the legislative branch, where he or she serves as the president of the Senate. The president of the Senate's role on January 6 is set forth in clear terms in our Constitution's 12th Amendment: "The President of the Senate shall, in the presence of the Senate and House of Representatives, open all the certificates, and the votes shall then be counted. The person having the greatest number of votes for President shall be the President."

This seems like a very straightforward instruction. And in almost all instances, it is. On January 6, Mike Pence's role was purely ministerial, purely procedural. He could not change the result of the election. Our Constitution unambiguously instructed him to open envelopes so the electoral votes could then be counted. Period.

Donald Trump did not have the power to instruct Mike Pence to do something different than that. Mike Pence could not refuse to open the envelopes; he could not prevent the counting. Mike Pence could not determine that a particular set of official state electoral votes was not to be counted. Mike Pence could not decline to do what the Constitution required because he didn't like how the recounts had gone in a certain state, or because he disagreed with how state and federal courts, including the US

Supreme Court, had resolved legal issues about an election in any state. He was simply required to open the envelopes so the votes could be counted.

Pence, in his role as president of the Senate, reached the correct conclusion that he could do none of those things on January 6. As he later said, "There is no idea more un-American than the notion that any one person could choose the American president."

Mike Pence's White House lawyer, Greg Jacob, knew Pence was right. Mike Pence's private lawyers, as well as those they consulted, knew he was right. Donald Trump's White House Counsel, Pat Cipollone—and every other White House lawyer who knew what was happening—knew that Pence was right. And evidence gathered by the January 6th Select Committee showed that even John Eastman, the lawyer advising Trump at the time, admitted in a meeting with Donald Trump himself that his and Trump's plan violated the law. Greg Jacob wrote this in a contemporaneous memo: "Professor Eastman acknowledges that his proposal violates several provisions of statutory law."

As Eastman wrote before the 2020 election:

The 12th Amendment only says that the President of the Senate opens the ballots in the joint session then, in the passive voice, that the votes shall then be counted. 3 USC §12 [of the Electoral Count Act] says merely that he is the presiding officer, and then it spells out specific procedures, presumptions, and default rules for which slates will be counted. Nowhere does it suggest that the president of the Senate gets to make the determination on his own. §15 [of the Electoral Count Act] doesn't either.

But Donald Trump would not accept the truth.

In fact, Donald Trump did not care about the truth.

In an email exchange between Greg Jacob and John Eastman during the violence, Jacob asked Eastman, "Did you advise the President that in your professional judgment the Vice President DOES NOT have the power to decide things unilaterally?" Eastman responded that Trump had been "so advised." Then Eastman continued: "But you know him—once he gets something in his head, it is hard to get him to change course."

Donald Trump would not accept Mike Pence's conclusion, as president of the Senate, that he could not legally do what Trump wanted him to do. So Trump reacted—persistently, with anger, and with repeated threats—to try to force Mike Pence into doing something that Pence and others had already told Trump was illegal.

Trump yelled at Pence in front of witnesses who later testified about it. Trump used profanities, including the "p-word." Trump tweeted at Pence again and again, telling the world that Mike Pence could deliver the presidency to him on January 6.

On January 5, Trump issued a statement he knew to be false: He claimed that he and Pence were in agreement that Pence could refuse to count electoral votes. The next day, Trump told an angry Ellipse crowd in clear and unequivocal terms that Mike Pence could deliver the election for Donald Trump. He then directed that crowd to march to the Capitol. And when Donald Trump already knew that the crowd had reached the Capitol and turned violent, and that none of his efforts to cow Pence had worked, Donald Trump attacked his VP once again, this time in a tweet accusing Pence of having failed to deliver the election. That triggered many in the crowd to surge forward into the Capitol as they hunted the vice president, chanting "Hang Mike Pence!"

No man who would do these things can ever be our president again.

Mike Pence did what was right. He deserves praise for standing up against a plan that was obviously illegal.

The day after the violent assault, White House lawyer Eric Herschmann counseled Trump's lawyer John Eastman:

I said, "John, now I'm going to give you the best free legal advice you're ever getting in your life: Get a great f'ing criminal defense lawyer—you're gonna need it." And then I hung up on him.

According to federal judge David Carter, Donald Trump's plan to pressure Mike Pence "likely" violated multiple federal criminal statutes.

After Greg Jacob's initial interview, we had no doubt that Donald Trump knew that what he was demanding Mike Pence do was illegal.

Jacob also described working with Pence to prepare a public letter that would announce Pence's decision on January 6 — that the Constitution prevented him from doing what Trump wanted. According to Jacob, Pence said the letter was "the most important thing I ever say." It probably was. Of course, that letter is what led Donald Trump to put Pence's life at risk less than two hours later with his 2:24 p.m. tweet.

———

The letter that Mike Pence issued at approximately 1:00 p.m. on January 6 said exactly the right thing about his role as president of the Senate: Pence lacked the authority to refuse to count electoral votes. But the letter also contained what seemed to be a political compromise. It suggested that Congress had the power, through its objections process under the Electoral Count Act, to determine who could be president.

The framers of our Constitution did not give a majority in Congress the authority to veto the outcome of a presidential election by opting not to count electoral votes from whatever states they choose. If that were so, and if Republicans had held a majority of the House and Senate on January 6, 2021, they could have declared Trump the winner no matter what the final tally of Electoral College votes was. A future Democratic bicameral majority might similarly attempt to pick a Democrat for president even if a Republican won.

Mike Pence was reading the simple text — "The President of the Senate shall, in the presence of the Senate and House of Representatives, open all the certificates and the votes shall *then* be counted" — correctly, on one hand, to say he personally had only a ministerial role. But then Pence read the same text incorrectly to say that Congress had some authority on January 6 to object and potentially reverse the election outcome by refusing to count electoral votes.

On January 6, there was no ambiguity about what that simple sentence required: We had only one certified electoral slate for each state; each slate had to be counted. Indeed, it appeared to us that Pence's own counsel, Greg Jacob, may not have shared Pence's view about objections. At the very end of his recorded Committee interview, Jacob said this:

In my view, a lot has been said about the fact that the role of the Vice President in the electoral count on January 6th is purely ministerial, and that is a correct conclusion. But if you look at the Constitutional text, the role of *Congress* is purely ministerial as well. You open the certificates, and you count them. Those are the only things provided for in the Constitution.

———

Americans must not lose sight of an appalling fact. Certain Republican members of the House of Representatives—including many members of the Freedom Caucus—fully supported what Donald Trump was trying to force Mike Pence to do. That is a crucial point: A significant number of House Republicans thought they could ignore the Electoral College result and find a way to reinstall Trump as president. As Judge J. Michael Luttig explained at our June 16 hearing,

> I believe that had Vice President Pence obeyed the orders from . . . the President of the United States of America during the joint session of the Congress of the United States on January 6, 2021, and declared Donald Trump the next President of the United States . . . that declaration of Donald Trump as the next President would have plunged America into what I believe would have been tantamount to a revolution within a Constitutional crisis in America.

At the close of our June 16 hearing, Judge Luttig described the prevailing state of affairs this way: "Donald Trump and his allies . . . are a clear and present danger to American democracy."

And as Judge Carter had concluded: "President Trump's pressure campaign to stop the electoral count did not end with Vice President Mike Pence. It targeted *every tier* of federal and state elected officials."

The next hearing of the January 6th Committee would tackle precisely that issue.

47. CONSPIRACY THEORIES AND
THUG VIOLENCE

WE HAD A NUMBER OF goals for our June 21 hearing. First, we wanted to show the astounding amount of effort Donald Trump had devoted to trying to change state electoral votes from Biden to Trump. Trump called legislators in every state at issue, and election officials in virtually every state at issue. He tried to persuade them, he tried to pressure them, he threatened them.

One of those conversations was caught on tape. In it Donald Trump presses Georgia Secretary of State Brad Raffensperger "to find 11,780 votes" for Trump, "informing" Raffensperger that he may be criminally liable if he does not. (A similar call, reportedly with then-Governor Doug Ducey of Arizona, came to light in 2023.)

Among other things, Trump wanted to change the election outcome by having state legislatures replace the Biden electors with Trump electors. This was illegal, as even John Eastman had acknowledged in writing before the 2020 election.

In the end, despite the Trump pressure, not a single Republican governor or secretary of state relented, and not one state legislature tried to alter the official and lawful electoral votes.

You might think Trump's failure to persuade state legislatures to illegally upend the election would have ended his efforts to overturn the election. It did not. He continued with his plot regardless.

We also knew it was imperative to reveal what else had transpired in each state during Trump's effort to apply pressure on individuals to abandon their oath. Individual state office holders, individual election workers, and legislators, along with their families, were subject to threats of violence, intimidation, and harassment. The threats began in November and December 2020, and they were publicized far in advance of January 6.

On December 1, 2020—more than a month before the attack on the US Capitol—Georgia elections official Gabriel Sterling pleaded with President Trump in an extraordinary and emotional speech at the Georgia state capitol. He began with this: "It has all gone too far. All of it."

Then Sterling elaborated with specifics:

A twentysomething tech in Gwinnett County today has death threats and a noose put out saying he should be "hung for trea-son" because he was transferring a report on batches from EMS to a county computer, so he could read it. It has to stop, Mr. President. You have not condemned these actions or this lan-guage. Senators, you have not condemned this language or these actions. This has to stop. We need you to step up. And if you are going to take a position of leadership, show some....

This is elections. This is the backbone of democracy. And all of you who have not said a damn word are complicit in this.

Sterling further urged the president to "stop inspiring people to com-mit potential acts of violence. Someone is going to get hurt, someone is going to get shot, someone's going to get killed. It's not right."

This was all the warning Donald Trump or anyone else needed that the Trump strategy could lead to violence—clear as a bell, more than a month before January 6. But nothing stopped. Nothing changed.

In addition to what Trump had said on the private call with Georgia Secretary of State Brad Raffensperger, Trump also attacked Raffensperger publicly. Raffensperger described the vile messages and harassment tar-geting his family:

And so I was getting texts [from] all over the country. Then eventually my wife started getting texts, and hers typically came in as sexualized texts, which were disgusting....And so they started going after her, I think, just to probably put pressure on me....

Then some people broke into my daughter-in-law's home, and my son has passed and she is a widow and has two kids.

As our hearing evidence showed, similar situations were playing out in several other states where Donald Trump was pressuring local officials. Many of them faced threats or harassment, prompted by Trump. We played testimony from Michigan, for example, where Secretary of State Jocelyn Benson described angry Trump protestors surrounding her home while she was inside with her son, and threatening clerks and election officials across the state.

Election deniers also made violent threats against Stephen Richer. He is a longtime Republican who successfully ran for election as the Recorder of Maricopa County, Arizona, in 2020. After taking office, and after Trump and his supporters lodged false complaints about a rigged election in this key Arizona county, Richer investigated the facts himself in his new role. He had no motive to cover up any problems with the election—his election opponent was the incumbent in 2020 and had overseen the election. But after an exhaustive review, he concluded that Biden had fairly won the vote in Maricopa County. He published an open letter to Republicans to explain—in great detail—why the election results were valid. Ever since, he and his family have been subjected to abusive, violent threats from individuals across the country. But he continues to stand firm on the facts.

Speaker of the Arizona State House of Representatives, Rusty Bowers, testified live. I had met Bowers once before, at the Kennedy Presidential Library when we were both honored with a "Profile in Courage" Award. I had tremendous respect for his devotion to the principles of honor and justice, and his deeply held religious faith.

Donald Trump and Rudy Giuliani had both called Speaker Bowers on multiple occasions, urging him to reverse or cast doubt on the election result in Arizona, where Biden had won by over 10,000 votes. Bowers asked Giuliani repeatedly for hard evidence that the election had been corrupted. Bowers testified that Giuliani eventually admitted, "We've got lots of theories, we just don't have the evidence."

Speaker Bowers' testimony made it clear he had no ax to grind:

Q: And did you tell the President [Trump] in that second call that you had supported him, that you voted for him, but that you were not going to do anything illegal for him?

SPEAKER BOWERS: I did, sir.

Speaker Bowers also described becoming a target of the same type of intimidation tactics that we had seen Trump supporters use elsewhere:

[V]arious groups come by and they have had video panel trucks with videos of me proclaiming me to be a pedophile and a pervert and a corrupt politician and blaring loudspeakers in my neighborhood and leaving literature . . . on my property.

Among the worst incidents of Donald Trump's political-intimidation campaign was what he and Rudy Giuliani did to Georgia election workers Shaye Moss and her mother, Ruby Freeman. Moss, too, had received a "Profile in Courage" award, and I had met them both at the ceremony where Rusty Bowers was also honored. Trump and Rudy Giuliani had a theory, hatched from watching a video, that Moss and Freeman had somehow utilized a thumb drive to corrupt the machines tabulating votes in Fulton County, Georgia. The video in question showed Freeman handing Moss something small.

It was not a thumb drive.

It was a ginger mint.

But Donald Trump attacked both Moss and Freeman relentlessly on a national stage, describing Ruby Freeman as "a professional vote scammer and hustler." Our hearing described how a group of Trump supporters had appeared at Freeman's house, barged through her front door, and tried to perform a citizen's arrest. In the wake of the incident, the FBI cautioned Freeman that it was no longer safe for her to remain in her own home.

Freeman recounted the traumatic episode this way:

> There is nowhere I feel safe. Nowhere. Do you know how it feels to have the President of the United States target you? The President of the United States is supposed to represent every American, not to target one. But he targeted me, Lady Ruby—a small-business owner, a mother, a proud American citizen who stood up to help Fulton County run an election in the middle of the pandemic.

In July 2023, eager to settle the defamation case against him brought by Freeman and Moss, Rudy Giuliani admitted in court documents that his statements about them were false.

After their testimony, Chairman Bennie Thompson and I walked over to the witness table and thanked Ruby Freeman and Shaye Moss for their courage. Nobody with any sense of honor or dignity would have treated them the way Donald Trump, Rudy Giuliani, and others working on Trump's behalf had done. Just as there is no excuse for provoking violence against our Capitol, there is no defense for targeting a statehouse or state official, a courthouse, a judge or justice, or any election worker.

————

In addition to the pressure Trump and his allies exerted on state election officials, this hearing addressed another vital topic: Donald Trump's scheme to create fake electoral slates. Evidence indicated that the White House Counsel's office was concerned about the plans for fake slates. By December 2020, in fact, multiple lawyers on the Trump campaign understood it was illegal and refused to participate in the effort.

Despite this, the Committee showed that Trump plowed ahead, personally asking RNC Chairwoman Ronna McDaniel for assistance. McDaniel testified to the Committee that she had directed her RNC staff to help the campaign assemble the fake electors. On December 14, McDaniel was able to report to President Trump that the fake Trump electors had met and voted in states Biden had won.

One of our witnesses testified that he "absolutely would not have [participated in the fake electors scheme] if I had known that the three main lawyers for the campaign that I had spoken to in the past...were not on board."

The plan was that Vice President Pence could rely on the fake electoral slates on January 6 to rationalize not counting the genuine electoral votes. As the Select Committee explained, "Dr. [John] Eastman told a Trump campaign representative that it did not matter that the electors had not been approved by a state authority....[T]he fact that we have multiple slates of electors demonstrates the uncertainty of either. That should be enough."

One key point about the fake electors slates is this: Even after no state had attempted to reverse its lawful election outcome, even after no court of law had ruled in a way that could overturn any election, Donald Trump and his team still sent the false slates to the executive branch and to Congress, intending that they be utilized in Congress's official proceeding to count electoral votes.

The slates were knowingly false, and the action was intended to obstruct the legitimate count of certified state electoral votes. It was all part of a larger conspiracy to steal the election. Donald Trump and everyone involved knew that the slates were fraudulent.

The fake electoral slates were one of many issues the Committee considered as we later drafted our criminal referrals. We believed at the time that the Department of Justice would certainly pursue this: It was a straightforward, unambiguous example of criminal conduct. And in fact, DOJ special counsel Jack Smith's indictment of Donald Trump did take this up directly.

This June 21 hearing was ably led by Democratic Congressman Adam Schiff. His scrupulous attention to the evidence, as well as his careful and respectful questioning of the witnesses, helped to ensure that the American people understood the full picture of Donald Trump's pressure campaign on state officials.

———

My sense was that our hearings were having a broad impact. Tens of millions of Americans were watching live. We were reaching people, and we were revealing facts almost entirely through Republican witnesses — the people who knew Donald Trump the best, the people who had worked with him the most closely. Each of our hearings had been conducted without partisan squabbling or posturing.

It was clear, though, that no amount of evidence would ever convince a certain segment of the Republican Party. Throughout the 18 months of our work, certain Republican House members and senators who knew better elected to play to that audience anyway. Senator Tom Cotton, for example, went on conservative commentator Hugh Hewitt's radio show at one point and disparaged the hearings as a partisan exercise — and therefore inconsistent with "Anglo-American jurisprudence."

Senator Cotton then admitted that he had not watched any of the hearings. I respected Tom, and we had worked together over the years on a number of foreign-policy and national-security issues. He knew the truth about what Trump had done, and was continuing to do, and I didn't want to let him get away with such a cheap shot at the Committee's work. I responded in a tweet:

Hey @SenTomCotton — heard you on @hughhewitt criticizing the Jan 6 hearings. Then you said the strangest thing; you admitted you hadn't watched any of them. Here's a tip: Actually watching them before rendering judgment is more consistent with "Anglo-American jurisprudence."

While I knew that most of my colleagues didn't actually believe Donald Trump's lies, millions of others did believe them. We needed to take advantage of the progress we were making in presenting the facts—largely through Republican witnesses—and push for even more critically important testimony.

48. IT MAY HAVE SPIRALED US INTO A CONSTITUTIONAL CRISIS

BY THE TIME WE BEGAN our hearings in June 2022, Donald Trump's dealings with Department of Justice official Jeffrey Clark had already gotten some press. The DOJ's inspector general had reportedly been investigating, and a Senate committee had interviewed some of the people involved. My opening statement at our first hearing had highlighted how we thought Trump's dealings with Clark fit into Trump's larger plans to overturn the election.

On June 22, 2022, as we were preparing for our hearing on this topic, the Justice Department served a search warrant on Clark at his home in the suburbs outside Washington. It was now apparent that DOJ was following the same path as our committee.

A number of facts relating to the Trump-Clark story are important. First, the context: By late December of 2020, it was clear to Donald Trump that the Department of Justice investigations had found no significant election fraud. Attorney General Bill Barr, Acting Attorney General Jeff Rosen, and Acting Deputy Attorney General Richard Donoghue had all told him so repeatedly. At the same time, none of Trump's efforts to persuade state legislatures to flip Biden electoral votes was working. A member of the House Freedom Caucus, Scott Perry, was apparently telling Mark Meadows and others that Jeffrey Clark could help fix both of those problems.

The idea was that Clark could draft a letter, to be sent from the Department of Justice to the key state legislatures, beginning with Georgia's. The letter would falsely announce that the Department of

Justice had "identified significant concerns that may have impacted the outcome of the election in multiple States..."

Second, the letter would recommend a very specific course of action, which was almost exactly what Trump and John Eastman were simultaneously urging legislators in Georgia to do: "In light of these developments, the Department recommends that the Georgia General Assembly should convene in special session" and consider approving a new slate of electors.

Clark's draft letter was originally written for Rosen's and Donoghue's signatures, but both of them refused to sign it. Donoghue confronted Clark, telling him the letter was "not based on fact"; that it was not something the Justice Department should ever do; and that it could have "grave consequences for the country. It may very well have spiraled us into a constitutional crisis." In an email, Donoghue warned Clark that the draft letter "could have tremendous constitutional, political, and social ramifications for the country."

During our June 22 hearing, Rosen and Donoghue sat at our witness table and carefully explained all of this. The hearing was led by Adam Kinzinger, who presented the evidence and led much of the questioning in a clear and compelling way.

Once it became clear that neither Rosen nor Donoghue would sign the letter, Donald Trump resolved to replace Rosen with Clark, so Clark could sign and issue the letter himself. Clark had several conversations with Trump, including on January 3, and White House call logs referred to Jeffrey Clark as *Acting Attorney General* because Trump had already appointed him.

When Rosen learned what was happening with Clark, he was determined to put a stop to it. Rosen called White House Counsel Pat Cipollone, and an urgent meeting was set with the President for the evening of Sunday, January 3.

Rosen, Donoghue, and Steve Engel (who had served in the Trump Justice Department for most of the administration), along with White House lawyers Pat Cipollone, Pat Philbin, and Eric Herschmann, attended the Oval Office meeting in addition to Clark. My sense is that Cipollone was integral to making this meeting happen, and that he, along with Herschmann and others, knew there was only one way to make Trump back down: They had to convince Trump that naming Clark as attorney general would harm Trump personally.

After a lengthy discussion trying to persuade Trump that Clark was not qualified to be attorney general, they all threatened to resign if Clark took over as AG. They told Trump that virtually all of his other appointees in the Justice Department would resign as well. This would quite likely be followed by a wave of resignations by Trump officials in other agencies. In short, appointing Clark would cause a blowup with significant ramifications for Trump personally and politically.

That ultimately worked: Trump backed down as to Clark's appointment as acting attorney general.

One other key fact was clear from the June 22 hearing. Acting Deputy Attorney General Donoghue testified that Trump had told him this in a phone call: "Just say it [the election] was corrupt and leave the rest to me and the Republican congressmen." Elsewhere in the call, Trump mentioned Representatives Jim Jordan and Scott Perry specifically. In early August, about five weeks after this hearing, the Department of Justice served a search warrant on Perry and seized his cell phone.

Although Cipollone, Rosen, and others were successful in reversing Trump's appointment of Jeffrey Clark, they could not persuade Trump to stop pursuing the fake stolen-election allegations. And they did not manage to stop Trump's other plans for January 6, which continued to gain steam as that date approached.

As the Clark hearing wound down, we were also working to bring in yet more evidence about what was happening inside the White House during the violence of January 6. Chairman Thompson announced that the next hearing would take place "in the coming weeks." The press interpreted that to mean we would adjourn until July. That is not what happened.

49. HIDEAWAY 2.0

THE WATERGATE SCANDAL LEADING TO President Richard Nixon's 1974 resignation resulted in the prosecution and conviction of multiple members
of Nixon's White House staff. The crimes included obstruction of justice
and perjury—lying under oath in an effort to conceal what individuals in
the White House had known about the break-in and the role Nixon had
played in its cover-up. I wanted to believe that at least some of those serving in the Trump White House were familiar with the history of the
Watergate scandal and would know they could not get away with lying
about what happened before, during, and after the attack of January 6.

Ultimately, we found a number of honest people who told the unvar-
nished truth.

One of those people is Cassidy Hutchinson, who had served as Mark
Meadows' principal aide in the White House. She had been interviewed
twice by the Committee earlier in 2022; as mentioned, upon reading portions of her testimony in a brief we filed as part of our litigation with Mark
Meadows, Hutchinson recognized that she needed to find a way to provide the Committee with additional information. Counsel for the
Committee had set up a third interview with her at the end of May so she
could answer additional questions.

Most of the Committee's interviews were conducted in the O'Neill
House Office Building, where the Committee staff had office space.
Knowing this, reporters routinely staked out the building entrances to
monitor who was coming and going. We knew that Cassidy was already

facing tremendous pressure from the Trump camp. She was also well known to many members of Congress and their staffs because she had worked directly with many of us over the last few years. We didn't want to create any additional pressure on her, so we needed to find a discreet place to conduct the interview.

Jamie Fleet provided us with a small conference room on the third floor of the Cannon House Office Building, tucked in beside an elevator bank. Even though journalists and camera crews were permanently posted just down the hall in the Cannon rotunda, none noticed as Cassidy got off the elevator, turned a corner, and entered the small office.

Cassidy provided us with additional important information, but she was obviously nervous about her Trump-affiliated lawyer and initially gave only short answers. Our Committee counsel and I took turns asking her specific questions, and following up in areas where we sensed she had more detail. We drew out additional details piece by piece.

At the close of the session, as Cassidy and her lawyer were leaving, she paused and turned back to me. I gave her a hug, and I thanked her. "I want you to know," I said, "that I have three daughters who are about your age. If they ever had to face what you have, I can only hope they would show the same courage you have."

Tears welled in her eyes. It was obvious that Cassidy was under tremendous stress. It was equally obvious that she was determined to do what was right.

Our Committee counsel walked Cassidy and her lawyer to the exit. I learned later what Cassidy had quietly told our counsel on the way out:

"I'm about to get f'ing nuked."

She meant the Trump team would soon learn what she had done—and attempt to destroy her and her reputation. Her instinct proved correct.

———

Cassidy later explained to us, on the record, what happened next: Her lawyer, who she had recently confirmed was paid by a Trump-affiliated group, answered a call from a *New York Times* reporter in the cab as they were leaving the interview, even though Cassidy asked him not to. A short while later, that newspaper's senior political correspondent Maggie Haberman tweeted: "Former MEADOWS aide Cassidy Hutchinson went back to the J6 committee under subpoena for a second [sic] interview today, per people briefed."

Against Cassidy's wishes, her lawyer also called counsel for at least one other Trump witness to report on the interview. We already knew what type of pressure had been applied by Trump and his team to Shaye Moss, Ruby Freeman, Speaker Bowers, Secretary Raffensperger, and many others. Cassidy had just told us in the Cannon interview room about several conversations she overheard during the violence of January 6, describing Donald Trump as unwilling to instruct his supporters to leave the Capitol. We worried about her safety.

As Cassidy testified in a later Committee interview, she sought advice from a number of people about what to do about her Trump-funded lawyer, including from a Republican member of Congress who was not on our committee. Cassidy, like all witnesses, deserved counsel who would give her independent and objective advice — including about what to do with respect to her existing lawyer. According to one report, she consulted with former Republican Congresswoman Barbara Comstock, too, who offered to help start a legal defense fund "so that Ms. Hutchinson would not have to rely on a lawyer paid for by Trump affiliates."

Not long after this third interview, Cassidy contacted me directly. She told me that she was inclined to represent herself going forward. I was very sympathetic to her situation, but I did not want our committee to be advising her on what she should do next. I told Cassidy that she could consult another lawyer, and seek his or her independent advice on how best to move forward. Every witness deserves an attorney who will represent their interests exclusively.

Ultimately, Cassidy decided to retain two new lawyers, both with prior experience in the Justice Department. One had been appointed a few years earlier by President Trump to oversee the Justice Department's civil division. The other had served at Justice during the George W. Bush administration. They represented Cassidy pro bono — that is, without charging her anything.

———

In mid-June, in the midst of our hearings, Cassidy's new lawyers notified the Committee staff that she had further information to share. We set Cassidy's next interview for June 20, when the House would be out of session for Juneteenth. We suspected that almost no one would be in the Capitol Building that day.

Two things worried me: Cassidy's security and Committee leaks. Key investigative material had already been leaked. Any leaks about a new Cassidy interview could be harmful to her, and to our investigation. Cassidy had already been contacted by people in the Trump orbit, warning her, among other things, that "Trump reads the transcripts" and pays close attention to what witnesses are saying.

We decided to hold this June interview in my Capitol basement hideaway office—the same room where Alyssa Farah, Sarah Matthews, and I had met several months earlier. Members of my Capitol Police security detail and our Committee counsel met Cassidy and one of her new lawyers and escorted them to the basement office, where I waited with Committee counsel and staff from the office of the Clerk of the House, who transcribed all our interviews. No reporters saw Cassidy enter.

My hideaway office was cramped. The office itself was maybe 10 feet across and perhaps 15 to 20 feet long, with a narrow table running lengthwise, and a small sofa and chair filling up much of the remaining space. There were no windows. The ventilation wasn't great.

Those who viewed the January 6th Committee hearings have seen witnesses such as Bill Barr seated at a table in a large interview room, surrounded by a team of lawyers. When you watch Cassidy's testimony from June 20, you see her sitting at that narrow table. Her lawyer sat beside her. We made room at one end of the table for the House stenographer and at the other end for the video camera. Committee counsel and I sat across from Cassidy.

From the beginning of that interview to the end, Cassidy provided further significant detail to supplement everything she had told us before. She was exacting, noting with careful precision what she could and could not remember. She had careful notes and referred to them often. She obviously wanted to get this right. We explored a greater range of topics than in any prior interview.

As soon as the interview ended, Cassidy was escorted out by Capitol Police—again without anyone in the press spotting her. I instantly recognized that we had just gathered much important new material, as did our committee staff and counsel.

Before this interview, our tentative plan had been for Cassidy Hutchinson to appear at our final hearing of the summer—scheduled for the second half of July—possibly along with two other former members of the White House staff, Sarah Matthews and Matt Pottinger. We thought these witnesses would provide powerful testimony about what happened in the West Wing during the violence, and why Donald Trump had failed to act. But Cassidy's new testimony went further than that of either Matthews or Pottinger, and it was more detailed. Cassidy was giving us specific insight about Trump and Mark Meadows, and about what White House Counsel Pat Cipollone and other senior staff had urged President Trump to do during the violence. By that point, we had met informally with Cipollone, but he had repeatedly declined to give us any recorded testimony.

My sense, as we sat in the basement hideaway, was that we would not be able to keep this testimony secret for very long. Everything we did as a committee was under an intense spotlight. Every hearing was viewed live by millions of people, covered by virtually every major news broadcast, and consumed hours of programming on cable news. Reporters were calling nearly everyone involved with the investigation, desperately seeking information. We had suffered many leaks already, some harmful to our effort.

But now a leak wouldn't harm just the Committee; it could also place Cassidy Hutchinson in a difficult and possibly dangerous situation. The longer we delayed, the higher the risk. Other witnesses—including a number of national security and military staff posted at the White House—had likewise identified concerns about retribution from Donald Trump and his allies, and the Committee had taken special measures to protect their security.

But Cassidy's name was already out there in published press reports.

Cassidy's testimony might fit better in our planned late-July hearing, but we couldn't reasonably ask her to wait that long. We needed to act quickly. After some initial discussions with senior staff on the evening of June 20, 2022, we began to formulate plans for a new hearing—a hearing that no one in the press or on our committee had anticipated.

———

A key part of Cassidy Hutchinson's testimony related to what White House Counsel Pat Cipollone had said and done during the violent attack on the Capitol. My instinct was that Cassidy's public testimony would make it even harder for Cipollone to refuse to appear for a taped interview. Pat might still be coaxed to testify voluntarily, we believed, because he probably wanted the public to know that he had tried to do the right thing. Pat had vehemently disagreed with the nonsense being spouted by Rudy Giuliani and others, and he probably wanted that fact on the historical record. There was no question that Pat Cipollone had crucial information about what had happened inside the White House on January 6.

We were in the process of preparing for two additional hearings that week, and I decided to use my closing statement at the June 21 hearing to launch a more public effort to persuade Cipollone to come forward and testify on camera. That evening, Phil and I worked to draft language that might sway him. I began by listing other high-ranking Trump administration witnesses who had already testified, including Bill Barr and Jeff Rosen, both of whom were Pat's close friends. Then I said this:

> But the American people have not yet heard from Mr. Trump's former White House Counsel, Pat Cipollone. Our committee is certain that Donald Trump does not want Mr. Cipollone to testify here. Indeed, our evidence shows that Mr. Cipollone and his office tried to do what was right. They tried to stop a number of President Trump's plans for January 6th....
>
> [I]n our coming hearings, you will hear testimony from other Trump White House staff explaining what Mr. Cipollone said

and did, including on January 6th. But we think the American people deserve to hear from Mr. Cipollone personally. He should appear before this Committee, and we are working to secure his testimony.

A few days later, the Chairman and a small group of Committee staff crowded around a laptop in my hideaway office to watch portions of the video of Cassidy's June 20 testimony. Everyone present immediately realized that her latest testimony was a dramatic step forward.

By Friday, June 24, most members of the Committee had left town to spend the weekend in their districts. Many Committee staffers had been working day and night on the June 21 and 22 hearings, and they deserved a break. Except for Chairman Thompson and the handful of Committee lawyers and staff now squeezed into my hideaway office, almost no one knew what we were contemplating doing.

We now had interview material from Cassidy that could easily fill a three-hour hearing. Everyone present shared my fears about her security, and about leaks. We knew we couldn't wait. We began to plan a hearing for the following Tuesday.

50. KETCHUP ON THE WALL

I HAD ALREADY SHARED SOME of what we had earlier heard from Cassidy Hutchinson in my June 9 opening statement: that Donald Trump thought Mike Pence "deserved" to be hanged, and that Donald Trump did not think his violent supporters were doing anything wrong. But Cassidy's recent interview had produced much more detailed information. For example, after Meadows told Pat Cipollone that President Trump "doesn't want to do anything" about the violence, Cipollone had replied, "Something needs to be done or people are going to die — and the blood is going to be on your f'ing hands."

Cassidy was aware of the many Republicans, both inside and outside the White House, who had been desperately trying to get Donald Trump to appear on television and demand that the violent mob stand down and *leave the Capitol.* And she knew how frustrated senior White House staff were when Trump refused to do what virtually all of them thought was imperative.

But Cassidy also possessed many other insights directly relevant to what Donald Trump and White House Chief of Staff Mark Meadows were thinking—information that could make Meadows a key witness for any Justice Department investigation of Trump. Cassidy testified, for example, that the White House had begun receiving information about the threat of violence even before President Trump's Ellipse speech, and that Meadows had recognized in advance that January 6 could be violent. She testified that President Trump understood there were weapons in the crowd before he instructed his supporters to march to the Capitol. She testified that President Trump's White House legal team was worried about the contents of his Ellipse speech. And Hutchinson had heard in detail from other White House staff that President Trump was obviously and demonstrably angry—both in the presidential limo and upon his subsequent return to the White House—after being informed by Secret Service agents that he could not lead the crowd to the Capitol.

This last point was something we had heard from several others as well, including other White House witnesses, law enforcement, and off-the-record informants. (See pages 74 to 75 of the final report.) A national-security professional posted in the White House may have best summarized why Trump's intent to lead the crowd to the Capitol was relevant to how we thought about Donald Trump's conduct:

> To be completely honest, we were all in a state of shock.... we all knew what that implicated and what that meant, that this was no longer a rally, that this was going to move to something else if he physically walked to the Capitol. I—I don't know if you want to use the word *insurrection, coup,* whatever. We all knew that this would move from a normal, democratic, you know, public event into something else.

The most damning evidence of all, in my view, was that Trump had refused for hours to instruct the rioters to leave the Capitol. He had the ability to stop it all at the outset, but he wouldn't. He watched and let it happen. What type of man would refuse for hours on end to instruct a violent mob of his supporters attacking the Capitol and the police to stand down and leave?

Cassidy Hutchinson gave a sense of the answer to that question, too. She described a man who was uncontrollably angry with Bill Barr's statements refuting Trump's stolen-election allegations:

> The [White House] valet had articulated that the president was extremely angry at the attorney general's AP interview and had

thrown his lunch against the wall, which was causing him to have to clean up. So I grabbed a towel and started wiping the ketchup off the wall to help the valet out. He said something to the effect of, *He's really ticked off about this. I would stay clear of him for right now. He's really, really ticked off about this right now.*

For nearly two hours on June 28, 2022, Cassidy Hutchinson—at age 26—sat at a witness table before a congressional panel, alone in the national spotlight, answering question after question calmly and methodically. When a conservative commentator posted his story in *National Review* that evening, he wrote: "Things will not be the same after this." Millions of Americans shared this conclusion.

Cassidy Hutchinson had shown more courage and patriotism than White House officials in positions senior to hers, with many more years of experience. As we expected, her willingness to tell the truth made her the target of intense attacks in the media from Donald Trump and his supporters. I wondered whether the onslaught would have been as fierce had she been a man. I suspect not.

Cassidy never wavered. I was proud of her. As an American, and as a mother, I was also deeply grateful for her love of country.

Until Cassidy testified, we'd had no luck in persuading Pat Cipollone to testify. The day after her testimony, the Committee sent Pat Cipollone a subpoena. Pat immediately changed course. He appeared for a recorded interview a little over a week later.

51.   WE DID OUR DUTY AND WE STOOD FOR TRUTH

THE MORNING AFTER OUR JUNE 28 hearing, I flew to southern California for a speech at the Ronald Reagan Presidential Library. I had been to the library many times, including as a member of the House Armed Services Committee for the annual Reagan National Defense Forum. On a prior visit, I had been walking through the exhibits about Reagan's life when I was surprised to hear my dad's voice. I turned a corner to see a video playing of the eulogy he gave for President Reagan. I stood and watched. Speaking in the Capitol Rotunda, my dad recalled the words of President Reagan's second inaugural address:

> Ronald Reagan spoke of a nation that was "hopeful, big-hearted, idealistic, daring, decent, and fair." That was how he saw America, and that is how America came to know him. There was a kindness, simplicity, and goodness of character that marked all the years of his life.

In his eulogy, he also talked about Reagan's will and his love of freedom:

> More than any other influence, the Cold War was ended by the perseverance and courage of one man who answered falsehood with truth, and overcame evil with good.

I was reminded of what it felt like to have a president who was kind and good, a president your children could look up to. And I was moved to see my father talking about Ronald Reagan. Those were the men who exemplified the Republican Party I had joined.

The Reagan Library had invited me to speak as part of its "A Time for Choosing" series highlighting leading Republicans talking about the future of our party and country. When I had spoken at the library previously, the audience had always been warm and welcoming. Now, however, I wasn't sure how the mostly Republican crowd would respond. Notices had appeared online that Trump supporters were organizing to protest and disrupt the speech, but none of that happened. When I walked into the packed auditorium, I was surprised to receive a standing ovation.

I cast my first vote in a presidential election at age 18 in 1984—for Ronald Reagan. Today, I still believe that President Reagan has, perhaps better than almost any US president since Abraham Lincoln, expressed the nobility and honor of our great nation.

I began my speech by remembering how President Reagan's vision of American freedom had transformed the world. He had inspired millions, and he taught us what was required of us all in the defense of freedom. In 1983 Reagan had warned:

> It is up to us in our time to choose and choose wisely between the hard but necessary task of preserving peace and freedom, and the temptation to ignore our duty and blindly hope for the best while the enemies of freedom grow stronger day by day.

The choice confronting Republicans in the aftermath of January 6 was clear, although it could be painful for them to accept:

> Republicans cannot both be loyal to Donald Trump and loyal to the Constitution. . . . I come to this choice as a mother, committed to ensuring that my children and their children can continue to live in an America where the peaceful transfer of power is

guaranteed. We must ensure that we live in a nation that is governed by laws and not by men.

And I come to this choice as an American, as a citizen of the greatest nation God has ever created on the face of this earth.

And I come to this choice as a person of faith, as someone who believes deeply that our rights come from God, not from the government. And always mindful that we must pray as though everything depends upon God, because it does. And we must work as though everything depends upon us, because it does.

I remembered those last lines from the sermon delivered by the Navy chaplain at the Camp David presidential retreat on the first Sunday following 9/11. They are from a prayer of St. Ignatius.

Near the end of the speech, I recalled Cassidy Hutchinson's testimony from the January 6th Committee hearing the day before: "Her bravery and her patriotism yesterday were awesome to behold. Little girls all across this great nation are seeing what it really means to love this country and what it really means to be a patriot."

The crowd interrupted me and applauded Cassidy and her courage.

In closing, I asked everyone listening to resolve to do what was necessary to defend our great country:

So let us all, as we leave here tonight, let us resolve that we will embrace the grace and the compassion and the love of country that unites us. Let us resolve that we will fight to do what is right. And that we will be able to look back on these days and to say in our time of testing, *We did our duty and we stood for truth.* Ultimately, that is what our duty as Americans requires of us, that we love our country more, that we love her so much, that we will stand above politics to defend her, and that we will do everything in our power to protect our Constitution and our freedom paid for by the blood of so many.

I was later told that most of the crowd — all of whom had to reserve tickets — were regular attendees at Reagan Library events. I was speaking to a largely Republican audience, and they had been watching our hearings. And they fully understood the courage of the young woman who had appeared alone on national television the day before.

Cassidy watched the speech a few days later. When she heard the Reagan Library's overwhelming response as I mentioned her name, she confided to me later, she couldn't hold in the tears.

———

A few hours after my Reagan Library speech, I flew to Wyoming for the one and only primary debate for my House race. Wyoming covers nearly 100,000 square miles and has one member of Congress. In a Republican primary there would usually be between 100,000 and 125,000 voters. Two years earlier, I had won the Republican primary with 73 percent of the vote. In the general election that followed, I had received nearly 70 percent of the vote. Donald Trump had done a couple of percentage points better. No state in the country had given him a larger margin of victory.

The people of Wyoming are tough. They have grit. I've always been proud of my family's Wyoming heritage. My maternal grandmother was the first woman to serve as a deputy sheriff in Natrona County. My ancestors walked across Wyoming on the Mormon Trail in the middle of the 19th century, before Wyoming became a state. One of my great-grandfathers left home in Missouri in the early 20th century, finding work first as a cowboy near Lysite, Wyoming, in 1907, and then in the Salt Creek Oil Fields outside Casper. He and my great-grandmother raised their five children in a hard-sided tent on the edge of the oil fields. Political opponents who accused me of not being from Wyoming almost never had roots in the state as deep as mine were.

I was honored to represent this incredible place, and I was very proud of what my staff and I had accomplished for Wyoming since my election in 2016.

Donald Trump, his family, and most of his closest advisers are from Eastern cities. At the outset of the Trump administration they were happy to help my state, but often did not know what the issues were or how to do what was needed. Beginning during the 2016 presidential transition, we had helped the new administration form its team in the federal agencies that mattered to Wyoming. And we had worked very closely with that team, introducing and passing legislation and steering policy. During the Trump administration, important policies changed in areas such as land use and energy policy. I was pleased to introduce and cosponsor a number of pieces of legislation in these areas that were signed into law. Wyoming prospered.

But 2022 was very different. I had watched thousands of hardworking, good-hearted people across Wyoming fall prey to Donald Trump's lies. Some truly believed the falsehoods he was spreading. Others knew the truth but chose to perpetuate the lies.

The Wyoming congressional debate was held at the Whitney Center for the Arts at Sheridan College. All five candidates were there. There was no anger at any point, either before or during the debate. I visited with all the candidates backstage beforehand, hugged those I knew and their families, then took the stage.

The other candidates echoed Trump's stolen-election claims. My principal opponent, Harriet Hageman, had been endorsed by Donald Trump. She was an attorney and a member of the Wyoming Bar. I was surprised that she didn't have more respect for the rule of law. She didn't seem at all concerned about parroting the very election lies that had caused other attorneys in Trump's orbit to be sanctioned and disbarred.

At the close of the debate, I wanted to describe—in clear terms—how I saw my duty:

> I will never put party above my duty to the country. I will never put party above my duty to the Constitution. I swore an oath under God and I will abide by that oath. I won't say something that I know is wrong simply to earn the votes of people, to earn political support.... So I'm asking for your vote, and I'm asking

you to understand that I will never violate my oath of office. And if you're looking for somebody who will, then you need to vote for somebody else on this stage because I won't. I will always put my oath first.

My constituents deserved the truth, even if it wasn't what many of them wanted to hear.

52. PRESIDENT TRUMP IS A 76-YEAR-OLD MAN. HE IS NOT AN IMPRESSIONABLE CHILD.

PAT CIPOLLONE SAT FOR HIS recorded interview on July 8, 2022. The January 6th Committee had not planned to make any public statement following his interview, but that changed once we began to see leaks about the interview from Trump lawyers. We issued a suitable and measured response, summing up how important Cipollone's testimony had been. The Committee, we said, "received critical testimony [from Cipollone] on nearly every major topic in its investigation, reinforcing key points regarding Donald Trump's misconduct and providing highly relevant new information that will play a central role in its upcoming hearings."

Our next two hearings demonstrated that this was exactly right: Pat Cipollone's testimony was a central feature of both of them. "If you've watched these hearings," I said as we began our July 12 hearing, "you've heard us call for Mr. Cipollone to come forward to testify. He did, and Mr. Cipollone's testimony met our expectations."

By the time the Committee reached its July 12 hearing, a number of Trump's defenders had begun to change tactics yet again. It was important to address this shift directly in my opening statement:

> Today's hearing is our seventh. We have covered significant ground over the past several weeks. And we have also seen a change in how witnesses and lawyers in the Trump orbit

approach this Committee. Initially, their strategy, in some cases, appeared to be to deny and delay. Today, there appears to be a general recognition that the Committee has established key facts, including that virtually everyone close to President Trump—his Justice Department officials, his White House advisers, his White House Counsel, his campaign—all told him the 2020 election was not stolen.

This appears to have changed the strategy for defending Donald Trump. Now, the argument seems to be that President Trump was manipulated by others outside the administration. That he was persuaded to ignore his closest advisers, and that he was incapable of telling right from wrong. This new strategy is to try to blame only John Eastman, or Sidney Powell, or Congressman Scott Perry, or others, and not President Trump. In this version, the President was "poorly served" by these outside advisers. The [new] strategy is to blame people his advisers called "the crazies" for what Donald Trump did.

This, of course, is nonsense. President Trump is a 76-year-old man. He is not an impressionable child. Just like everyone else in our country, he is responsible for his own actions and his own choices. As our investigation has shown, Donald Trump had access to more detailed and specific information showing that the election was not actually stolen than almost any other American. And he was told this over and over again. No rational or sane man in his position could disregard that information and reach the opposite conclusion.

Our July 12 hearing began with testimony from high-level Trump administration officials—including Labor Secretary Gene Scalia, White House Counsel Pat Cipollone, Ivanka Trump, Attorney General Bill Barr, and others. They all believed that Donald Trump should have conceded the election by December 14—the date on which the Electoral College met and voted and declared Joe Biden the victor.

Featuring testimony from Trump White House staffers, the July 12 hearing demonstrated *yet again* that Trump had been told repeatedly that there was no evidence to support the stolen-election claims. Trump did not care. He ignored all of them. He made a conscious choice to continue with his January 6 strategy. He hosted a wild and highly contentious showdown at the White House on December 18 between his White House legal team, on one hand, and Sidney Powell, Mike Flynn, Rudy Giuliani, and conspiracy theorist Patrick Byrne on the other. Shortly after that meeting ended, in the early hours of December 19, Trump sent his tweet inviting supporters to come to Washington for a "wild" event on January 6. This tweet immediately triggered planning by militia groups and many others, and led to the violence two weeks later.

This hearing, which was expertly led by Jamie Raskin and Stephanie Murphy, also walked in detail through the involvement of the Proud Boys and Oath Keepers on January 6 — in particular, how they planned for that day, and how they led the crowd that Donald Trump had sent to the Capitol into the building. Key members of both groups have since been convicted of the crime of seditious conspiracy.

We continued with poignant testimony by former Trump supporters, including Ohio resident Stephen Ayres, a self-described "family man" who accepted Donald Trump's invitation to come to Washington for January 6. These men and women ruined their lives by following Donald Trump, by doing what he wanted them to do. Ayres walked the panel through his experience that day, explaining that he was following every word of Donald Trump's instructions. Ayres would not have violated the law nor later lost his job, he said, had Trump simply instructed the rioters to leave at 1:30 p.m. (by which time Trump knew that violence had erupted). Ayres further testified that Trump's 4:17 p.m. video and tweet, at long last instructing his supporters to leave, had a dramatic effect on him and others: "We literally left right after that come out." As did many of the other rioters.

As the January 6th Committee brought its July 12 hearing to a close, I needed to do one more thing. We had learned that following our prior hearing, Donald Trump had attempted to contact a committee witness — a witness we had not yet identified in any hearing. I announced publicly that we had alerted the Department of Justice to Trump's call. We would not stand for efforts by Donald Trump or anyone else to try to intimidate or tamper with our witnesses.

———

Our last hearing in July—on Thursday the 21st—may well have been our most important. All Americans should watch it. We now had testimony from White House Counsel Pat Cipollone leaving no doubt that all of Trump's senior White House staff were saying essentially the same thing during the violence: They were desperately trying to persuade President Trump to instruct his supporters to leave the Capitol. This evidence cannot be rebutted.

In the hearing, we walked systematically through the three-hour period while rioters attacked police and invaded the Capitol. We walked through phone calls begging Trump to help. We walked through a cascade of important texts from Trump's supporters and family. We examined all the tweets. We scrutinized what Donald Trump's staff and his family had said. There was a staff-written note begging the president to instruct the rioters to leave the Capitol.

The mounting violence had clearly frightened House Minority Leader Kevin McCarthy, Trump son-in-law Jared Kushner told the Select Committee: When he couldn't persuade Trump to help, Kevin desperately called Trump's family and begged them to intervene. Virtually everyone knew what needed to be done. And yet the evidence showed that Trump was making phone calls instead, belatedly still trying to convince senators to further delay the electoral count.

There is only one reasonable conclusion from this mountain of evidence: Donald Trump wanted the electoral count to stop, and he knew the rioters were the only thing stopping it. This is why Trump did not pick up the phone and order federal law enforcement or the military to intervene. This is why he would not instruct his supporters to stand down and leave.

We also showed that Trump was fully aware of the ongoing violence when he sent his infamous 2:24 p.m. tweet attacking Vice President Pence for cowardice. One of our witnesses, former Deputy White House Press Secretary Sarah Matthews, said this about Donald Trump's tweet:

> You know, I worked on the campaign, traveled all around the country going to countless rallies with him. And I've seen the impact his words have on his supporters. They truly latch on to every word and every tweet that he says. And so I think that in that moment for him to tweet out the message about Mike Pence, it was him pouring gasoline on the fire and making it much worse.

Even Trump's far-right ally Ali Alexander, who was outside the Capitol Building, texted, "POTUS is not ignorant of what his words would do."

Not one person we interviewed on President Trump's White House staff could find any excuse for that tweet. They universally condemned it.

Well after all this, during his May 2023 CNN town hall, Donald Trump admitted that his supporters follow every word he says. And, as the Select Committee concluded, on January 6, Donald Trump was trying to threaten and endanger Pence's life in order to pressure him to violate the law. During the violent chaos and even after it, Trump and his lawyers Rudy Giuliani and John Eastman all continued to pressure Congress and Mike Pence to delay the electoral count.

In our committee's final report, we cited a legal analysis by Professor Emeritus Albert Alschuler, one of our country's leading professors of criminal law. As a law student at the University of Chicago in the mid-1990s, I had taken Professor Alschuler's course in criminal law. Alschuler suggested that Donald Trump's intentional failure to stop the violence could constitute "assisting or giving aid or comfort" to an insurrection, under the US criminal code. The Committee concluded that Trump knew what was happening at the US Capitol, and knew what he needed to do to stop it. He refused.

Leading the questioning in the July 21 hearing were Congressman Adam Kinzinger and Congresswoman Elaine Luria, both military veterans. Before being elected to Congress, Elaine had served in the Navy for 20 years, including as a nuclear-trained Surface Warfare Officer, and had risen to the rank of Commander. I had gotten to know her during our time together on the Armed Services Committee, where we had all benefited from her expertise and her dedication to serving her constituents and our country. Chairman Thompson asked them to lead this hearing in part because he knew their experiences serving in the military brought an important understanding to issues related to the dereliction of duty by our commander-in-chief.

The hearing also demonstrated the shameful immorality of those, like Senator Josh Hawley, who first provoked the riotous crowd with a raised fist, then ran from the crowd once he realized what was happening. A member of the Capitol Police told us that Senator Hawley's fist pump, from behind police lines, bothered her greatly because he "riled up the crowd" and was "doing it in a safe space, protected by the officers and the barriers." When the Committee showed footage of Hawley's gesture, then followed it immediately with footage of Hawley running down a Capitol hallway, the hearing room erupted in laughter.

Hawley deserved it.

"[S]upporting Josh and trying so hard to get him elected to the Senate was the worst mistake I ever made in my life," legendary former Missouri Republican Senator Jack Danforth said after the January 6 riots.

———

In my closing statement, I intended to make several points—not just about the evidence we had presented over the past two months, but about how we had uncovered the truth over the past year:

We've seen bravery and honor in these hearings. Ms. Matthews and Mr. Pottinger, both of you will be remembered for that. As will Cassidy Hutchinson. She sat here alone, took the oath, and testified before millions of Americans. She knew all along that she would be attacked by President Trump, and by the 50-, 60-, and 70-year-old men who hide themselves behind executive privilege.

But like our witnesses today, she has courage, and she did it anyway. Cassidy, Sarah, and our other witnesses—including Officer Caroline Edwards, Shaye Moss, and her mother, Ruby Freeman—are an inspiration to American women and to American girls. We owe a debt to all of those who have and will appear here.

And that brings me to another point. This committee has shown you the testimony of dozens of Republican witnesses, those who served President Trump loyally for years. The case against Donald Trump in these hearings is not made by witnesses who were his political enemies; it is instead a series of confessions by Donald Trump's own appointees—his own friends, his own campaign officials, people who worked for him for years, and his own family.

I also intended to address people like Hugh Hewitt, on whose nationwide radio program for conservative listeners I had appeared many times. I was convinced that people like Hewitt agreed with most of what I was saying about Trump but could not say so without risking a revolt by their listeners.

It seemed a number of conservative writers, analysts, and media personalities clung to whatever rationale they could to attack what I was doing, and to avoid engaging with our evidence. They urged their viewers not to watch our hearings because, for example, we *had no cross-examination*. Ironically, this was Kevin McCarthy's doing: He had chosen to withdraw all five of his Republican nominees to the Committee a year earlier.

Nor was this a circumstance where we relied on testimony from Donald Trump's political opponents. We had intentionally structured our hearings around dozens of unimpeachable witnesses: Donald Trump's own supporters, his own appointees, his own advisers. I wanted conservatives who were finding excuses to ignore us to ask themselves a key question:

For those of you who seem to think the evidence would be different if Republican Leader McCarthy had not withdrawn his nominees from this committee, let me ask you this: Do you really think Bill Barr is such a delicate flower that he would wilt under cross-examination? Pat Cipollone? Eric Herschmann? Jeff Rosen? Richard Donoghue? Of course they aren't. None of our witnesses are.

Of course, the larger and much more important issue for this hearing was what Donald Trump failed to do during the attack. I focused on that in my concluding remarks:

In our hearing tonight, you saw an American president faced with a stark and unmistakable choice between right and wrong. There was no ambiguity. No nuance. Donald Trump made a purposeful choice to violate his oath of office, to ignore the ongoing violence against law enforcement, to threaten our Constitutional order. There is no way to excuse that behavior. It was indefensible. Every American must consider this: Can a president who is willing to make the choices Donald Trump made during the violence of January 6th ever be trusted with any position of authority in our great nation again?

This is exactly the question we still face as I write *Oath and Honor*, more than a year after our July 2022 hearings concluded. I believed then (and still believe today) that we are dealing with a larger question—not just one man's effort to subvert our Constitutional republic but the commitment of all Americans to the rule of law and the premises of our Constitution. As we ended, I tried to put the issues we'd been tackling in a larger historical context:

In this room in 1918, the Committee on Women's Suffrage convened to discuss and debate whether women should be granted the right to vote. This room is full of history, and we on this committee know we have a solemn obligation not to idly squander what so many Americans have fought and died for. Ronald Reagan's great ally, Margaret Thatcher, said this: "Let it never be said that the dedication of those who love freedom is less than the determination of those who would destroy it."

Let me assure every one of you of this: Our Committee understands the gravity of this moment, the consequences for our nation.

———

In the days that followed, Trump defenders largely went silent. Most national media fully grasped what we had showed. One commentator wrote that the Committee's presentation proved that we had "understood the assignment." That our job was not to grandstand or gloat, but to create a "thorough historical record" that all Americans could understand.

To this day, the evidence from this final summer hearing is among the most potent information I can share with Americans who still think that Donald Trump has been railroaded, or that January 6 was a sightseeing visit by "tourists" engaged in "legitimate political discourse." Most people who will take the time to listen realize that there is no excuse or defense for Donald Trump's unwillingness to step to the microphone and instruct the rioters to leave. A man who would behave that way when his character is tested lacks the sense of right and wrong that most Americans learn from their parents.

53.   FREEDOM MUST NOT AND WILL
NOT DIE HERE

DURING WORLD WAR II, THE Heart Mountain Relocation Center was located about 15 miles outside Cody, Wyoming. Following the attack on Pearl Harbor, the United States government began forcibly evacuating and detaining individuals of Japanese ancestry. More than 110,000 Japanese Americans were incarcerated in 10 camps in isolated areas of the country. Heart Mountain was the destination for over 14,000 of them.

Among those detained at Heart Mountain was a 10-year-old boy who had been born in California. When he boarded the train with his family in San Jose in the spring of 1942, he was wearing his Cub Scout uniform and carrying his baseball bat and glove. Military sentries confiscated the bat as a potential weapon. By November, Norman Yoshio Mineta and his family had arrived in the Heart Mountain camp.

The Scout troops in the camp tried to get troops from the nearby towns of Cody and Powell to join them for activities. All the other troops declined the invitation except one from Cody, where a young Alan Simpson was a member. Al Simpson and Norm Mineta formed a lifelong friendship.

Simpson, a Republican, grew up to represent Wyoming in the United States Senate. Mineta, a Democrat, was elected to Congress and served in the Cabinet of two American presidents—one Democrat and one Republican. On the morning of September 11, 2001, Secretary of Transportation Norm Mineta sat with my father, Vice President Richard Cheney, in the secure bunker underneath the White House, orchestrating the unprecedented effort to get every American commercial aircraft out of the sky while our nation was under attack by al-Qaeda.

A few days after our last July hearing, I was honored to participate in a ceremony at the Heart Mountain camp to break ground for the Mineta-Simpson Institute celebrating the lifelong friendship of these two men. Hundreds of family members of those who had been interned, as well as a few camp survivors themselves, gathered under a large tent on the high plains where the Heart Mountain Relocation Center had once stood. I sat on stage next to Senator Simpson and Norm Mineta's wife, Deni.

When I was introduced, the audience rose in a loud, sustained ovation. I hadn't expected this, and it was overwhelming. It was a very emotional moment for me. I spotted my father in the audience, standing with the crowd. It was emotional for him, too.

Many of the people who came up to me afterward expressed a gratitude informed by what their families had suffered. They were Americans who had lost their freedom, who had seen everything taken from them by their own government. Given what their families had endured, their deep love of the United States was humbling. And their warnings about how quickly it could all be lost resonated with me deeply.

Later that same day, David and Kristine Fales hosted me at a meet-and-greet at their home. Chairs had been set up on their front lawn; off to one side was a table with punch and snacks. Near the microphone set up for my remarks stood an American flag and a large, beautiful photograph of a bald eagle, taken by one of their four sons. It was a perfect Wyoming summer evening, with friends and family, Democrats and Republicans together, talking about our love of America and all we must do to protect her.

The Fales are the parents of 11 children. As a mother of five, I don't often meet parents with more children than Phil and I have, and I always take the opportunity to compare notes. As the event was winding down, Kristine and I were talking about our children. "I've realized something about you," she said. "You will never stop fighting for America, because you have a mother's love for our country." It was the highest compliment I could imagine.

———

With just a few weeks to go before the primary election, we decided to make two final ads. I knew I had a steep uphill climb. I had not charted my course with the goal of being reelected. I was doing my duty. I wanted the language of the ads to explain why the truth matters, and why the lies about the 2020 election were so dangerous: "If we do not condemn these lies, if we do not hold those responsible to account, we will be excusing this conduct—and it will become a feature of all elections. America will never be the same."

A substantial majority of Wyoming Republican primary voters would disagree with that sentiment, I knew when we ran the ad. This was no way to win an election in Wyoming. But I refused to hedge the truth.

The final ad of the campaign featured Dick Cheney wearing his Stetson and speaking directly to the camera about the threat our country faced:

> In our nation's 246-year history there has never been an individual who is a greater threat to our republic than Donald Trump. He tried to steal the last election using lies and violence to keep himself in power after the voters had rejected him. He is a coward—a real man wouldn't lie to his supporters. He lost his election, and he lost big. I know it. He knows it. And deep down, I think most Republicans know it.
>
> Lynne and I are so proud of Liz for standing up for the truth, doing what's right, honoring her oath to the Constitution when so many in our party are too scared to do so. Liz is fearless. She never backs down from a fight. There is nothing more important she will ever do than lead the effort to make sure Donald Trump is never again near the Oval Office. And she will succeed.

———

The Wind River Reservation occupies more than two million acres near the center of Wyoming. It is shared by two tribes, the Northern

Arapaho and the Eastern Shoshone. During my time in Congress, I worked closely with tribal members and leaders to learn about the challenges they faced, and to do everything I could to ensure I was an effective representative for them. I had worked especially closely with tribal Chairmen Lee Spoonhunter and Jordan Dresser, who led the Northern Arapaho Tribe during my time in office. In July they told me the tribe would like to honor me during its annual powwow on the reservation at Ethete, Wyoming.

Before the ceremony, I talked with a young woman who had been one of the recipients of a scholarship my parents had endowed at the University of Wyoming for students to study abroad. A member of the Arapaho tribe, she was a law student at UW and had used some of the scholarship funds to visit the United Kingdom.

She described visiting a British Museum warehouse on the outskirts of London. Curators there had brought a sacred item out of storage: a headdress once worn by Chief Yellow Calf, the last chief of the Arapaho. She was the first member of the Arapaho tribe to see the headdress in over 100 years. Now she was doing all she could to secure the return of the headdress to the Arapaho tribe.

Though my term would be up in months, I worked to help. As I write this, the headdress remains packed away in that museum warehouse. Given the artifact's significance to the history of the Northern Arapaho, that seems especially wrong.

The Honor Ceremony in Ethete that day was very moving. A woman wrapped a red blanket with white fringe, made for this ceremony, around my shoulders. Drums sounded as tribal elders and leaders escorted me in a solemn walk around the arena. Members of the tribe stepped down from the stands to shake our hands and join the procession.

———

On August 8, 2022, a team of federal agents conducted a lawful search of Donald Trump's Mar-a-Lago residence in Florida. At the time, we didn't know the full extent of Donald Trump's obstruction of efforts by the DOJ to retrieve classified documents from him. But Trump's response to the raid was no surprise: He claimed he was a victim.

Trump's victim strategy had enjoyed ringing success in deep-red states such as Wyoming. And at least one violent assault on an FBI field office had ensued. But now he weaponized that strategy by working to publicly disclose a number of the FBI agents who had been involved in the search.

Mobilize the anger, put people's lives at risk, make them pay: How many times had the January 6th Committee seen precisely that tactic before? I suspected that the agents and their families—agents who had devoted their lives to law enforcement and were simply doing their jobs—would face the same type of harassment we had seen inflicted on Speaker Bowers, Shaye Moss, Ruby Freeman, and dozens of others. And other Republicans were joining in, following Donald Trump's lead, attacking the integrity of FBI agents involved in the search. Donald Trump's outing of the agents had been purposeful and malicious. In public remarks a few days later, I warned of the danger to law enforcement and to our nation as a whole:

> Today, our federal law enforcement is being threatened, a federal judge is being threatened. Fresh threats of violence arise every-where. And despite knowing all of this, Donald Trump recently released the names of the FBI agents involved in the search. That was purposeful and malicious. No patriotic American should excuse these threats or be intimidated by them. Our great nation must not be ruled by a mob provoked over social media.

Of course, today we know far more about that document search. And Donald Trump has now been indicted, including for obstruction of justice and violations of the Espionage Act. One of the allegations—that Trump caused his lawyers to provide a false certification to the Department of Justice—reminds me of the type of deceit our January 6 investigation uncovered. And Donald Trump is also now attacking, and endangering, the Department of Justice lawyers prosecuting him.

———

As the Republican primary in Wyoming approached, friends, family, and staff gathered in Jackson Hole. The night before the election, we hosted a dinner in a restaurant on the Jackson town square. It was clear what the outcome would be the next day, but the mood was neither sad nor somber. I was proud of, and humbled by, the support of these wonderful men and women.

We had been through a lot together over the last many months. Members of my staff—both on Capitol Hill and in Wyoming—had weathered harassment, including from family members who were angry that they had stayed with me. Before joining my team, many of these staffers had worked in Republican politics, or in Republican offices on Capitol Hill; it would no doubt have been easier for them to keep their heads down and quietly go to work for someone else. I certainly would have understood. I felt grateful—and honored—that we had stood together.

In the shadow of the Grand Tetons outside Jackson, Wyoming—on some of the most beautiful land in America—sits the Mead ranch. Nestled against East Gros Ventre Butte, the cattle ranch has been in the Mead family for over 100 years. When Phil and I got married in Jackson 30 years ago, our rehearsal dinner was at Spring Creek Ranch, atop the butte overlooking the Mead ranch.

The Mead family has been involved in service to Wyoming for generations. Matt Mead was US Attorney for Wyoming, then governor of the state from 2011 to 2019. His grandfather, Cliff Hansen, served as the state's governor and as one of our senators in the 1960s and 1970s. After a young Dick Cheney visited the older man in his Senate office on Capitol Hill in the late 1960s, Senator Hansen wrote to my grandparents to say what an impressive young man he had found their son to be. I still have that letter.

The Meads had graciously agreed to host our Election Night event. As the sun sank behind the mountains at the end of that summer day, the few clouds were lit by pink dusk light. I had never seen a more beautiful evening in Wyoming.

Donald Trump's refusal to concede a political campaign that he had resoundingly lost was un-American and dishonorable, and it had devastating consequences for our country. Resolved to concede my own race definitively and unconditionally, I began my Election Night speech this way:

> Two years ago, I won this primary with 73 percent of the vote. I could easily have done the same again. The path was clear, but it would have required that I go along with President Trump's lie about the 2020 election. It would have required that I enable his ongoing efforts to unravel our democratic system and attack the foundations of our republic. That was a path I could not and would not take.
>
> No House seat—no office in this land—is more important than the principles that we are all sworn to protect, and I well understood the potential political consequences of abiding by my duty. Our republic relies upon the goodwill of all candidates for office to accept honorably the outcome of elections. And tonight, Harriet Hageman has received the most votes in this primary. She won. I called her to concede the race.

My congressional race was over, but our work to defend our democratic republic was only just beginning. Because America's democratic system has endured longer than any in history, it can be easy to take its survival for granted. Sometimes people would tell me that January 6 wasn't so bad, because, after all, our institutions had held. I would remind them that our institutions don't defend themselves. The institutions held only because of a handful of Americans who did their duty and refused to yield to Donald Trump's pressure. And because of the men and women in law enforcement who literally defended our democracy when it came under attack.

American freedom is precious and rare, and active vigilance is required from all of us to defend it. As I spoke that night, we were facing a particular danger in the form of candidates who were still refusing to accept the outcome of the 2020 presidential election. Should any of these "election deniers" be elected governor or secretary of state in swing states such as Arizona or Pennsylvania, they could inflict enormous damage in 2024—by, for example, honoring election results only if their preferred candidate won. They had to be defeated. Describing how fragile and rare our freedom is, I continued:

> Most of world history is a story of violent conflict, of servitude and suffering. Most people in most places have not lived in free- dom. Our American freedom is a providential departure from history. We are the exception. We have been given the gift of freedom by God and our founding fathers. It has been said that the long arc of history bends toward justice and freedom. That is true—but only if we *make* it bend.
>
> Today, our highest duty is to bend the arc of history to pre- serve our nation and its blessings. To ensure that freedom will not perish. To protect the very foundations of this Constitutional republic. Never in our nation's 246 years have we seen what we saw on January 6. Like so many Americans, I assumed that the violence and the chaos of that day would have prompted a united response, a recognition that this was a line that must never be crossed, a tragic chapter in our nation's history to be studied by historians to ensure that it can never happen again. But instead, major elements of my party still vehemently defend those who caused it. At the heart of the attack on January 6 is a willingness to embrace dangerous conspiracies that attack the very core premise of our nation: that lawful elections—reviewed by the courts when necessary, and certified by the states and Electoral College—determine who serves as president.
>
> If we do not condemn the conspiracies and the lies, if we do not hold those responsible to account, we will be excusing this conduct—and it will become a feature of all elections. America will never be the same.... Our nation is barreling, once again,

toward crisis, lawlessness, and violence. No American should sup-port election deniers for any position of genuine responsibility, where their refusal to follow the rule of law will corrupt our future.

Our nation is young in the history of mankind and yet we're the oldest democracy in the world. Our survival is not guaran-teed. History has shown us over and over again how poisonous lies destroy free nations.

I knew my address would also be carried by national and interna-tional media. I wanted to explain to the crowd—and to all those watch-ing—why I had decided to take this course, and what I saw as our essential next steps:

Our duty as citizens of this republic is not only to defend the free-dom that's been handed down to us. We also have an obligation to learn from the actions of those who came before, to know the stories of grit and perseverance of the brave men and women who built and saved this union. In the lives of these great Americans, we find inspiration and purpose.

In May of 1864, after years of war and a string of reluctant Union generals, Ulysses S. Grant met General Robert E. Lee's forces at the Battle of the Wilderness. In two days of heavy fight-ing, the Union suffered over 17,000 casualties. At the end of that battle, General Grant faced a choice. Most assumed he would do what previous Union generals had done: retreat. On the evening of May 7, Grant began to move. As the fires of the battle still smol-dered, Grant rode to the head of the column. He rode to the inter-section of Brock Road and Orange Plank Road. And there, as the men of his army watched and waited, instead of turning north— back toward Washington and safety—Grant turned his horse south toward Richmond and the heart of Lee's army. Refusing to retreat, he pressed on to victory.

Lincoln and Grant and all who fought in our nation's tragic Civil War, including my own great-great-grandfathers, saved our Union. Their courage saved freedom. And if we listen closely, they are speaking to us down the generations. We must not idly squander what so many have fought and died for.

America has meant so much to so many because we are the best hope of freedom on earth.

Last week in Laramie, a gentleman came up to me with tears in his eyes. "I'm not an American," he said. "But my children are. I grew up in Brazil. I know how fragile freedom is, and we must not lose it here."

A few days ago, here in Jackson, a woman told me that her grandparents had survived Auschwitz. They found refuge in America. She said she was afraid that she had nowhere to go if freedom died here.

Ladies and gentlemen, freedom must not, cannot, and will not die here. We must be very clear-eyed about the threat we face, and about what is required to defeat it.

I have said since January 6 that I will do whatever it takes to ensure Donald Trump is never again anywhere near the Oval Office, and I mean it.

This is a fight for all of us together. I'm a conservative Republican. I believe deeply in the principles and the ideals on which my party was founded. I love its history. And I love what our party has stood for. But I love my country more.

So I ask you tonight to join me. As we leave here, let us resolve that we will stand together—Republicans, Democrats, and Independents—against those who would destroy our republic. They are angry and they are determined, but they have not seen anything like the power of Americans united in defense of our Constitution and committed to the cause of freedom. There is no greater power on this earth. And with God's help, we will prevail.

Thank you all. God bless you. God bless Wyoming. God bless the United States of America.

By the time I left the stage, the sun had set behind the mountains. I waded through the crowd, hugging supporters who had stood with me for years—Paul and Judy Cali from Cody; John and Mary Kay Turner and Jackie Montgomery from Jackson; my dear college friend Liza Pohle and her daughter, Eliza; and many other close friends. We all knew that we were standing at the beginning, not the end, of the work that will be necessary to defend our Constitution.

54. YOU'RE WELCOME, @KARILAKE

FOR MONTHS, POLLSTERS HAD PREDICTED that Republicans would retake the US House of Representatives in 2022 by double digits, with some estimating gains as high as 30 congressional seats. History seemed to support that prediction for an off-year election: Normally, the party in the White House loses seats in Congress. As the election approached, some pollsters also had the Arizona Republican candidate for governor—Kari Lake, an election denier—up by at least a few points.

To combat election deniers and help educate voters about all that was at stake, I formed a political action committee (PAC) called the Great Task, named for Lincoln's description from his Gettysburg Address of "the great task remaining before us": to ensure that "government of the people, by the people, for the people, shall not perish from the earth."

I had accepted an invitation to speak at the McCain Institute at Arizona State University on October 5, 2022. During the event, I was asked about Kari Lake and another election denier, Mark Finchem, who was running for secretary of state. They had both fully embraced election denialism, and they posed a significant threat.

My speech was covered in Arizona, but as the election drew closer, the Great Task cut an ad using clips from my Arizona speech and ran it, beginning about a week before Election Day:

> I don't know that I have ever voted for a Democrat, but if I lived in Arizona I absolutely would. You have a candidate for governor, Kari Lake, and you have a candidate for secretary of state, Mark

Finchem, both of whom have said that they will honor the results of an election *only if they agree with it*. And if you care about the survival of our republic, we cannot give people power who will not honor elections. We must have elected officials who honor that responsibility.

Lake fired off a sarcastic open letter in response, thanking me for my "generous in-kind contribution" to her campaign and suggesting that my ad would move even more people to vote for her: "In fact, my team tells me that your commercial should add *another* 10 points to our lead!... Thank you again for the huge boost to our campaign....P.S. Make Arizona Great Again." Lake seemed to think she was already up by 10 points over her Democratic opponent, Katie Hobbs. I doubted it, but polling did suggest that Lake was in the lead.

Yet when the votes were counted the next week, Kari Lake lost. So did Mark Finchem. Whatever Lake's lead in the polls may have once been, it disappeared during the last week of her campaign.

When Lake's defeat was officially announced, I responded to her earlier sarcastic thank-you letter with a tweet: "You're welcome, @KariLake."

———

During each of my three terms in the House, I had served on the Armed Services Committee. Armed Services is different from other House committees in a number of important ways. Many members on the committee are veterans themselves or have a background in national security or intelligence. The work of the committee has historically been less overtly partisan than that of some other House committees.

During my years on the Armed Services Committee, I got to know a core group of colleagues who happened to be women — Democrats and Republicans — who were serious and knowledgeable about the issues. We certainly didn't always agree, but I respected their expertise, and their dedication to serving their constituents and our country.

One of these Armed Services Committee colleagues was Democrat Elissa Slotkin of Michigan. Elissa had served at the Central Intelligence

Agency, the Defense Department, and on the National Security Council. She worked for President Bush and President Obama. Her Republican opponent was an election denier who had refused to accept the results of the 2020 presidential election—and declined to say whether he would honor the outcome of the 2022 congressional election.

Despite our policy disagreements, I was honored to endorse Elissa. It was the first time I had ever endorsed a Democrat, but I knew that no policy debate was as important as standing together—across party lines—on behalf of democracy. On November 1, 2022, I traveled to East Lansing and spoke at an event on Elissa's behalf. Elissa won her race.

Another Democrat I endorsed in 2022 was Abigail Spanberger. Abigail had worked as a CIA officer for many years. I respected her level-headedness and devotion to public service. I knew she understood how perilous this moment was for our nation. She was exactly the kind of person the country needed in Congress.

Abigail faced a tight reelection race in 2022. Her opponent was an election denier who had been endorsed by Donald Trump on October 27. A week later, I endorsed Abigail: "We need our elected leaders to be honest, serious, and responsible," I said, "which is why I would urge voters in Virginia's 7th District to support Abigail Spanberger." Abigail prevailed, garnering 52 percent of the vote to her opponent's 48 percent.

As these two races demonstrate, 2022 did not turn out to be a typical midterm election. The expectations that Republicans would flip dozens of seats in Congress, as expert pollsters had maintained right up until Election Day, collapsed. Election deniers were defeated in many races.

From all of these races I recognized that a significant number of Americans—Republicans, Democrats, and Independents—would never embrace the lies of Donald Trump or other election deniers.

55. THEY KNEW

THROUGHOUT THE SUMMER OF 2022, it became increasingly clear that text messages among Secret Service agents on January 6 had been destroyed. We had seen reports that a criminal investigation had been initiated relating to the missing texts. The deletion of these texts was certainly suspicious, and it made our job much more difficult. Department of Homeland Security (DHS) Secretary Alejandro Mayorkas called Chairman Thompson and me, as well as others on the Committee, and pledged to help in any way he could. Among other things, he appointed a former DHS general counsel, Steve Bunnell, to help us navigate these and related issues with the department. (Joe Maher had joined my Committee staff from the department, and he was recused from any matters connected to DHS; so I dealt with much of this directly.)

I had been in Wyoming for a good portion of August, and I was concerned that the January 6th Committee was not making much progress with Homeland Security's offers to help us. I spoke with Congresswoman Zoe Lofgren about this, and we set up a call with Bunnell and DHS General Counsel Jonathan Meyer over the Labor Day weekend. Bunnell and Meyer moved quickly to ensure the Committee received additional Secret Service emails and other electronic messages. We could not recover the destroyed text messages — although they could have been incredibly valuable, they were apparently gone forever — but we could do the next best thing by obtaining and reviewing the emails and other messages that DHS made available to the Committee.

Within the next few weeks, we received approximately one million new emails, radio transmissions, chat messages, and other documents from the Secret Service. We recognized that this was an extraordinary step for the Homeland Security Department: The Secret Service normally refuses to produce this type of material, which included intelligence- and law-enforcement–sensitive information, and does so only when compelled by a court. Their decision to provide it to the Select Committee reflected the gravity of the issues we were addressing.

As the material began to arrive, I was trying to jump-start our team to plow through these critical new documents. Jamie Fleet worked with my chief of staff, Kara Ahern, to dedicate additional resources and staff to review the newly produced documents. I went to the staff offices in September to help sift through the materials myself.

What we found was important.

There was no doubt about it: In the days leading up to January 6, and on that morning itself, the Secret Service was receiving warnings about the potential for violence—and the White House personnel interacting with them knew it.

They knew.

This was not just a single stray report, or one isolated intelligence analysis. Instead, the signs were many. The potential for violence should not have been a surprise; indeed, based on communications among Trump supporters identified in the intelligence and threat reporting, it was entirely predictable.

The White House knew more than enough to cancel President Trump's Ellipse speech on January 6. They knew more than enough to realize that sending the Ellipse crowd to the Capitol could be exceptionally dangerous. This was obviously a disaster waiting to happen. Rational people in the White House—or a rational president—easily could have prevented it.

To be clear, the issue was *not* that the Secret Service failed to brief those up the chain at the White House about the threat. It appeared to the Committee that this information *was* being conveyed up the chain, including directly to Mark Meadows and President Trump. We presented explicit testimony about that topic in our hearings. With the weight of the intelligence we received via Homeland Security, it is exceptionally difficult to believe that anyone in the White House with access to this information could have failed to recognize this obvious menace.

It is also extremely difficult to believe that Mark Meadows, Donald Trump, and others were not briefed. I was concerned, *even without access to this intelligence,* about what might happen on January 6—so concerned, in fact, that I hired private security for that day. I would invite anyone who still harbors doubts to read the *Final Report of the Select Committee to Investigate the January 6th Attack on the United States Capitol,* and in particular to download and read the November 29, 2022, recorded examination by Chief Investigative Counsel Tim Heaphy of White House Deputy Chief of Staff Tony Ornato. They knew.

The bottom line is this: Donald Trump never should have summoned his supporters to Washington for January 6. And as it became clear that they were angry and could suddenly turn violent, he should have canceled his Ellipse speech and told them to leave town. He never should have addressed the crowd the way he did. He never should have instructed them to march to the Capitol. And once the violence erupted, he should have intervened and instructed them to leave the Capitol immediately—certainly when he was informed that a riot was underway. Certainly at the moment Pat Cipollone and others on his staff pleaded with him to do so. And Donald Trump never should have poured gasoline on the fire by tweeting his attack on Mike Pence at 2:24 p.m.

At 2:44 p.m. on January 6, at the height of the deadly violence, Ashli Babbitt attempted to invade the House chamber, climbing through the shattered glass window of a locked door—ignoring the warnings of a lone Capitol Police officer guarding the door with his weapon drawn. Other officers with weapons drawn were defending a second door from rioters attempting to break in. Members of Congress were in the chamber at the time, while others were being evacuated through the far door.

In the prior one to two hours, Metropolitan Police had found firearms on Trump supporters in the streets. The rioters outside the Capitol had begun physically assaulting police officers, and their numbers were so overwhelming that they had severely injured many officers. More than

1,000 rioters—and possibly as many as 2,000—had already forced their way inside the Capitol. Some were hunting Mike Pence. Others were trying to infiltrate the House and Senate chambers. An armed standoff was playing out at the chamber's north door. Suffocating tear gas swirled through the Capitol Rotunda.

If a riotous crowd like this had breached the White House grounds, was attacking police, was breaking windows to gain entry to the White House itself, and then had entered the White House through a broken window, the Secret Service would have been fully justified in using lethal force, as the Capitol Police officer did here.

Donald Trump has repeatedly said he blames Ashli Babbitt's death on the Capitol Police. Yet if anyone other than Ashli Babbitt is responsible for her death, it is Donald Trump. She died trying to keep Donald Trump in office. She died because she believed Donald Trump's lies. Donald Trump could have and should have put a stop to all of this before she died. This was his responsibility.

56.   STATE OF MIND

THE JANUARY 6TH COMMITTEE CONDUCTED a business meeting on October 13, 2022. The Committee had a number of options for structuring this meeting. We had secured new documentary evidence from the National Archives and the Secret Service. We also had heard new evidence directly relevant to Donald Trump's intent, including from Trump confidant Steve Bannon and conservative activist Tom Fitton. And we also now had video from Fort McNair, where the most senior Democratic and Republican leaders had been evacuated during the violent riot.

By this point in the fall we were confident that the Department of Justice was pursuing the same investigative paths we were. We wanted to be certain that they had the benefit of our thinking. We also thought that some state prosecutors had begun to look into the topics we were covering.

We thought our most important role now might be to put all of our most important evidence, new and old, in its proper context—that is, to show precisely how it fit into the larger evidentiary picture. The easiest way to do that (and the way we thought might be most helpful to criminal prosecutors) would be to itemize key evidence relevant to Donald Trump's *intent*—his state of mind.

The addition of evidence relating to Trump advisers Steve Bannon, Tom Fitton, and Roger Stone was particularly relevant: It confirmed that Donald Trump's Election Night strategy had been *premeditated*.

During the Select Committee's meeting on October 13, 2022, we also showed the public a number of the newly obtained Secret Service documents. These bore directly upon the depravity of Donald Trump's actions on January 6, proving that those in the White House knew there was a substantial risk of violence. We also presented other evidence demonstrating that Trump had been aware his election claims were false — including new evidence of conversations with Mark Meadows revealing what Trump knew and thought.

————

The January 6th Committee also decided to issue a subpoena to Donald Trump. Over the course of our committee's work, Trump had challenged members of the Committee to debate him and suggested that he would be more than happy to testify. The time had now come for Trump to either appear before the Committee or admit that he had been bluffing.

To bolster the Committee's request for Trump's testimony, we presented material from a series of witnesses, among them General Flynn and Roger Stone. Each of them had invoked their 5th Amendment rights in declining to answer questions about their direct communications with the president.

We had long suspected Trump and Meadows of having communicated with Flynn and Stone in advance of January 6. Both Flynn and Stone had been seen with members of the Proud Boys and Oath Keepers. We had direct testimony indicating that Trump asked Meadows to call Flynn and Stone on the night of January 5. But because Flynn and Stone took the 5th, and because Meadows refused to testify and Justice declined to prosecute, we had no further details about those communications.

Both the Proud Boys and the Oath Keepers had played key roles in the Capitol assault. Members of each of those two far-right militias had been convicted of seditious conspiracy. We all suspected there was more to this story. For these and other reasons, the Committee did not feel that we could close our investigation of January 6 without seeking direct testimony from Donald Trump.

As it turned out, Donald Trump's earlier posturing was just posturing.

57.   NEVER AGAIN

OUR COMMITTEE'S MANDATE REQUIRED THAT we conduct an investigation, and that our investigation inform future potential legislation. That's exactly what we did.

What Donald Trump attempted to do in 2020 and 2021 was unconstitutional and illegal under existing laws, but what if the plan was different next time? What if one or more sitting state governors refused to certify a lawful election result? What if a state's secretary of state opted not to report the lawful outcome of the popular vote? Congresswoman Zoe Lofgren and I, assisted by my senior counsel, Joe Maher, and Giancarlo Pellegrini and Sean Wright, from the House Administration Committee, discussed how we might fill these holes—including introducing legislation to modify the 1887 Electoral Count Act.

Consulting with legal scholars from across the political spectrum, Zoe's team produced a strong initial draft. Phil, Joe, and I worked to edit it. Here's how I characterized the resulting proposed bill on the House floor on September 21:

> Commentary from conservatives on our bill has been exceptionally positive. Here are a few examples: Judge Luttig, a widely respected conservative legal expert, wrote that our bill was "masterfully drafted to ensure we never have another day anything like January 6th, and to avert other future efforts to overturn our nation's democratic elections." The *Wall Street Journal* editorial board offered a range of positive comments, including explaining

that the House bill would make it harder "for partisans in Congress who want to get C-SPAN–famous to lodge phony Electoral College objections," or for them to raise objections on the House floor because "somebody had a funny feeling about the vote totals in west southeastern Pennsylvania." The conservative Cato Institute said this: "In some respects, this bill is more conservative and originalist than the existing Senate bill." Conservative commentator Quin Hillyer said in *The Washington Examiner*, "The House bill adds to the work already done by the Senate and fills in almost all gaps with admirable and sensible specificity." There are many other examples from conservative commentators, as well. I urge my Republican colleagues to read those articles and editorials in full.

Before the process was over, we had to iron out some differences with the Senate's version of the same bill. I thought ours was stronger, but the Senate bill was good. Ultimately, the Senate version of the bill passed both houses of Congress. The new law may have addressed future January 6 turmoil, but I knew that we still faced a significant threat: a possible second Trump term as president.

58. UNFIT FOR ANY OFFICE

As soon as our October 2022 hearing ended, the January 6th Committee shifted full-time into working on its final report. During my time in government, I had seen many reports assembled after congressional hearings. Most of them have no impact. They take an immense amount of time to create and are generally read by very few people.

We decided at the outset of our hearings that we would need to explain how all of Donald Trump's various efforts to overturn the election fit together. This was a principal goal of my opening statement on June 9, 2022, and it was why we had organized our hearings around that seven-part plan. Our report would need to clearly detail the complexity of that plan. We also expected that a fair number of Select Committee staffers would depart before we had finished, pursuing other legal opportunities or Hill positions. This would be an intense process in a brief span of time, carried out by our remaining dedicated staff.

Evidence had been the prime, almost exclusive, focus of our hearings. Our report also had to avoid exaggeration; we wanted its every paragraph and section to be meticulously sourced and supported.

We also aimed to produce a carefully drafted criminal referral. After Judge Carter's first ruling in March of 2022 (finding that it was likely Donald Trump and John Eastman had violated two criminal statutes), I believed there was no doubt the Committee would make such a criminal referral.

By early November, we had further concluded that we would need some form of executive summary — something that would stand alone yet effectively present our key findings and evidence. In the many months since the report's December 2022 publication, I have talked to hundreds of people who've read the executive summary—including college students studying the institutions of democracy. The executive summary served its purpose, and the chapters and appendices that follow provided substantially greater detail.

Chairman Thompson had asked the four Committee members who were attorneys—Zoe Lofgren, Jamie Raskin, Adam Schiff, and me—to serve on a subcommittee to make recommendations to the full Committee concerning criminal referrals. John Wood, with substantial help from Tim Heaphy and many others, spent a great deal of time drafting and editing the section on criminal referrals in our report. Others, including Brittany Record, had also been of crucial help on these issues. Our hearings had spotlighted many specific moments when Donald Trump, presented with a clear choice, *chose* to act unlawfully and in direct contravention of his duty. In my speech about Meadows' contempt a year earlier, I had quoted the words of the criminal statute about obstructing or impeding an official proceeding, 18 USC §1512(c)(2). Judge Carter had relied on that and, in the John Eastman privilege case, on another provision, concerning anyone who conspires to commit an offense against the US (18 USC §371). But there were several other potentially applicable provisions of criminal law as well, from the straightforward (transmitting falsely certified electoral votes to the Executive Branch and Congress, 18 USC §1001) to the more complex (assisting, or aiding and comforting, the ongoing violence at the Capitol, 18 USC §2383).

By this time, we also recognized that both the Department of Justice and Georgia's Fulton County District Attorney might utilize other theories. For example, the department's *Justice Manual* lays out multiple options for prosecuting defendants who interfere with elections. And from what we were hearing, we thought Fulton County might be pursuing something like the Georgia equivalent of a RICO (or racketeering) theory.

The Committee had also heard all manner of straw-man arguments, which seemed to turn on Donald Trump's speechwriter having inserted the word *peacefully* in one place in the president's January 6 Ellipse speech.

The ploy didn't sway us, for it was obvious what (or rather *who*) had motivated the deadly violence: Trump supporters involved in the havoc told us the same thing over and over again. And our criminal referrals were not solely, or even largely, based upon the words of incitement in Trump's Ellipse speech. The Committee's referrals were much broader and more comprehensive: We had uncovered far more inappropriate and illegal conduct over the prior year.

As we drafted the executive summary and criminal referrals, Tom Joscelyn was working with Kristin Amerling, Dan George, and the key remaining Committee investigators to draft and edit the report's chapters. Tom also structured and wrote the final chapter—a detailed anatomy of the attack. James Sasso, Marcus Childress, and David Weinberg also made important contributions, including in producing this portion of the report. We wanted to be certain that the historical record included a clear description of each phase of the assault. This was crucial to combating disinformation and making sure the American people learned the truth.

Given the sensitivity of (and media interest in) our work, plus the ongoing danger of leaks, we assigned each member of the Committee a separate binder that would remain locked in the Committee's reading room—an ornate space in a corner of the Capitol's ground floor that Speaker Pelosi had set aside for the Committee's use. Members could review updated sections of the report, and ask questions or provide comments on a rolling basis.

Committee staffer Jacob Nelson was tasked with ensuring that members' edits were incorporated and their questions were answered. This work, overseen by Kristin Amerling and Dan George, was no small task; we were working to complete our report before the 117th Congress adjourned. In cases where members had conflicting comments, or questions about input from other members, Jacob elevated those issues so they could be resolved.

Jamie Fleet, Jacob Nelson, and I set up shop two floors below the reading room, in my hideaway office in the Capitol basement. We spent many long hours around the same table where months earlier we had conducted those vital witness interviews with Sarah Matthews and Cassidy

Hutchinson—going page by page through each section of the *Final Report*. Jacob shuttled back and forth between the hideaway and the member reading room as we finalized the document.

On one of our last evenings in the hideaway, Terri McCullough, Speaker Pelosi's chief of staff, surprised us with a delivery of midnight snacks. She knew we'd been down there around the clock, working to meet our deadline. I looked up from the pages of the report to see that Terri was sporting a TEAM CHENEY hoodie.

It made me smile. It was a touching symbol of the unprecedented alliance we had formed, beyond partisan politics, to do what had to be done for our country.

———

As we prepared the *Final Report* for publication, we also got ready to release the Committee's interview transcripts. We ultimately released all but a handful.

Only for certain Secret Service, national-security, and military witnesses was the January 6th Select Committee obligated, as a condition for obtaining testimony, to return the transcripts to the government entity involved. In the few cases of this type, the Committee requested that the government entities perform whatever redactions were necessary to safeguard sensitive national-security information, then supply the edited transcripts to the National Archives.

Committee staffers also released transcripts to the Department of Justice, and earlier still they had been briefing prosecutors about specific witness testimony and other elements of our evidence. Our transcripts will remain accessible at the website of the US Government Publishing Office.* They will also be preserved for history in the National Archives.

Occasionally, people such as Tucker Carlson would make transparently false claims about evidence supposedly in the Committee's possession.

———

* https://www.govinfo.gov/collection/january-6th-committee-final-report

At one point, Carlson alleged that a mass of secret Capitol Hill videos, apparently released to him on Kevin McCarthy's orders, revealed that our committee had been lying to the public.

This was intentional disinformation.

In an order entered in the obstruction-of-an-official-proceeding prosecution of Jacob "QAnon Shaman" Chansley, Senior United States District Judge Royce Lamberth explained Tucker's lies this way:

> Finally, the Court would be remiss if it did not address the ill-advised television program of March 6, 2023. Not only was the broadcast replete with misstatements and misrepresentations regarding the events of January 6, 2021, too numerous to count, the host explicitly questioned the integrity of this Court—not to mention the legitimacy of the entire US criminal-justice system—with inflammatory characterizations of cherry-picked videos stripped of their proper context. In so doing, he called on his followers to "reject the evidence of [their] eyes and ears," language resembling the destructive, misguided rhetoric that fueled the events of January 6 in the first place.
>
> The Court finds it alarming that the host's viewers throughout the nation so readily heeded his command. But this Court cannot and will not reject the evidence before it. Nor should the public. Members of the public who are concerned about the evidence presented in Mr. Chansley's case and others like it may view the public docket and even attend court proceedings in these cases. Those of us who have presided over dozens of cases arising from, listened to hundreds of hours of testimony describing, and reviewed thousands of pages of briefing about the attack on our democracy of January 6 know all too well that neither the events of that day nor any particular defendant's involvement can be fully captured in a seconds-long video carelessly, or perhaps even cynically, aired in a television segment or attached to a tweet.

————

On December 19, 2022, the Select Committee held its final public meeting. We had several purposes for this meeting, including announcing our criminal referrals and the imminent release of the *Final Report*. But I also wanted to underscore the historical context for what we were doing, and how I viewed our labors of the last 18 months. In almost every generation, Americans have given their lives to preserve the ideals of our founders. Each generation in our nation must be a steward of our history. But American history is not just *our* legacy. The United States is proof that human freedom can survive what has destroyed other democracies over millennia of human history. At no *prior* point in my life had I believed that we were on the precipice of losing that legacy. Virtually everyone on either side of the aisle had agreed with the fundamental ideals that built our republic.

But all that had changed on January 6 of 2021.

We seemed in danger of losing what so many in previous generations had sacrificed for:

In April of 1861, when Abraham Lincoln issued the first call for volunteers for the Union Army, my great-great-grandfather, Samuel Fletcher Cheney, joined the 21st Ohio Volunteer Infantry. He fought through all four years of the Civil War, from Chickamauga to Stones River to Atlanta. He marched with his unit in the grand review of troops on Pennsylvania Avenue in May of 1865, passing a reviewing stand where President Johnson and General Grant were seated.

Silas Canfield, the regimental historian of the 21st Ohio Volunteer Infantry, described the men in the unit this way: He said they had a just appreciation of the value and advantage of free government and the necessity of defending and maintaining it, and they enlisted prepared to accept all the necessary labors, fatigues, exposures, dangers, and even death for the unity of our nation and the perpetuity of our institutions. I have found myself thinking often, especially since January 6th, of my great-great-grandfather and all those in every generation who have sacrificed so much for the unity of our nation and the perpetuity of our institutions.

When you serve in Congress, you have the privilege of walking through a shrine to our history every day—through the Capitol Rotunda, through Statuary Hall, past reminders of those who have come before. I did that on January 5, 2021, again on the evening of January 6, and repeatedly during the investigation. The statues and paintings have a purpose: They are there to remind elected representatives *why* they are serving. If we are so inclined, we can descend into pettiness, into the day-to-day muck of partisanship. And surely, some of that is unavoidable—on many issues, the people of the United States are not united. But when the fundamental ideals of our nation come to bear, we must be united. When our country faces a crisis, we must find our noble purpose. Some things are beyond partisanship. That is the reason we all take an oath.

One thing was now unavoidably apparent to any objective observer: Donald Trump had demonstrated that he is unfit for any office.

Of course, our investigation never could have succeeded without the willing participation of many Republicans, including those working in the Trump administration: "Many of our Committee's witnesses showed selfless patriotism, and their words and courage will be remembered." I also recognized that "[t]he brave men and women of the Capitol Police, the Metropolitan Police, and all the other law-enforcement officers who fought to defend us that day saved lives—and our democracy."

Nothing in our hearings, in our investigation, or in our *Final Report* would have been possible without the dedication of our expert staff, nor without the commitment, the full attention, and the leadership of Chairman Thompson and the members of the January 6th Committee. This had not been an easy road, and it was not a road that was guaranteed to end in success. For various reasons, many members of the January 6th

Committee would not be returning to Congress in the coming weeks. But we knew that what we had done was right, and we knew that it had been necessary. I ended with this:

> Finally, I wish to thank my colleagues on this Committee. It has been a tremendous honor to serve with all of you. We have accomplished great and important things together, and I hope we have set an example. And I also want to thank all of those who have honorably contributed to the work of our Committee, and to our report. We have accomplished much over a short period of time. Many of you sacrificed for the good of our nation. You have helped make history—and, I hope, helped to right the ship.

Epilogue

Thomas Jefferson was the first president to take the oath of office in Washington, DC. On March 4, 1801, he was sworn in at the US Capitol Building—which at the time consisted of a single small structure that would eventually become the north wing of the building we know today. Among the visitors in attendance was Margaret Bayard Smith, wife of the owner of one of Washington's major newspapers. She wrote this to her sister-in-law:

> I have this morning witnessed one of the most interesting scenes a free people can ever witness. The changes of administration, which in every government and in every age have most generally been epochs of confusion, villainy, and bloodshed, in this our happy country take place without any species of distraction or disorder.

Four years earlier, President George Washington had handed power to President John Adams, but this was the first time power had passed from one party to another. And those watching understood what a momentous—indeed, miraculous—thing it was for that to happen absent "confusion, villainy, and bloodshed." Until January 2021, every American president had fulfilled his solemn obligation to safeguard the peaceful transfer of power. Every four or eight years, down through our history, candidates of both parties have put aside personal ambition and political battles for the good of the nation—even after the closest of presidential races.

As I was writing this book, I found—pasted onto the pages of one of

my Grandmother Cheney's scrapbooks—President Ford's concession statement from November 1976. Ford lost the presidential election that year to
Jimmy Carter. The final tally in the Electoral College was 297 to 240.

During the closing days of that campaign, President Ford had lost his
voice. The morning after the election, when he placed the call to Jimmy
Carter to concede the race, Ford handed the phone to his 35-year-old chief
of staff, Dick Cheney, to read the concession statement to President-elect
Carter. In the statement my father read, President Ford congratulated
Carter on his victory, then looked to the future:

> As one who has been honored to serve the people of this great
> land—both in Congress and as President—I believe that we
> must now put the divisions of the campaign behind us and unite
> the country once again in a common pursuit of peace and
> prosperity.

Despite the policy differences between the two men, President Ford
assured Carter that he would have Ford's "complete and wholehearted
support" as he took the oath of office. Ford also pledged that he and all
members of his administration would do everything they could to ensure
Carter began his term "as smoothly and effectively as possible." Gerald
Ford's statement ended, "May God bless you and your family as you
undertake your new responsibilities."

One leader ceding power to the next, gracious in defeat, pledging
unity for the good of the nation—that is what is required by fidelity to
the Constitution and love of country. We depend upon the goodwill of
our leaders and their dedication to duty to ensure the survival of our
republic. Only a man unacquainted with honor, courage, and character
would see weakness in this.

———

In a just world, the January 6th Select Committee investigation, and
the criminal prosecutions that have now followed, would be the end of a
dark period in our nation's history. The man who mobilized a violent

assault on our Capitol — who attempted to overturn an election and seize power — would have no political future. Donald Trump and those who aided him would be scorned and punished. But as I write this in the fall of 2023, Trump is running for president of the United States once again, and he holds a sizable lead among Republican contenders. Today, none of us can tell if the story of January 6 is nearing its end or is only just beginning. We may have many darker chapters ahead.

When I questioned Jared Kushner during his appearance before the January 6th Committee on March 31, 2022, the presidential son-in-law attempted to suggest that those criticizing Donald Trump were making the mistake of taking his words literally — that Trump often made hyperbolic and provocative statements as a kind of sport. But the events of January 6 demonstrated that Donald Trump *meant* what he said. He actually intended to achieve the most extreme things he was suggesting. And on the morning of January 6, 2021, he believed that his schemes would allow him to continue in the presidency despite having lost the election.

Today, we must take Donald Trump's statements literally. Trump has told us that he thinks the Constitution can and should be suspended when necessary, that what happened on January 6 was justified, that in a second Trump presidency he would seek retribution. And much more. Some have suggested that "the normal U.S. checks and balances" of our constitutional system would constrain Trump. They won't.

We have seen what a group of dishonest and unscrupulous lawyers will do in service to Donald Trump. An American president surrounded by people like these could dismantle our republic. It would not necessarily all happen on the first day of a second Trump term. But step by step, Donald Trump would tear down the walls that our framers so carefully built to combat centralized power and tyranny. He would attempt to dismantle what Justice Antonin Scalia called the "real constitutional law." Perhaps Trump would start by refusing to enforce certain judicial rulings he opposed. He has already attacked the judiciary repeatedly, and ignored the rulings of scores of courts. He knows that judicial rulings have force only if the executive branch enforces them. So he won't.

Certainly, Donald Trump would run the US government with acting officials who are not, and could not be, confirmed by the Senate. He would obtain a bogus legal opinion allowing him to do it. He would ensure that the Senate confirmation process is no longer any check on his authority.

The types of resignation threats that may have kept Trump at bay before—that, for example, convinced him to reverse his appointment of Jeffrey Clark as acting attorney general—would no longer be a deterrent. Trump would be eager for those who oppose his actions at the Justice Department and elsewhere to resign. And, at the Department of Defense (where a single US senator, one of Donald Trump's strongest supporters, is doing great harm to America's national security by refusing to allow the confirmation of senior civilian or military officials), Trump would again install his own team of loyalists—people who would act on his orders without hesitation.

This is not speculation.

This is what Donald Trump has already told us he will do.

This is what he has already done.

Step by step, Donald Trump would tear down the other structures that restrain an American president. No Pat Cipollone, no Mike Pence, no Greg Jacob, no Bill Barr, no Jeff Rosen—none of them would be there to stop what Donald Trump attempts. The assumption that our institutions will protect themselves is purely wishful thinking by people who prefer to look the other way. Those loyalists and lawyers who step up to help Trump unravel our republic would do so knowing that they would be pardoned. That they would face no risk of prosecution. And Donald Trump would not hesitate to pardon himself. Any who step forward to oppose Trump will face the types of threats, retaliation, and violence we have already seen—but this time with the full power of an unconstrained American president behind them.

We have also now learned that most Republicans currently in Congress will do what Donald Trump asks, no matter what it is. We cannot rely on them to check his power. A Senate of Josh Hawleys certainly won't stop Trump. Neither will House Republicans led by a Speaker who has made himself a willing hostage to Trump and his most unhinged supporters in Congress. I am very sad to say that America can no longer count on a body of elected Republicans to protect our republic.

Meanwhile, those in the media who have willingly spread Donald Trump's dangerous claims and propaganda for profit will continue to propel him forward. They know that what he says and does is wrong. They know the consequences of what they are doing. But they do it anyway.

Donald Trump will be on trial as he runs for the presidency in 2024. We cannot know for certain what the next year holds. But we have already seen enough to know what might happen.

———

In November 1800, John Adams wrote to his wife, Abigail, after he had spent his first night in the White House. His letter included a prayer, which is now inscribed above the fireplace in the White House state dining room. It reads, in part, "May none but honest and wise men ever rule under this roof." Adams knew that the character of our leaders mattered. He and our other founders knew that the institutions of self-government could not sustain and protect themselves. It would fall to the people of this nation—and to our elected leaders—to do that. The perpetuation of our institutions and the defense of our Constitution now depend on us.

At some point, a genuinely conservative Republican Party—a party that stands for limited government, a strong national defense, and the rule of law—can reemerge and win the presidency. But if Donald Trump is the Republican nominee in 2024, we must do everything we can to defeat him. If Trump is on the ballot, the 2024 presidential election will not just be about inflation, or budget deficits, or national security, or any of the many critical issues we Americans normally face. We will be voting on whether to preserve our republic. As a nation, we can endure damaging policies for a four-year term. But we cannot survive a president willing to terminate our Constitution.

If you visit the National Archives in Washington, DC, you can see America's founding documents on display. Look down through the glass at our Constitution and you will notice immediately that the first three words of the document, written in 1787, are larger than all the others. Those words—*We the People*—describe our power and our responsibility.

In the era of Trump, certain members of Congress and other Trump enablers—many of whom carry the Constitution in their pocket but seem never to have read it—have attempted to hijack this phrase, to claim it gives them authority to subvert the rule of law or overturn the results of elections. They have preyed on the patriotism of millions of Americans. They are working to return to office the man responsible for January 6.

We the people must stop them. We are the only thing that can stop them. This is more important than partisan politics. Every one of us—Republican, Democrat, Independent—must work and vote *together* to ensure that Donald Trump and those who have appeased, enabled, and collaborated with him are defeated.

This is the cause of our time.

ACKNOWLEDGMENTS

During my time in Congress, I worked alongside a group of dedicated and extremely talented individuals on my staff. As the events described in this book unfolded, I was honored that so many of them stood with me to serve the people of Wyoming and our country. This tremendous team included Kara Ahern, Jeremy Adler, Will Henderson, Caroline Boothe, Ryan O'Toole, Michael "Sully" Sullivan, Elizabeth Pearce, Luke Sullivan, Hayley McGhee, Parker Reynolds, Morgan Anderson, and Andrew Meyer. My team in Wyoming was led by Tammy Hooper and Karmen Rossi. Along with Amy Edmonds, Esther Wagner, Holly Kennedy, Lindy Linn, and Ally Garner they worked tirelessly to serve the people of Wyoming.

The work of the January 6 Select Committee would not have been possible without the contributions of an outstanding group of professionals, beginning with Jamie Fleet and Terri McCullough who were indispensable. I am grateful to Joe Maher and John Wood for their leadership, advice, counsel, and invaluable contributions to every aspect of the Committee's work. Our committee staff was also skillfully led by David Buckley, Kristin Amerling, Hope Goins, Tim Heaphy, Tim Mulvey, Lisa Bianco, and Candyce Phoenix. Tom Joscelyn was vitally important as we produced the Committee report. I am very grateful for his years of friendship, his willingness to take on this assignment, and for the outstanding contributions he made to the Committee's investigation and historical record. Barry Pump, Evan Mauldin, Steve Devine, William Danvers, David Weinberg, and many others provided important professional expertise in many areas of the Committee's work. I'm also grateful for Gus Coldebella's expert advice.

ACKNOWLEDGMENTS

The American public is now familiar with the excellent witness exams conducted by many of the skilled Select Committee attorneys, including Tim Heaphy, Marc Harris, John Wood, Dan George, Soumya Dayananda, Sean Tonolli, and many others. The public has also seen the outstanding videos compiled and narrated by Committee attorneys, including Casey Lucier, Josh Roselman, and Alejandra Apecechea. The Committee benefited from the talents of incredibly bright young lawyers, like Brittany Record, James Sasso, and Marcus Childress, who will, no doubt, accomplish many other notable things in their careers. I am also grateful for the important work done by Jacob Nelson, Lizzie Obrand, Hannah Muldavin, Jacqueline Colvett, and Eddie Flaherty.

James Goldston and his team of experienced and talented producers were instrumental in helping the Committee present the facts to the American people in a series of historic and impactful hearings. I am grateful for their important contributions.

I am thankful for the sage advice and friendship of Eric Edelman, Dr. Jon Reiner, Dr. Gigi el Bayoumi, Scott Carpenter, and Jeff Larson. I also want to thank Kevin Seifert, Brenda Gianiny, Sheryl Jahns, Amy Womack, John Drzewicki, Bev Shea, Kristin Loucks, Max Becker, Jen Simon, and Karissa Akin for their hard work and support. Even when it wasn't politically convenient or beneficial, they chose to stand on the right side of history.

I have been blessed by the support of friends across Wyoming, including Al and Ann Simpson; Toni Thomson and her daughters Laura and Jennifer; Mary Kay and John Turner; Tad and Jenn True; Chuck and Joanne Tweedy; Judy and Don Legerski; Becky Constantino; Joanne and Shane True; Landon Brown; Marilyn Kite; Byra Kite and Candy Paradis; David and Christine Fales; Jackie Montgomery; Lois, Jackie, and Ruth Van Mark; Judy and Paul Cali; Tim and Susan Stubson, Joe McGinley, and so many others. I also want to say a special thank you to Liza and Chris Pohle for their many years of friendship, and to Kris and Kevin Poole, Sarah and James Eaton, and Juana Gonzales. I thank them all.

Kara Ahern, Will Henderson, and Michael "Sully" Sullivan have been crucial to this book project. Sully has expertly overseen the research and fact-checking, and they have all spent months processing huge amounts of information and answering questions at all hours with thoroughness, accuracy, and speed. My daughter, Elizabeth, and my son, Philip, also provided important research assistance.

For this book, as with each of the others in which I've been involved over the last fifteen years, I was superbly represented by Bob Barnett. I benefited greatly from his advice, judgment, and deep knowledge of and experience with every aspect of this process. He is so good, in fact, that I've decided to forgive him for playing the role of Dick Cheney in the Democrats' vice-presidential debate prep sessions in 2000 and 2004.

I'm grateful for the work of the entire team at Little, Brown. Bruce Nichols helped guide this book through each step of the process and provided important insight and suggestions to shape the story. Pat Jalbert-Levine oversaw all elements of the production with professionalism and patience. The jacket was designed by the talented Mario Pulice. Allan Fallow tirelessly copyedited. I would also like to thank Sabrina Callahan and Bryan Christian for their work overseeing the press and sales strategy, along with editorial assistant Annie Martin.

David Kennerly has been a friend for over forty years and I am indebted to him for his unmatched talent and skill. I'm so grateful to my sister, Mary, for sharing many of the memories in David's photos and for agreeing to let me dig them out. Thank you to the University of Arizona Center for Creative Photography for the use of David Kennerly's photographs. I'm also grateful to David Bohrer for his friendship and the wonderful photographs he captured during eight years as the vice president's photographer. Thank you also to Marty LaVor and Adam Amick for the use of their photographs.

Thank you to all the members of law enforcement and of the US military who answered the call on January 6, including the Capitol Police who defend our Capitol and our democracy every day. Supervisory Special Agent Sean Camp and Special Agents Warren Leap, Christy Webb, Abbey Barthe, Anthony Booth, Brandon Exum, Fred Lent, Joe

Nemeth, and Reggie Straughn served as members of my detail over my last two years in Congress. I'm grateful for their professionalism, dedication, and good humor.

During my time in the House, I served on the House Armed Services Committee. It was a tremendous honor to work with the men and women who wear the uniform of our nation and defend our freedom every day. I particularly want to thank the 20th Chairman of the Joint Chiefs of Staff, General Mark Milley, and his wife, Hollyanne. General Milley found himself standing in the breach when many elected officials—including members of Congress serving on the House Armed Services Committee—failed to fulfill their obligations to the Constitution. America owes General Milley a debt of gratitude for his unwavering leadership and devotion to the Constitution.

Finally, the greatest thanks go to my family. To my parents, Lynne and Dick Cheney, and to my five children, Kate, Elizabeth, Grace, Philip, and Richard: You stood with me at every fork in the road and reminded me daily of what was right and what was so dramatically wrong during this dark period of our history. To my husband, Phil: I cannot imagine accomplishing any of this without you.